LEADING LADIES

LEADING LADIES

An Affectionate Look at
American Women of
the Twentieth Century

ELECTA CLARK

 STEIN AND DAY/*Publishers*/New York

We gratefully acknowledge permission to excerpt
the following copyrighted material:

From *Lillian Hellman, Playwright* by Richard Moody,
Copyright © 1972 by the Bobbs-Merrill Co.

From *Times Three* by Phyllis McGinley,
Copyright © 1946 by Phyllis McGinley, reprinted by
permission of the Viking Press.

First published in 1976
Designed by Ed Kaplin
Printed in the United States of America
Stein and Day/*Publishers*/Scarborough House,
Briarcliff Manor, N. Y. 10510

Library of Congress Cataloging in Publication Data

Clark, Electa.
    Leading ladies : an affectionate look at American women
    of the twentieth century.

    Includes index.
    1. Women—United States—Biography.   I.   Title.
CT3260.C57   920.72'0973   75-34263
ISBN 0-8128-1909-8

To Three Little Ladies: Yvonne Janine Clark
Christina Anne Leet
Heather Elizabeth Leet

AUTHOR'S NOTE

Undoubtedly, readers of *Leading Ladies* will protest, "But why did you leave out the life story of that actress, and this businesswoman, and those political leaders?"

I can only reply, "Lack of space."

I wish I could have given the recognition they deserve to poets Elinor Wylie and Marianne Moore, authors Gertrude Stein, Fannie Hurst (different though they be!) and Joyce Carol Oates, to actresses Laurette Taylor, Ruth Gordon, Joan Crawford, Marilyn Monroe, and Barbra Streisand; to Bessie Smith and Lily Pons, Beverly Sills and Carol Channing; to artist Neysa McMein and sculptor Malvina Hoffman, and dozens of other zealous and talented women.

Any six authors who set out to write about important women would come up with six different lists of names, and then, forced to trim the lists, would differ on which names to eliminate.

To all who should have been included in this volume and were not, my apologies.

E. C.

Contents

The 1900s

THE DEAR LITTLE WOMAN   11
  Let Us Be Correct
  The Darlings of the Theater
  Maxine Elliot and the King
  Winds of Change
  Woman's Sacred Shrine: Stuff and Nonsense!
  Straight Road to Fame
  True Women
  Princess Alice
  New Americans
  "... Keep On Keeping On"
  The Two Faces of Isadora Duncan
  The Elusive, the Magical ...
  Ladies of Fiction
  The New Woman
  Back to Real Life
  When Carry Nation Takes Her Hatchet,
    Demon Rum's A-Going to Catch It!
  The Suffrage Movement

The 1910s

FEMINISTS ON PARADE   53
  The New Broom
  The Returnees
  Survival Problems
  Struggles for Peace
  Meanwhile, Back at the White House
  "Woman at Work"
  Ardent Reformers
  Radiant Rebel

Artist from the Prairie
Pussy Jones Makes Good
Fashion and Frivolity
America's Sweetheart
Voice of Velvet

The 1920s

CALL IT A SPADE   90
The It Girls
Segments of the Society
Patterns for the Period
Two Governors for the Price of One
Wittiest Woman in New York
Fabulous Ferber
She Played It Cool
Golden Vessel of Great Song
The Achievers
"Behind a Veil of Silver Chiffon"
Other Charmers
The Power, the Glory, and the Hoax

The 1930s

THE DESPERATE DECADE   120
New Designs for Living
China Observer
Chicago Prodigy
Such Good Company!
South of Mason-Dixon
The "One-Woman Team"
Fighter for the Underdog
First Ladies of the Theater
Helen the Queen
Eva the Dynamo
Escape from the Big, Bad Wolf
Woman with a Pencil
Margaret Bourke-White
The Lady Who Would Be Queen

All in One Year ...
Her Soul Was Anchored in the Lord
Café Society

The 1940s

ROSIE THE RIVETER   161
    Frenzy of War
    "The Manpower Question Has Been Solved
      by Womanpower"
    Woman without a Flaw
    Nobody Called Her Frances
    "She Wrote Like an Angel"
    "Silence Gives the Proper Grace to Women"
    Women in the Arts

The 1950s

THE CALM BEFORE THE MARCHING   186
    The Building Boom Was On
    Woman's Place
    The Middle-Class Woman Goes to Work
    The Eisenhower Years
    She Joined a Gentlemen's Club
    Glorious Eccentric
    Harden Your Heart
    Gift from Anne Lindbergh

The 1960s

STORM AND STRUGGLE   206
    The Black Rebellion
    Freedom Singer
    "You Can't Trust Anyone Over Thirty"
    Scientist and Poet in One Package
    Articulate Professor
    Rebel in the Theater
    First Lady

On the Literary Scene
The Women's Revolution
The Opposition

The 1970s

THREE-QUARTER MARK   233
Stars of the Seventies
Political Women and Church Women
Women's Liberation Movement
The Equal Rights Amendment
The Turn of the Century
Index   247

THE DEAR LITTLE WOMAN

"Humanity marches on into the new and glorious 20th century!" exults a daily paper in its first issue of 1901. "Come, oh century, child of hope!" begins a long poem on page one. Another column trills, "We are 20th century women ... with the dower of privilege and responsibility which enriches women in this wonderful era!"

The quotations are from the *Republican,* of Columbus, Indiana, then the center of population of the United States. All across the country, journalists, preachers, and ordinary folk rejoiced with the same exuberance. The nation was rich and would grow richer! Railroads were faster and better every day, factories were busier, cities were larger, people were cleverer, life was more stimulating than ever before!

Of course a few evils remained to be righted: child labor, sweatshops, epidemics—but the greatest country in the world would quickly set those right.

Americans believed in America.

Women were pleased with themselves. "Our grandmothers and great-grandmothers," boasts the *Republican,* "were handicapped in girlhood by a thousand prejudices and cast-iron traditional rules from which we are emancipated."

Among the new freedoms was the freedom to join clubs, if their papas or husbands permitted. Most of these were self-improvement clubs in which the ladies read works of Browning or Dante, enjoyed the hostess's tea and cookies, and returned refreshed to their family duties.

The Columbus newspaper coos over one such meeting in its first issue of 1901: "The Culture Club celebrated the last day of the year at the hospitable old home of Mrs. Hinman." Readings and discussions on the progress of the world occupied the afternoon, and at the close of

11

the program, ice cream, coffee, and cake were served on beautifully decorated tables in the dining room, where "toasts were given and sociability reigned supreme."

A few clubs, more serious, worked to establish a juvenile court or a public library or a day nursery, and members endured the scoffing of townsfolk who labeled them do-gooders, radicals, or women trying to wear the pants of the family.

In New York City in 1903 Mrs. J. Borden Harriman, Mrs. Richard Irwin, Mrs. John Jacob Astor III, and Mrs. W. S. Rainsford daringly founded a women's club in imitation of clubs that men had enjoyed for a century. Known as the Colony Club, it was such a novelty that people all over the world threw up their hands in horror. Those American women with all that freedom! Former President Grover Cleveland expressed general opinion when he piously cautioned, "[Woman's] best and safest club is her home."

One evening Mrs. Thomas H. Perkins, whose sons were club presidents, sailed gaily into the dining room of the Colony Club and called out to the assembled ladies, "I've waited for this evening all my life. I've just telephoned the boys, 'Don't wait dinner. I'm dining at my club.' "

Other women bent over their reams of paper, pouring out the stories that they were compelled to tell. When young Ellen Glasgow of Virginia took her first manuscript to a New York editor, he handed it back to her unread. He knew there wasn't a chance of its being accepted by anyone. "The best advice I can give you," he told her benignly, "is to stop writing and go back to the South and have some babies."

This typical rejection must have been enough to stop many a girl from trying to fight the system. Not Ellen. A rebel against masculine supremacy and stuffy tradition, she did go back to the South, but only to her desk. She wrote steadily through the decades—nineteen splendid novels, which were gladly accepted by publishers more open-minded than her first critic.

In the early years of this century, ladies—in spite of all that self-congratulation in the Columbus *Republican*—were expected to be productive of babies, embroidery, and ice-cream socials, but not to compete with men in the professions or the arts. Those who succeeded in this competition, or who fought for social reform, had one quality in common: a fanatic's zeal that kept them forging, relentless and single-minded, toward their goals.

Such women were exceptional. The average woman, of course, did not trample fences down. The ideal lady of 1901, while never idle, strove to appear fragile and elegant. She was a stern mother, but gentle and submissive to her husband. She was smiling and content in whatever milieu God had chosen to place her. She was a dear little woman.

Let Us Be Correct

Fashion drawings at the turn of the century show an interesting bust: it swells down grandly to the waistline; there the figure is tightly belted and seems to be no more than a hand-span around. This belt is not horizontal, but low in front and high in back so that the lady's little round behind is hoisted up in the air. She tips stylishly forward and her next step will surely send her crashing right down on her face.

It is a relief to observe that a photograph of a live woman of 1901 always shows her standing straight up like any human being.

The lady of the fashion drawing is short-legged. Her skirt flares out like a bell. On her head is a coquettish hat, for no lady ever appears out-of-doors hatless, and the hat is rather large (small hats are going out) worn tipped to one side and loaded with flowers or feathers.

The dear little woman strained to follow fashion's laws exactly, and she guided her life along iron rails of propriety, for correctness was next to godliness. Your table must be set correctly, your manner correctly modulated according to whether you addressed the president of the Culture Club or the Irish girl who came in to help with the laundry.

There was a rule for everything. A nice girl accepted only flowers, books, bonbons, or music from a male friend. Subjects such as pregnancy were never mentioned in mixed company, even in the family. Taboo words were "corset," "underwear," "toilet paper," any words referring to concealed or internal part of the human body, and sex.

There were rules about when to pay calls, upon whom, how long to stay, and how many cards to leave. Incidentally, it would have been unpardonably gauche to visit a hostess's bathroom during a call. What?—admit to owning a body with biologic functions beneath those layers of correct clothing?

An unmarried girl of the upper class had to be chaperoned while attending the theater or a ball. In very strict circles, a young lady at a ball dared not grant several dances in succession to any one young man unless he was her fiancé, or unless he hotfooted it to her parents' home next day and asked for her hand in marriage; otherwise she was "compromised."

The use of first names was reserved for family and friends and people one had known since childhood. Ladies helped each other through childbirth, the pangs of errant husbands, and difficult crochet patterns, yet addressed each other to the death as Mrs. White and Mrs. Green.

There were rules for the wearing of mourning. It was correct for a widow to wear unrelieved black, including a heavy black crepe veil, for one year; then black garments with a lighter veil the second year. In the third year she might dispense with the veil entirely, but she must wear only black, white, lavender, or gray. She was looked upon sternly if she remarried in less than three years. (A light woman, that one!)

No nice girl wore face powder or other makeup, or even dyed her hair. A good woman never, never wore black underwear or nightgown; they signified membership in a profession that shall remain nameless.

Gentlemen in an elevator swept off their hats if a woman entered. If a lady and a gentleman met on the street and stopped to talk, he took off his hat and did not replace it until they parted.

These pretenses that the ladies were delicate treasures to be preserved upon pedestals existed side by side with the unromantic truth that the exquisite creature, unless she was well-to-do, worked like a drayhorse at running her household; and the still drearier truth that women were kept unenfranchised, uneducated, and unfree.

The real purpose of this game of worshiping the ladies was to persuade women that their position was not humiliating but enviable. Most women played their part in the charade willingly.

But a new wind was blowing, a fresh, exciting breeze. Young women lifted their submissive heads and breathed in a new scent. Freedom? Rebellion? They began striding with a freer step. Some of them spoke up in bold voices. They sat down and crossed their knees. Old gentlemen bleated, "Whatever has become of the old-fashioned girl?"

There were disturbing signals, as the decade progressed, that the dear little woman might be superseded by a new ideal.

The Darlings of the Theater

Playgoing was the delight of the decade. Theater tickets cost from 50 cents to $2. There were forty-one legitimate houses on Broadway in 1900, more than in any other city in the world. That year the street

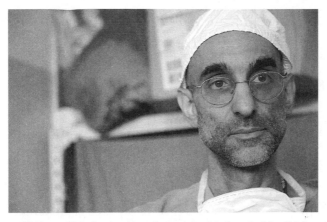

The incredible Doctor Tom Catena, at his hospital in Gidel.

the courtyard on mats on top of the dirt. It was a little like being in a MASH unit, only ten times worse. Everything felt urgent, everyone needed attention.

Dr. Tom had chosen a group of young local men for us to train to make the arm, and they joined us as we toured the facility. We set up our equipment in a room adjacent to the hospital office and got ready to make some arms.

The room was crowded—in addition to the men whom I was going to train, it seemed like everyone in the village had crowded in to see these miracle machines. A lot of these folks had never seen a computer before, let alone a printer, let alone a 3-D printer. Because the ceasefire had ended, and because our trip had been delayed, the fourteen days we'd planned to spend in Gidel had turned into five. There was so little time and so much to do. Occasionally throughout the day, I would have to ask people to leave because it would get so crowded. One of the villagers, a young man named Achmed, always hung in the wings whenever everyone was asked to leave. Achmed was a happy but persistent fellow, with a quiet but forceful personality.

I started the class with the absolute basics—this is a drill, this is how you load the drill. This is filament, this is how you load the filament into the printer. This is how you call up the 3-D files on the computer. This is how you print a comb; this is how you print a bracelet. This is how you print an arm.

Achmed was still there, but I figured someone who was that motivated to help just might be useful. And sure enough, he turned out to be one of the best arm-makers we had.

Just goes to show you, asking forgiveness is always easier than asking permission.

We worked through the day, using Daniel as a model. That first day, a Saturday, I was really just teaching them the basics. Sunday was a down day, because that's the day everyone either went to church or to see family members who lived out of town. Monday was our first real day, and slowly but surely, they started understanding how to make a hand. They had to take on so much, and they learned so much in such a short amount of time: heating water over charcoal to soften the molding plastic, using tools they'd never seen before. One of the men had never held a drill before, and when he turned it on, it startled him so that he dropped it, and all the men laughed. Working on computers when they'd never touched a computer before. And, of course, the computers came loaded with some American music; these men had no access to music, and they played the songs over and over and over until I screamed. I mean, there's just so much Kesha a man can take.

But little by little, it was happening. People who had never used a computer before learned to print a hand on a 3-D printer.

It kind of takes your breath away.

◆

The next day, I was teaching the Robohand class again, and feeling pretty great, when Dr. Tom came barging in. "A ten-year-old boy was just admitted who had his arm blown off by a bomber," he said.

The boy had been brought in by his uncle, who had related the terrible tale: They'd been out in the field the day before, when the MiGs came. The bombs killed the boy's seven- and eight-year-old earned its nickname, "The Great White Way," because of the brilliant street lights just then going up.

Audiences were unsophisticated and enthusiastic, especially in provincial theaters. They stamped their feet and whistled as they applauded, and they hurled bouquets onto the stage. If they were very uninhibited, they even shouted encouragement to favorite actors, hissed the villain, and called warnings to heroines in distress.

Of course New York theatergoers were more formal than that. One actress, speaking of the New York theater, recalled: "Going to a play was a major event that called for pomp and ceremony. The women wore gorgeous evening gowns and the men were always in formal attire, their white shirts and waistcoats gleaming in the darkness. And I shall never forget the wave of perfume that wafted across the footlights to us on the stage. How happily we basked in it!"

"It was a superb theater to be young in," wrote a drama critic. "It was a great world to be alive in!"

Ethel Barrymore was a favorite of this exuberant public. She sprang to stardom in 1901 in New York, on the first night of Clyde Fitch's gay little comedy, *Captain Jinks of the Horse Marines*.

Until that night, Ethel had never had a success. When the play opened in Philadelphia, it had been a disaster. One critic wrote, "If the young lady who plays Madame Trentoni"—that was Ethel—"had possessed beauty, charm, or talent, this play might have been a success."

As long as the actress lived, she remembered that review word for word.

The company played three weeks of one-night stands to cold audiences. Then the play was to open at the Garrick in New York.

"Don't do it, Mr. Frohman," Ethel implored the producer. "Please don't do it." But he would do it. She had to face another humiliation. She went onstage physically sick with opening-night panic. All through act I she was too terrified to lift her eyes from the floor.

But when the curtain rose on act II, by some magic of the theater, or some mysterious heritage from the Drews and the Barrymores, she was transformed. Her chin lifted. So did her eyes. Her voice became firm, her gestures graceful and sure. She was the radiant Madame Trentoni. At the end of act III the audience stood up to applaud.

Ethel had an ovation.

The great dramatist Sir Arthur Wing Pinero once said to her, "My dear child, you are the most natural thing I have ever seen on the stage!"

Theatrical fashions were changing. Bombast and melodrama were going out; simplicity and realism were coming in. Though she didn't plan it that way, Ethel's casualness was in vogue.

One night early in her career, she and her brother John walked from her boardinghouse on Thirty-sixth Street to the Garrick before the evening performance. Ethel glanced up and clutched John's arm. "Look at that!" she whispered.

There on the marquee was her name in lights: ETHEL BARRYMORE in CAPTAIN JINKS OF THE HORSE MARINES. She burst into tears and cried all the way to the theater.

But, as the years passed, the shy and graceful girl of 1901 developed into a commanding woman with the Barrymore hawk profile and the bearing of an empress. One evening, after years of success had accustomed her to arrogance, a group of people strolled into their stage box when her play was under way. They made a commotion, whispering and rustling their programs.

On the stage with the star was an elderly character actor named Charles Cherry, who was a little deaf.

By and by Miss Barrymore stepped down to the apron, made an apologetic little gesture to the audience and said, looking up at the box, "Excuse me; I can hear every word you are saying, but Mr. Cherry is slightly hard of hearing. I wonder if you would speak up for him?" Then she stepped back and went smoothly on with the play.

Critics and playgoers loved her, but a more remarkable triumph came to her. She had free access to all social circles. When she acted in England she was the "toast"—that delightful Edwardian word—the toast of London. She was the friend of a duchess and a guest in the homes of the titled. In America, she was a valued addition to dinner parties of the wealthy elite, and a friend of Alice Roosevelt's.

Don't think she attended house parties and great dinners without happening to notice the honor. She loved every title and every million, as her autobiography naïvely attests, and she was aware that no other Broadway star of the decade was accepted by society as she was.

In the summer of 1903, Mrs. Cornelius Vanderbilt, a society leader, gave one of her splendid parties at the family estate in Newport. It was a fête of roses, with thousands of American Beauties in the décor. Guests entered the estate through a specially built archway twenty-five feet wide and eighteen feet high.

Entertainment included a Punch-and-Judy show, Negro dancers, and other acts suggesting an amusement park. The climax of the entertainment was the first act of a Broadway musical, *The Wild Rose*, with its entire cast, starring Marie Cahill, Eddie Foy, and Irene Bentley; full orchestra; and all the first-act scenery transported from the Knickerbocker Theater, closed for that evening, to Newport.

After the show, supper was served to the Vanderbilt guests in the house, while actors and musicians, being only a notch above servants, dined on the same food, but under a tent of their own erected at the end of the midway. Guests eagerly visited this alien and fascinating Bohemia, but the performers knew their place. Of course they did not approach the house.

Next day the party had four and a half columns in the New York papers, while Theodore Roosevelt's political tour had one column.

Lillian Russell, queen of comic opera and one of the most beautiful women of the American stage, figured in a society party of a different sort. In 1900 a group of young New York clubmen caused a delicious furore in the newspapers and in their own social set by giving a men's party at Sherry's, at which all the guests were actresses.

Town Topics, a news sheet that was grandfather to a later generation's gossip columns, reported this "fast and furious ball" with sanctimonious horror: "Among the 'ladies' who graced the occasion were Miss Anna Robinson, Miss Nina Farrington, Miss Lillian Russell. . . ." No word could have denoted the actresses' social position so accurately as those quotation marks around the word ladies.

"The giving of such a ball by young men who are members of New York's leading clubs," continued the report, "shows that the morals of New York society have become . . . weakened," and added that the men would not have dared give this party five years earlier. It was said that Mrs. Ogden Mills, Mrs. Stuyvesant Fish, and other ladies of the smart set boycotted the young men who dared to sponsor the disgraceful ball.

Maxine Elliott and the King

In 1908 Maxine Elliott was an actress of thirty-seven, a great beauty with a sumptuous figure and masses of shining black hair. Whistler had called her "the girl with the midnight eyes." She was a star of the American stage and she was wealthy, but she wanted one thing more: to be a member of the social circle around King Edward VII. She had no intention of meeting the king as Lillian Russell and the other "ladies" had met the young clubmen. She was ambitious to be an eminent society hostess, respectable and correct. With the implacability that characterized the other female winners of this decade, she set out to get what she wanted.

Knowing that she could not break through the close and jealous circle of hostesses who surrounded the king in London, she made other plans. He "took the waters" at Marienbad, and it followed that she too felt the need of restoring her health at the same spa—accompanied, of course, by another lady.

She learned that the king, while in Marienbad, stayed at the Weimar Hotel. And she learned his daily routine: each morning he and his party sauntered from the hotel, through a courtyard, and on to the Kurhaus to drink the beneficial waters.

It would not do for the two ladies to take rooms at the Weimar; that might look as if they were trying to force a meeting with the king. Instead, they booked their suite in the hotel across the courtyard from the Weimar.

At the appropriate hour one morning Miss Elliott strolled from her hotel, book in hand, and seated herself in the sun. She wore a stunning, pure-white costume.

The king's party emerged from the Weimar. As the gentlemen drew near, she slowly lifted those magnificent eyes and her gaze drifted over them. They paused. The king murmured to his friends. The party moved on, but one of the group stepped over to her, hat in hand.

"His Majesty believes you are the Miss Elliott he admired so much in your play. He would be delighted with your presence tonight for dinner. Mrs. Arthur James is giving a dinner in His Majesty's honor. Your invitation will of course be delivered to your hotel."

Was the plan working too smoothly?

That afternoon Maxine dressed her hair, put on her loveliest white dinner dress and white satin slippers, invisible makeup, jewelry, perfume.

She waited.

The invitation did not arrive.

Hidden behind her window curtain, she watched carriages begin to arrive at the Weimar. Time passed. By now the king must have entered Mrs. James's suite. Miss Elliott continued to sit without moving.

At Mrs. James's the new-fashioned cocktails were passed. By and by the hostess asked His Majesty to lead her guests in to dinner.

He lifted his eyebrows. "But Miss Elliott has not arrived."

"The invitation! It must have fallen behind my desk." Dismay, confusion, a flurry of apologies.

From behind her curtain, Miss Elliott saw a footman hurry out of the Weimar, large white envelope in hand. He knocked on her door. She admitted him, read the card unhurriedly, drew on her white wrap, and composedly followed him out of her hotel, across the courtyard to Mrs. James's suite.

No one could have behaved more charmingly than she. Not for a moment did she drop the pretense that she accepted Mrs. James's story of a lost invitation. Perfectly at ease, she was presented to His Majesty. He insisted that dinner must wait while she had her cocktail. As he did not sit down, she could not sit either, and her feet, in those white evening slippers, were killing her. No one else could sit down either, and their feet were killing them. For twenty minutes the party was held on its feet while Miss Elliott chatted graciously with the king.

As Mrs. James's efforts to snub the actress had failed and she now had the king's favor, she could not be excluded from his social group. She had got exactly what she wanted and went on to become a famous hostess of the international set.

Years later Maxine discussed the story of the "lost" invitation with her two young nieces, who hotly declared that they wouldn't have accepted such a humiliation. They would have ripped off the white evening gown; they would have refused to go to that hateful woman's dinner.

Their Aunt Maxine fixed them with a steely eye. "But," she said, "I wanted to be there."

Speaking of those "new-fashioned cocktails," Gertrude Atherton, the California novelist, tells in her autobiography of dining one evening in England with a friend. (*What* friend? We wish she had named this friend!) Mrs. Atherton asked the headwaiter if he knew how to make the new American cocktails. "Certainly, madam," he replied, as if offended. Presently he brought reddish concoctions in liqueur glasses. The two tasted their drinks and hastily put them down. Summoning the headwaiter, they asked him the contents of these remarkable cocktails. "Scotch," he replied loftily, "and raspberry syrup."

Winds of Change

Hundreds of American girls were burning with an ambition as fiery as Maxine Elliott's, but their ambition was to go to college.

"Restless!" scolded their mothers. "Bluestocking!" jeered their brothers. "Who'll want to marry you?" fumed their fathers. Even the family doctor shook his head.

Dr. S. Weir Mitchell filled a page in the sometimes liberal *Ladies' Home Journal* with warnings. "Of one hundred men of eighteen, almost all will be fit to stand the trials of college work," he wrote. "Of one hundred women, far fewer. I often stop women who wish to go to college, thinking them physically unfit. It is very rare that I give a similar verdict to a young man. Girls, do not conclude that the whole mass of you can assume the man's standard as to what you do in the way of mental labor. It will be at your peril! There will be days when to use the mind persistently will be a danger!"

A 1908 article in *Good Housekeeping* sputters with rage against the college woman, "that heavy, incongruous product." The writer slings furious adjectives at her: supercilious, pedantic, dictatorial, hard, brainy, fisty. She is dull in conversation, cold, austere, knows not how to dress, has no charm, no manners, no social grace. College women's children have no manners, "even if they can quote Shakespeare at the age of eight."

Almost as angry is another magazine article by "A Mother" who asks whether colleges give girls the kind of education they need. "Courses of study cover every branch of learning from the language spoken by the Ninevites to the measurement of a gnat's foot. All the little Janes and Pollies come together to learn whatever they may choose, whether it be Sanskrit, the ancient Irish tongues, or the embryology of the verte-brates. These are useful if the girls are to become teachers—if they are to pack the rudiments of a dozen uncomprehended sciences into the empty brains of other Janes and Pollies, or if they propose to study medicine."

Dr. Mitchell refers to the college graduate's "wild craving for what girls call a career.... The result is neglect of duty, ungratified ambitions, discontent; and so what was meant to make life fuller ends in lessening the sum of happiness."

An unsigned editorial in a 1901 *Ladies' Home Journal* comments, "It is only the dogged obstinacy of man that is able to keep [women] out of the Cabinet and out of the White House." Woman, scolds the author, wants to take up "new occupations of art, reform, and money-making [and give up] her own real work as a homemaker, wife, and mother [in that household] which she makes beautiful and sacred for her husband and sons." Not, it seems, for her daughters.

Though marriage was the career that girls were encouraged to pursue, critics of the college girl were angry if she did marry. "All that money spent on schooling, and she threw it away by getting married like any other girl!"

Few of the girls who went to college took jobs afterward. At an eastern women's college in 1907, only one-third of the graduating class expected to support themselves.

Woman's Sacred Shrine: Stuff and Nonsense!

One of the rebels who paved the way to college for many women was Martha Carey Thomas. Even as a young Quaker girl in high button shoes, she was a spirited feminist.

She once wrote in her diary, "My *one* aim and concentrated purpose *shall be* and *is* to show that women *can learn, can reason, can compete* with men in the grand fields of literature and science and conjecture . . . without having all [their] time engrossed by dress and society."

A later entry in the diary tells of a friend of her father's who talked about "the sacred shrine of womanhood," saying that "no matter what splendid talents a woman might have, she couldn't use them better than by being a wife and mother . . . completely forgetting that all women ain't wives and mothers, and they, I suppose, are told to fold their hands and be idle, waiting for an eligible offer. Stuff! Nonsense!"

Carey knew that she could never marry. A wife's first duty was to her husband's wishes, so that one could not be simultaneously a career woman and a good wife, and a career Carey must have. At twenty she fell in love, but she uprooted this unsuitable emotion and threw it away.

She had decided that Cornell was the college she must attend. Social prejudice was against her, of course, but much more dire was the absolute "No" of her father.

He opposed her notion in the first place because at college she would meet all sorts of men, would probably fall in love, and would insist upon marrying some unsuitable person. If she escaped this horror, years of study would make her discontented with marriage and motherhood, and naturally homemaking was the sphere of woman's true happiness. Most terrible of all, in Cornell's free-thinking atmosphere she might lose her religious faith.

Carey's mother had longed for education herself and been denied it, and she was determined that her brilliant eldest daughter should go to college if that was where her talents directed her. She and Carey fought side by side.

Dr. Thomas was driven back from defense to defense. At last he entrenched himself in an impregnable position: he could not afford it. Not four years of college for a daughter! Carey knew that if she had been a son her father would have found the money somehow. She promised to earn her degree in two years. No. He could not afford even two years.

Mrs. Thomas, however, had one weapon which she abhorred and which she had never used before. It violated her sense of dignity, but employ it she must in a cause as important as this one.

"Nothing is left us but tears," she said to Carey. "Reason will not move thy father. We will see whether he can hold out against our weeping. We shall both have to cry day and night, thee as well as I."

And so, separately and together, they wept. Dr. Thomas pleaded with them, he called them unjust, he locked himself in his room, he stayed away from home. Wife and daughter continued in silence to weep whenever he appeared. He surrendered at last. Carey prepared to enter Cornell.

No one believed she could earn a degree in two years, and in fact she did it only by utilizing every minute. She had to cover freshman and sophomore courses while attending junior and senior classes. Often she worked all night. When her room grew too cold to stay in at night, she took her books down to the cellar and sat in front of the furnace. She opened the furnace door so that the embers cast a glow on the pages of her book, bright enough for reading. By grinding effort, she passed all her examinations.

Next Carey found that no university in the United States would confer an advanced degree on a woman, no matter how great her ability. Here was a locked door, and Carey Thomas had to force it open. She managed to go to Europe, and in Zürich she earned a doctorate—*summa cum laude*, an almost unheard-of triumph for man or woman.

All this she felt she achieved not for herself alone, but for women everywhere.

The next breakthrough was her appointment as professor of English and dean at the new Bryn Mawr College, and ten years later she bullied her way to the presidency. The woman who had battled so fiercely for her rights became an autocratic president under whose rule her faculty often fidgeted rebelliously; but generations of undergraduates loved the sight of Miss Thomas, who each morning at exactly 8:45 sailed with her rapid, limping steps (she was a little lame) down the aisle of the chapel, black gown billowing out behind her and mortarboard set at the back of her héad, pointing straight up in the air. She climbed to the platform, opened the Bible on the speaker's desk, and in her beautiful voice read some great passage, most often rolling, majestic stanzas from Isaiah, which she loved.

She closed the book and students listened, enchanted, while she talked briefly in her vivid, enthusiastic style, of a book she was reading, a news item that had caught her interest, or a play she had seen.

One of her good friends was Mary Garrett, who founded the prep school, the Bryn Mawr School for Girls, in Baltimore. While Carey Thomas was president of the college, she and Mary Garrett broke down another door.

Johns Hopkins University opened a hospital and planned to establish a medical school as well, but the trustees could not raise the needed money. Carey Thomas and Mary Garrett saw their chance at a dignified bit of skulduggery. They organized women's committees to raise money, and Mary, who controlled a tidy family fortune, offered additional large sums from her capital. They offered Johns Hopkins a gift totaling $500,000.

But the ladies made two stipulations. First, women were to be accepted as medical students on the same basis as men; and second, all candidates, both male and female, must have a bachelor of arts degree or its equivalent.

The trustees were aghast. They would admit women if they had to, but whoever heard of entrance requirements as high as these? Even in Europe, only a few medical schools had such standards, and in the United States no schools at all.

But the women were adamant. Johns Hopkins was anxious to establish that medical school. Doctors already engaged as teachers were receiving alluring offers from other schools and might be coaxed away. Four of the distinguished professors were Doctors Welch, Halstead, Osler, and Kelly. At last the trustees bowed their heads and accepted both the stipulations and the ladies' money.

"Welch," said Dr. Osler, "we are lucky to get in as professors. I am sure that neither you nor I could ever get in as students."

Seventeen candidates, three of them young women, entered the medical school in its first year, and in the second year there were forty new students, of whom eight were women.

Carey Thomas remained president of Bryn Mawr for twenty-eight years, and then stepped down only because it was her own rule that faculty members must retire at sixty-five.

Straight Road to Fame

Dr. Thomas, and most other outstanding women of this decade, were fortunate in having the devotion and support of one or both parents, who backed their winner with intense pride and loyalty. Ethel Barrymore, for example, had the entire Drew-Barrymore family to encourage her.

Of the spectacular women of the 1900s, however, few had the fanatical backing of Geraldine Farrar, who joined the Metropolitan Opera Company in 1906. Geraldine was born with two gifts: a fine voice and an indomitable mother.

Henrietta Farrar, herself a beauty and a soloist in the Unitarian Church choir of Melrose, Massachusetts, determined that her one child was to be a great singer. She was only eighteen when Geraldine was born, and the adored infant was "consecrated" (Geraldine's word) to fame, to fulfill the mother's thwarted ambitions.

The singer wrote two autobiographies, one published in 1916 and the other in 1938. You might expect this story of relentless ambition to be written in a terse, straightforward style. On the contrary, much of it is in a tone of heavy sentimentality, and reveals an impressive capacity for self-love, written with bland simplicity and a total lack of humor.

She writes of her mother with ardent admiration and of her father with courtesy. The father must have led a subdued life in a family dominated by two women of iron will.

Since his modest income could not finance the expensive training that a future star required, Mrs. Farrar, when her daughter was seventeen, coaxed a loan from a wealthy music patron of Boston. Then off the Farrars went to Europe to prepare for greatness.

Methodical and shrewd, mother and daughter advanced from mediocre teachers to fine teachers; from humble friends to helpful friends; to the great people of society and the opera world; and finally to Geraldine's debut at the Royal Opera in Berlin as Marguerite in *Faust*.

She was a smash hit in Berlin, aided by reports that she was "young, slender, and some said, beautiful." (Quotation is from her own works.)

During her second season at the Royal Opera she achieved the distinction of being presented to the Kaiser.

"A Hofmarschal from the palace presented himself at our apartment and officially 'commanded' my presence at the palace that night. I was notified that I must wear the prescribed Court dress, either lavender or black, with gloves and no jewelry."

Miss Farrar must have been thrilled, but she replied coolly that she never wore either black or lavender because they were unbecoming to her, and that she never wore gloves while she sang.

Shocked by this independence, the Hofmarschal stammered that he did not believe she could be received at the palace unless she conformed, but the young lady was adamant and he went away, much disturbed. Later that day, however, a second message came from the palace: Miss Farrar might wear what she chose, but attend she must.

Miss Farrar writes with superb simplicity: "I wore white."

She and her mother drove to the palace and were received "by various flunkies" and led to the hall where royalty and the diplomatic corps sat after dinner. She sang, she was complimented by the Kaiser, and presented to the Kaiserin.

"That meeting," she reports, "was the forerunner of many pleasant social gatherings at the palace, when Mother and I were honored guests."

After that bracing exercise in power comes the story of a little romance between her and the shy, charming crown prince. Miss Farrar writes of it with a bit of a simper, but after all, how many girls from Melrose, Massachusetts, have the opportunity to create tempests in the teapots of genuine European royalty? The romantic interlude caused a jealous stir in German society and much attention in the press.

She sang grand opera in Monte Carlo, Warsaw, Paris, and Stockholm, where, she tells us, King Oscar was among her admirers. Then—bull's-eye!—she was invited to sing at the Metropolitan in New York. This had been the target all along.

Did they rush to accept? Indeed no. Mother and daughter skirmished for months before achieving exactly the contract they wanted. After signing, back they came to New York, where Miss Farrar starred for sixteen years, until she retired, by her own choice, in 1922.

Surprisingly, she shows a certain sense of fun in an anecdote about a performance in Magdeburg, near Berlin, in the pre-Met days. Geraldine liked to invent bits of stage business (today called "hamming it up") and when she sang Violetta in *Traviata*, she had arranged to snatch a wine glass from Alfredo's hand, dash it to the floor, and then engage with the tenor in "a little intimate by-play." The glass smashed appropriately, but even before she and Alfredo could fly into each other's arms, a uniformed attendant walked stolidly onstage, whisk broom and dustpan in hand, looked at her darkly, bent down and swept up the shattered glassware, then stalked offstage while actors and audience stared in paralyzed silence.

Next day the American singer received a note from the management: "Glass Breakage—25 pfennigs."

In contrast to the success of Miss Farrar is the failure of Evelyn Nesbit, most notorious woman of the decade. She was an exquisitely beautiful showgirl married to the unbalanced and sadistic Harry K. Thaw. Driven berserk by jealousy, he dramatically murdered Stanford White, the gifted architect who had designed Madison Square Garden. Evelyn had formerly been mistress to both these wealthy men, turn and turn about, and finally, since White already had a wife, had married Thaw.

In the lurid murder trial, sensation of the 1900s, it seemed to be Evelyn and her scandalous life style that were on trial, as well as Thaw. He was at last adjudged not guilty by reason of insanity, and committed to a hospital for the criminally insane.

For Evelyn Nesbit, the following years were sordid ones. There were ugly money squabbles with the Thaw family, sorry love affairs, suicide attempts, and cabaret acts in drearier and drearier night spots. She died at eighty-two, poor and forgotten. In a tone that was, perhaps, maudlin, Evelyn said, "Stanny White was killed, but my fate was worse. I lived."

Imperious and single-minded, successful women of the decade had goals and drove straight toward them. Poor Evelyn flapped from one lover to the other, weakly trying to take advantage of the breezes of chance. And she had no family to back her up.

True Women

A true woman of the period spent her life in approved occupations for women: child rearing, housekeeping, and church work. Books and magazine articles used this term regularly—"a true woman." Since it was never defined, it follows that everyone knew what a true woman was.

Upon the death of papa and mama, if her hand had never been asked in marriage, this true woman retired to the home of sister or niece and became an unpaid drudge, helping to run another's household and helping to rear another's children. Presumably, the head of the house bent uncomplainingly under the burden of an added member of the household.

But young women of the 1900s began to scandalize their elders by choosing to escape the imprisonment of home, and going out to earn their living. Their choice of jobs was limited. A girl might become a schoolteacher; that was respectable. Or she could be a seamstress, a department store clerk, or a typewriter. (The instrument with which she worked was a typewriting machine; she was the typewriter.)

Of course no married woman of the middle or upper class went out to work. What a disgrace to her husband!

A widow could be a boardinghouse keeper without losing her reputation. There was nursing, too, for the single or widowed, but of course no *lady* went into nursing. That contact with the human body—not quite nice. But the work had to be done, and if the emancipated girl was poor enough and strong enough, society permitted her to try it.

The pay was $10 to $20 a month, and she didn't even have to pay board and room out of that. She would probably work twelve hours a day with one afternoon a week to spend all to herself. Besides giving medicines, helping in surgery, and giving baths, a nurse laundered bedding, cooked meals, and scrubbed floors.

A new profession for the emancipated woman was journalism. Edward Bok, however, distinguished editor of the *Ladies' Home Journal*, warned against it. He sent questionnaires to fifty newspaper-women and to fifty newspapermen asking their opinion. Of the women who replied, four said, Yes, they would permit their daughters, if they had any, to enter the newspaper world. The other women and all of the men who replied sent a flat No.

"A girl in the rough newspaper world loses her womanliness" is the burden of the negative replies. Also, "It dissipates her illusions." No one explains why illusions are desirable. "Unwholesome ... the work hardens her ... a young woman cannot remain sweet and modest ... the constant nervous strain will cause her to break down."

At that time, it was known that women—not women of the lower classes, of course, but the others—all possessed delicate nervous systems, easily shattered.

On the whole, Mr. Bok prefers that ladies busy themselves with china painting and trimming hankies with handmade lace. Or they might follow the instructions in one of the *Journal* articles and have "A Winter Evening's Fun With Egg-Shells"—making toy boats and things. Hilarious.

So strong was the prejudice against women's competing with men that many a girl must have scurried down the orange-blossom path to escape ridicule, for "the old maid" was a standard figure of fun. Everyone knew that *no* woman remained single from *choice*.

Under the code of sexual secrecy, many a woman entered wedlock with only the foggiest idea, or no idea at all, of what would be expected of her in bed. The conventional attitude toward sex was that a woman must stoically endure her mate's carnal appetites only for procreation and to keep him from straying into alien boudoirs.

Prejudice against women's working applied only to the middle and upper classes. Poor women worked as they have always worked, from the grim necessity to keep food in the kettle and shoes on the children's feet. In America, this group was composed largely of immigrant women and black women. They worked chiefly at farm and household drudgery or in factories, and the poor were so numerous that, throughout the whole population, one woman in five was employed.

Princess Alice

Neighbors watched each other narrowly and condemned any lapse from strict propriety. At the same time, they watched delightedly as the darling of the decade flouted the rules. Perhaps this was a way of escaping the tight corseting of their real lives, by identifying, in the safety of fantasy, with a gay, free spirit.

The nation's darling was Alice Roosevelt, oldest child of the president and "a chip off the old block"—a description that TR loved. She had his self-confidence, his vitality, his joy in life.

Alice could never resist a prank. At the time of her father's inauguration in 1905, the inaugural committee put placards on houses of prominent citizens and on public buildings to identify them for out-of-town visitors. Alice and a friend, Bertie Goelet, hung a sign on the house of Nicholas Longworth, the dignified congressman from Ohio. With fine simplicity the sign read, "I live here. Nicholas Longworth."

Indoors, Alice would maneuver Longworth to stand in the window directly over the sign while sightseeing buses paused, the occupants looked and read, then drove on, whooping with laughter.

Of course Alice rebelled against parental authority—but gaily. She smoked cigarettes at a time when few ladies did. When her father commanded her never to smoke under his roof, she went to the rooftop or knelt by the fireplace and sent the smoke up the chimney.

A color was named for her, and a popular song composed to go with it: "In My Sweet Little Alice-Blue Gown." Imagination boggles at relating high-spirited Alice to a sweet blue gown, but no matter, the tune caught on. A faster, more frolicsome melody followed: "Alice, Where Art Thou Going?" Everyone whistled and sang it. Whenever a band leader recognized the president's daughter in a crowd of lively young people, the music swung at once into the zestful "Where Art Thou Going?" With beautiful tact, Alice developed a technique of looking surprised, then amused, then pleased, every time it was played for her.

On a junket to Southeast Asia she learned to dance the hula—not the expurgated version considered proper for Westerners to see, but the sexy native dance.

During the same trip, she once jumped into the ship's swimming pool fully dressed and dared a fellow passenger to kick off his shoes and jump in too. (He did.) Afterward she remarked that there wasn't much difference between swimming in a sleeved and high-necked bathing dress and swimming in a linen skirt and waist.

Owen Wister, author of *The Virginian,* said testily to TR, "Can't you control your daughter?" And the president replied in the words that have been quoted hundreds of times, "I can do one of two things. I can be president or I can control Alice. I cannot possibly do both."

One winter day she was aboard a revenue cutter on her way down the bay to greet a friend arriving from Europe on the liner *Kaiser Wilhelm Der Grosse.* When the cutter nosed alongside, officers on the ocean vessel prepared to lower the gangway to the cutter for her. But Alice cupped her white-gloved hands and shouted up, "The ladder's all right! Never mind anything else!"

Sailors sent the twenty-five-foot Jacob's ladder down the ice-sheeted sides of the ship, and over her friends' protests Alice grasped the ladder and climbed nimbly up, up, up. When officers lifted her over the rail to the deck, the crowd of passengers cheered her lustily.

Her White House wedding in February, 1906, was the social event of the year. The bride wore white satin trimmed with lace that had been on her mother's wedding dress. Her gown had a long train of white and silver brocade.

After the ceremony she was photographed with husband and father.

There stands the bridegroom, Nicholas Longworth, formal in frock coat, bald, mustached, strictly serious, clasping his gloves in one hand. There is the bride's father, not formal at all. TR's head is bent to one side, his frock coat hangs loose, one arm is bent so that the fist seems to be resting on his hip.

Between them stands the bride, her head high under its pompadour; turned-back veil, tiny waist, those yards of heavy train. But her face . . . here is the Princess Alice paradox. Her face is closed, aloof, almost stern.

Among her friends, the girl was vivacious, bold, irreverent, witty. But she had the patrician's feeling that private emotions are never revealed to strangers. Among friends she might dance the wicked hootchie-kootchie or make fun of a pompous senator, and then stories of her stunts leaked to the press. But she faced a camera four-square, challenging. She never courted the public.

New Americans

While the very wealthy dressed, dined, and played elegantly, while professional people and wage earners worked in the cheerful expectancy of improving their lot in this best of all possible lands, life was grim indeed for the newcomers pouring across Ellis Island in their millions.

They filled the slums of New York, Philadelphia, Boston, Chicago, and the factory towns of Ohio and New England faster than the nation could absorb them into its economy.

In places such as New York's Lower East Side, from four to a dozen people slept in a single tenement room. They arranged dining-room chairs in rows to sleep upon; they slept four to a sofa, with rocking chairs aligned to support their feet. For warmth, windows were puttied shut, so that the air reeked with smells of food and sweat. Often, toilet facilities for the whole tenement were in the back yard, and the only water to be had came from a pump at a curb in front of the building.

Native-born Americans tended to look with contempt and dislike upon immigrants. These desperate outsiders accepted the lowest wages and the vilest working conditions to earn the few dollars needed to keep their families from starvation. They were blamed, therefore, for depressing the wage scale.

Second, the hunkies, wops, kikes, dagoes, and polacks yattered to each other in crazy languages that no American could, or wanted to understand. And they looked so foreign! Women wore heavy, flat-heeled boots. Instead of hats, they wore shabby scarves over their heads. Instead of wearing winter coats, they hugged dirty shawls around themselves. They looked stolidly upon the world. They never smiled. They stank.

Scandinavian women, even of the lowest class, were held in esteem by their countrymen. Slavic women, at the other end of the scale, were hardly more than chattels. In the eyes of all European peasants, American women enjoyed astonishing freedom and an incredibly high place in society.

For an immigrant woman of any background, life in America was hard. It wasn't the wretched housing or the hunger or the daily labor. These she had known in the Old Country. It was the mental disorganization.

She longed for her relatives—her old mother, her sisters, her cousins. She didn't know how to trade in American stores. She was frightened by the strange languages shouted by people on the streets. She needed a few square yards of dirt in which to grow her own cabbages and bring up a pig. She was adrift without religion, for probably her husband and the children threw off the Old World grip of priest or rabbi. Where was the children's respect for the elders? Her children laughed at her. They refused to obey. Her realities were swept away and she lost the path in a cruel world.

Never in history has there been a sadder or wider generation gap than the one between Old World women and their American children.

"... Keep On Keeping On"

In Illinois a shy and gentle young woman named Jane Addams was concerned about the misery of slum dwellers, and determined that her life's work must be to fight poverty. She was born into an intellectual family, was college-educated, and she had a little money; just enough, inherited from her beloved father, to be free from the need to earn her living.

A school friend of hers, Ellen Gates Starr, was fired with the same zeal to spend her life serving mankind; and the two girls, after a long search, found a once-gracious old mansion falling into ruins in the midst of Chicago's worst slums on South Halstead Street. Its original owner's name was Hull.

They couldn't afford to buy the house, but they rented the second story and the drawing room on the main floor. They scrubbed and scraped and painted until the rooms they would·occupy were restored to their original beauty and dignity.

It was the custom for families to sit outdoors on summer evenings, on porches or front steps, to greet friends who strolled past. On the first Sunday evening after moving in their furniture, Jane and Ellen and Mary Keyser, their housekeeper, sat on the wide porch of Hull House, viewing the world of Halstead Street as it slowly passed. They knew that the whole neighborhood was afire with curiosity about these strange ladies, who could surely afford to live wherever they liked, but who chose to live in the slums.

Many people strolled past, stealing glances at the three on the porch, but they were too bashful to stop. Then a cluster of school-age boys and girls paused at the gate, whispering and nudging each other. They saw the smiles of welcome on the ladies' faces. Pressed together, giggling, stumbling against each other, the children edged toward the porch.

Hull House had its first visitors.

Jane had a gift for putting people at ease and coaxing them to talk. Soon all the children were chattering away happily, telling her where they lived, what their school was like, even telling their heroic dreams of their future.

In the days that followed, adults called at Hull House. Some were hostile. ("What are these people after?") Some were eager and friendly. ("They want to know about us. All right, we'll tell them.")

To each of them Jane opened the front door herself and cordially invited each in for a cup of tea. They sat stiff and shy in the strange, beautiful drawing room, but soon they'd be telling her all about themselves and their work and their anxieties.

Jane and Ellen established a day nursery to care for little children who wandered in, with nowhere to go but the streets while their mothers were at work. Then a volunteer turned up who offered to set up a kindergarten as well. Other people came to Hull House and proposed the teaching of various subjects.

Soon Jane Addams was surrounded by a brilliant circle of workers. It was as if she stood quietly and attracted them as a magnet attracts. No matter how many teachers and workers were at Hull House, its unschooled neighbors always referred to it, with faultless instinct, as "the place where Miss Addams lives."

What did all these workers accomplish? They organized the first public playground in Chicago. They helped establish a women's Trade Union League, a pioneer effort at organizing women to improve working conditions.

They taught Americanization to immigrants, taught American cooking to young wives, gathered little girls into sewing classes, and held Saturday-night dances at the settlement house for young people who had nowhere to go except the saloon.

They forced Chicago authorities to see that only clean milk was sold; in consequence fewer babies died during hot weather. They vigorously fought the sale of cocaine in the neighborhood. They fought against the corrupt political machine of their ward—and lost.

Francis Hackett, later the biographer of Henry VIII and others, lived at Hull House when he was a young newcomer from Ireland. He wrote, "Hull House was not an institution over which Miss Addams presided; it was Miss Addams around whom an institution insisted on clustering. . . .

"I have been talking to her when, in answer to a ring at the door, she would let in a 'bum' who wanted a cup of coffee. And she herself would lead him into the Coffee House, and, with her curious air of earnest pleading politeness, would say, 'Mary, *would* you give this man a cup of coffee?' To the hobo and to Miss Addams, nothing seemed more natural, but these incidents of humanity never meant that Hull House interposed mere charity between itself and the rough-and-tumble world. Hull House lived in a bracing, not a mawkish atmosphere. It met the world vigorously."

It was not a pretty world, the South Halstead Street area, but Miss Addams, trim and composed, walked the cobblestone streets, which were crowded with vendors' carts and strewn with decaying garbage. In summer, the smell of humanity poured out of every door and window. But her duty was to know the home life and the working life of the people who came to Hull House for her help.

She had plenty of enemies, and not only among corrupt local politicians. The ruling class spoke of slum reformers as "unsettlement workers." Many who approved of Miss Addams's "nice charity work" were enraged when she encouraged strikers or tried to persuade employers to install safety devices in factories, because such acts were meddling in the world of profits. Mrs. Potter Palmer, among others, withdrew her financial support.

Such hard heartedness among the affluent hurt and discouraged

Miss Addams, but, outwardly serene and optimistic, she only reminded herself of the Hull House joke: "Sometimes there is nothing to do but to keep on keeping on."

There were, at the same time, women as dedicated to the arts as Jane Addams was dedicated to helping humanity. One of these was Isadora Duncan.

The Two Faces of Isadora Duncan

As a dancer, Isadora was a genius, passionately in earnest. In private life she was an unruly, irresponsible child.

The creative, disciplined Isadora danced Chopin and Wagner and Gluck and Schubert, and audiences wept. Her free and flowing motions were exquisite. The dramas that her body related stirred the soul. She performed the miracle of transforming music into a flow of movement.

She never danced *to* Chopin or Beethoven or the others. She *danced the music,* the first artist to do so. She was a revolutionary in art.

At the same time, the flamboyant, tempestuous, opinionated Isadora broke engagements to hide in an unfurnished studio with her current lover. She trailed about barefoot, clad in a gauzy tunic in the fashion of ancient Greece—this in an era when ladies armored themselves from chin to ankle in layers of thick clothing.

She insulted wealthy audiences from the stage and at the same time demanded money to support her art projects. "Give me the workers!" she stormed at them. "Give me the artist, the poor, they understand! I am not an amusement for the rich! Give me my friends, the artists. For them I created and danced 'The Resurrection.' "

After the Russian revolution, she danced "Ave Maria" in godless Russia—but, surprisingly, the Bolsheviks applauded her wildly—and in a red tunic she danced "The Revolution" and the call to arms of the oppressed at the correct and stately Metropolitan Opera House. In her outspoken autobiography, *My Life,* she remarks with uncharacteristic moderation that the latter "roused some storm in the audience."

The Duncan family traveled about together whenever they could: Isadora, her two brothers, her sister Elizabeth, and their naïve, happy-go-lucky mother. All devoted themselves to Isadora's career because they knew she was the family genius. She told them so. She told everyone.

When the family was in funds, they dined and wined elegantly and rode in carriages. Out of funds, they spent hours in museums and art galleries to keep warm. One cold dawn in London when the family had spent the night on park benches, Isadora decided that they must have shelter and rest. She commanded the others to follow her and say not a word. She led them into one of the city's fine hotels. (This story comes from her autobiography and the reader must use his own judgment about how much salt to use.)

Imperiously, Isadora wakened the night porter and told him that they had just arrived on the night train and that their luggage would come on from Liverpool, but that they would take rooms without waiting for it. Also, they wanted breakfast sent up to them at once.

All that day they slept in luxurious beds. Now and then Isadora telephoned the desk to complain that their luggage had not yet arrived. That evening they had to stay in their rooms, explaining huffily over the phone that they could not possibly emerge without a change of clothes.

At dawn next morning, deciding that the ruse was used up, they left the hotel modestly, without waking the night porter, and feeling "greatly refreshed and ready once more to face the world."

Years later, when Isadora was a world-famous dancer who had earned and frittered away thousands of dollars, her attitude toward money had not changed a bit. She and a woman friend once entered a Montmartre restaurant, where the patrons applauded the artist as soon as they recognized her.

Smiling, bowing, and waving her hand, she sallied to her table, then called in her sweet, childlike voice, "I am sure you all know how much I love champagne and possibly you are happy to see me only because you suspect that I might offer you some as well as drinking it myself. My friends, you are right! We must drink to France!"

With an extravagant gesture she signaled to the headwaiter to serve champagne to all, and as they cheered, she sat down and whispered to her companion, "Darling, have you got enough money?" Of course she had none herself.

She showered her friends with money (when she had it), with time, care, and love. Freely, she gave the most generous gift of all: unstinted admiration to rival artists. Hatred of ballet was the most frenzied hate of her life. Yet, when she toured Russia in 1905, being then at the top of her fame, and the spectacular ballerina Kschinsky called upon her and invited her to attend a gala performance at the opera that night, she accepted the invitation graciously. The Russian Ballet performed and Isadora wept at the beauty of Kschinsky's performance. She wrote that the ballerina "flitted across the stage more like a bird or butterfly than a human being."

Isadora's sex life shocked the conventional. A wanton, people called her, but this was unfair. She never skipped lightly from man to man. Each affair lasted months, sometimes years, and while it lasted she adored her lover passionately, she was delirious with joy in his presence, their relationship was the meeting of flame with flame; she was the helpless tool of ecstasy.

In one of her periods of frenzied love and broken theatrical engagements, her patient manager said of her and her lover, "At least I always know where to find them. They will be in bed."

Marriage she called an absurd and enslaving institution. She disdained the conventional attitude toward parenthood, too, which the rule books said belonged only to the married. Rubbish! said Isadora. She gave birth to two babies, Deirdre and Patrick, who had different fathers, each of whom she had worshiped dizzily in his turn, and she adored both children extravagantly.

By 1910 Isadora's life had risen to its height. She had success, adulation, love, children, and riches. Her current lover, Paris Singer, was wealthy. Three years later all that mattered to her came to an end in one terrible minute. Her children drowned.

Little Deirdre and Patrick were out driving with their nurse when the car stalled. At this point no fence or wall shielded the road from the River Seine. The chauffeur got out of the car to crank the engine, but left it in gear. The engine turned over, the wheels moved, the car rolled swiftly into the water and out of sight.

Onlookers dived at once into the river, but by the time they raised the car, it was too late. Children and nurse, all dead. Isadora was wild with grief.

The remaining fourteen years of her life make a sad story. She ate and drank too much. She grew fat. She aged. Yet audiences still wept at the heartbreaking beauty of her "Marche Slav" and "The Redemption." Who can regret that before she was fifty another auto accident took her life, even more quickly than the blunder beside the Seine took the lives of her darlings? She died in the very act of making one of her dramatic gestures. She flung a long, red scarf around her neck as she stepped into the passenger seat of a touring car. The driver started the car. One end of the scarf whipped around the right rear wheel. Isadora's head snapped back. Her neck was broken.

The Elusive, the Magical . . .

From its first New York performance in 1905, Broadway took *Peter Pan* straight to its tough, sentimental heart, along with its incomparable star, Maude Adams. This actress touched an audience with magic. That delicate gaiety of hers, the sweetness of her fleeting smile, her gentleness and grace reached across the footlights to give an aching sense of beauty almost—but never quite—caught in one's fingers.

She was a star before she was twenty-five, and played both modern roles and Shakespeare. But her charm and the Barrie whimsicality blended like moonlight and roses, so that Maude Adams and Barrie's *What Every Woman Knows* and *The Little Minister* were Broadway delights even before *Peter Pan.*

The Maude Adams of private life was as elusive as Peter. She never appeared in restaurants or at balls or in theater boxes. Offstage she was so shy that when strangers walked up to her on the street and spoke to her, she was tortured by embarrassment.

When her company was on tour, traveling of course by train, she often spent the whole day in her berth reading, with the green curtains closed around her. In her own house she surrounded herself with beautiful rugs, pictures, and china, spent her free time reading and studying—and everyone else in the household maintained a deep silence for her.

But onstage this gentle creature was as aggressive as the other winners. She rehearsed like a woman of iron to achieve the exact tone of voice, the precise flutter of the fingers and turn of the elegant little head that would express the mood of a scene, and she expected her company to work as tirelessly as she did.

She shied away from reporters, feeling that they infringed on her privacy. But as a young actress she granted an interview in which she said, "I haven't very decided opinions on the great questions of the day, but there's one thing I don't believe in, and that is woman's rights. I think the men have taken pretty good care of us all these years, and I don't see what is the matter with letting them keep it up. Any woman halfway clever can make the men do just as she wants to have them, and at the same time keep them thinking they are having their own way— and what more would she have?"

In this one speech, Miss Adams touched on two subjects that riled the feminists. Making a man do just what she chose was called by a womanly woman "winding him around your little finger," and filled her with glee. It was an accomplishment like tatting or making hairpin lace. A feminist, on the other hand, looked with disdain on this skill and called it an act of slave mentality; the sly, secret approach forced upon the inferior being. Why, stormed the feminist, can't man and woman face each other as equals? This made the "true woman" laugh. Who wanted equality?

The other subject touched upon so lightly by Miss Adams was the claim that "the men have taken pretty good care of us all these years." Feminists pointed out angrily that men not only closed the voting booth against women, and kept them out of the jury box, they also kept women out of the professions, except for a few stalwarts who forced their way, and once in the profession, they had to combat prejudice and ridicule for the rest of their working lives.

In many states women could not own property, had no legal jurisdiction over their children, and even had no right to the money they earned; a married woman's earnings belonged to her husband.

Law was strongly backed up by custom. Some cities had statutes prohibiting women's smoking in public, and where it was not illegal, restaurants sometimes ruled against it. Some hotels and restaurants closed their doors to women who were not escorted by men. People "talked" if young girls strolled together on the streets, especially in the evening. Why weren't they at home where they belonged?

Rules were not enforced with equal rigidity everywhere. Manners were stiff in the East and they relaxed somewhat on their way West. Also, girls had more freedom in cities than in small towns.

As for sexual morals, it was the massive middle class with its mania for respectability that observed the proprieties most fiercely. Slum dwellers sleeping six or a dozen to a room might literally shut their eyes in weariness to the goings-on in the next bed. At the other end of the scale, the very wealthy, with leisure to entertain themselves, played elegantly at amours, and the most admired lady might be the one with the most lovers of high degree *provided she kept herself free of scandal.*

But, between those two extremes, let the middle-class girl beware! Parents, neighbors, schoolfellows, all watched her (and each other) with piercing gaze; and instant disgrace crashed upon her head if she was caught breaking the sexual code. If she had an illegitimate baby, she never lived down the disgrace. Former friends had to turn their heads away in passing her house, lest they be embarrassed by seeing the sinner face to face, and have to stare at her without speaking.

Divorce was becoming more and more common, but was still difficult for a wife to obtain. A woman who sued for divorce had only a few grounds on which to base her suit; she had to possess money of her own to pursue the case, and if she won it, she had to have the hardihood to face possible disgrace. Many women endured wretched marriages rather than pay this awful price.

Martha Carey Thomas's Quaker parents once disagreed on the matter of a divorced woman. The woman was a dear friend of Carey's mother, who pointed out, pleadingly, that her friend had been compelled to sue for divorce because the husband's behavior had been very wrong, and that the woman was entirely free of blame. Dr. Thomas, the gentlest of men as a rule, leaned forward in his armchair and said sternly, "Understand this, Mary. I will not permit any divorced woman whatever to enter the doors of my house. I do not care what her husband may have done. How can thee know she was not to blame in the first place? Women often drive their husbands into temptation."

Nevertheless, the divorce rate was rising. The blame for its rise was variously laid upon sinfully increasing wealth, the move from farm life to urbanism, and turmoil over women's rights. After Sigmund Freud's visit to America in 1909, when all those shocking new ideas about sex were spread around, many people blamed psychoanalysis.

Whatever the cause, there was widespread anxiety that the nation was plunging into a moral abyss. The divorce rate presaged the destruction of pure family life. Young people no longer respected their elders and women were becoming bold as brass!

Ladies of Fiction

In the 1900s, nonfiction was still being written in a scholarly or a preachy style and had limited appeal; but both men and women were busy readers of fiction.

Graustark, by George Barr McCutcheon, was written in the late 1890s, but it was popular even beyond World War I. The story is constructed according to the best of formulas: glamorous royalty; an imaginary country; wicked intrigue and hair-raising danger; true-blue heroes who act only from the highest motives, and villains who act only from the vilest ones; and undying love.

Princess Yetive is Graustark's "girlish ruler," as the author likes to call her; and she typifies all that is truest and finest in woman. She is gentle and tender-hearted; stately but gracious; not brilliant (affairs of state weigh heavily upon her little head) but loaded with womanly intuition; sharp as a tack in drawing-room repartee; but of course she never says anything the least bit crude; and she is a real stunner for looks.

Let the little woman of 1901 match that if she can!

The girlish ruler is loved by a tall American named Lorry Grenfall, and one night on a balcony he sees her thus:

She was walking slowly toward the balustrade, not aware of his presence. There was no covering for the dark hair, no wrap about the white shoulders. She wore an exquisite gown of white, shimmering with the reflections from the moon that scaled the mountain top. She stood at the balustrade, her hands clasping a bouquet of red roses, her chin lifted, her eyes gazing toward the mountain's crest, the prettiest picture he had ever seen. The strange dizziness of love overpowered him . . . .

How long he revelled in the glory of the picture he knew not, for it was as if he looked from a dream. At last he saw her look down upon the roses, lift them slowly and drop them over the rail. [They were the gift of a vile prince who was trying to blackmail the girlish ruler into marriage to save her country from financial ruin.] [Lorry] advanced to her side, his hat in one hand, his stick . . . trembling in the other.

"I did not know you were here," she exclaimed in half-frightened amazement. "I left my ladies inside."

"And I am richer because of your ignorance," he said softly. "I have seen a picture that shall never leave my memory—never! Its beauty enthralled, enraptured. Then I saw the drama of the roses. Ah, your highness, the crown is not always a mask!"

This airy style is the charm of the novel. At one point the tall American exclaims, "Unhand me, Baron Dangloss! This is an outrage!" Of course, the baron is only trying to save the hero's life.

Later, when Lorry is made a prisoner in a monastery to protect him from the vengeance of the vile prince, he asks this same baron one night where Yetive is. Dangloss replies tartly, "Where all good women should be at nine o'clock—in bed."

When Lorry and a Graustarkian friend escape from the monastery on a moonlit night, the friend says, "I am sorely afraid, rash sir, that we cannot reach the castle unseen."

They do, however, and make their secret way to the apartment of the princess, only to have a second prince, who is also trying to force the girlish ruler into a loveless marriage, break in upon them and make coarse insinuations about the purpose of the tall American's presence.

The Princess Yetive's eyes "grew wide with horror, her figure straightened imperiously, and the white in her cheeks gave way to the red of insulted virtue."

The author spins a gratifyingly complicated tale, and all ends well. The whole book is a jolly good story. Our girlish ruler, however, helps us not to comprehend the qualities of real women of the time, for she is but a figment of romance and printer's ink. But she nicely reveals the fashionable pattern of womanhood, sheltered and reverenced.

The New Woman

Another novel whose appeal lasted through the decade and beyond was *Soldiers of Fortune* by Richard Harding Davis. It glorifies American engineers, who were favorite heroes of fiction until World War I. Setting for the story is a mythical South American country, and action revolves around a revolution, a popular gimmick in turn-of-the-century fiction. The revolution is put down tidily by our hero and his set. The plot has the same romance-and-adventure base as the other one, but it is out of the bread-and-milk class.

The heroine is wealthy and conventional Miss Langham, personification of the Gibson Girl. This lovely pen-and-ink girl, created by Charles Dana Gibson, was as well known across America and as lavishly admired and imitated as the live Alice Roosevelt or Ethel Barrymore. Charles Dana Gibson illustrated *Soldiers of Fortune*. He shows Miss Langham, and the author writes of her, as majestic in posture, splendidly broad of shoulders and chest, small head arrogantly high, no humor on the haughty features.

At first the reader is in sympathy with this lady, but wait! The author knows a trick or two. He switches heroines, and by the end of the story we and Mr. Clay, the tall engineer, are weary of Miss Langham and the artificialities of her society standards, and we are in love with her younger sister, Miss Hope.

As Miss Langham typifies self-control and austerity, underlaid with feminine meekness, Hope typifies the "new woman." She shakes hands vigorously with men, she talks to them about their work, she laughs out loud when things are funny. Yes, this book comes close to putting real men and women on the printed page.

At one time, when a carriage is stuck fast in the mud, Hope jumps out, splashes uphill, and while the men heave on the wheels, she helps to dislodge the vehicle by coaxing and tugging at the horses' bridles, careless of mud on her shoes and frock. Of course her sister remains correctly inside the carriage.

When the revolution explodes, the new woman throws herself into the action. In the crucial scene Hope is driving a carriage, and three of our tall friends are helplessly exposed on a moonlit beach, while the ruthless enemy, well armed, hides in a fringe of forest.

They all saw her distinctly now. She was on the driver's box and alone, leaning forward and lashing the horses' backs with the whip and reins, and bending over to avoid the bullets that passed above her head. As she came down upon them, she stood up, her woman's figure outlined clearly in the riding habit she still wore.

"Jump in when I turn," she cried.... She bent forward again and pulled the horses to the right, and as they obeyed her, plunging and tugging at their bits, as though they knew the danger they were in, the men threw themselves at the carriage.

Clay, gent that he is, leaps to the box, drops down beside Hope, and, reaching his arms around her, takes the reins in one hand, and with the other he forces her down to her knees upon the footboard so that, as she kneels, his body protects her from bullets. But the author, modern though he be, can't quite shake off the nineteenth century, and "something in her attitude at his feet held Clay in a spell."

Well, the girls can't get up off their knees all in one generation.

Back to Real Life

It took the full time of two people to operate a sizable house—say, seven rooms. Average family income during the 1900s was from $500 to $600 a year, but affluent families whose wage earner brought in as much as $1,500 a year hired a maid, if one could be had. Pay was from $3 to $4 a week for a full-time helper. "The servant problem" was a topic of endless discussion wherever women gathered: the difficulties of training one, her slovenliness, her ingratitude. The employer, for some reason, always expected gratitude.

It was only in the South or among the wealthy that she was called "a servant." The word was embarrassingly class-conscious. It was un-

American. The usual term was "the help," or, regardless of age, "the girl."

Young women were reluctant to enter domestic service. They preferred factory work, not only because it paid as well or better, but because it had more status. Wincing, they pointed out that hired girls were the constant butt of cartoons and rude jokes. Also, what chance had they of meeting men and marrying, especially if they "lived in"? In that case, they spent bleak evenings in the solitude of the smallest, coldest bedroom in the house, being not quite good enough to join the family downstairs, but kept by propriety from leaving the shelter of the house when their long day's work was finished.

The cult of delicacy was widely practiced by ladies. Letters to the editor in magazines and newspapers are full of such comments as "I have never been strong," "my health is delicate," "I am nervous and frail. . . ."

Bright-faced college girls might stride around in their turtleneck sweaters and long, swinging skirts, but a genteel lady prided herself on being fragile; and she had a theory about the servant problem: the best "girl," she said, was fresh from the Old Country. Such a girl would be muscular and tough. But the second-generation American would be as nervous and frail as her mistress.

Somebody in the house had to have stamina. Preparing three big, solid meals a day for a family was no rest cure. Chickens had to be cut up, sometimes killed and defeathered at home as well. Peas, beans, beets, spinach, and other vegetables in season had to be prepared by hand, though a few foods in tin cans were now available. Many women still baked their own bread, made jelly, and canned fruit and vegetables.

Laundry was a heavy, all-day job with water heated in great kettles on the stove or over a back-yard fire, and garments were scrubbed on a board. Washing was hung to dry on a clothesline in the back yard in sunny weather, or hung in cellar or kitchen in bad weather. If out-of-doors, sheets were pinned on lines nearest the sidewalk or alley, to screen private garments from the eyes of passersby. Some ladies hung underwear to dry modestly concealed inside the pillowcases.

Then the ironing: that occupied a whole day every week. A *Good Housekeeping* article of April, 1907, comments: "That woman who will not give to the care of her 'fine linen' as anxious thought as she gives to its purchase is not a true lady in the best sense of the word. . . . A wonderful American house-mistress who never allows anyone but herself to iron her fine linens uses on her tablecloth and napkins . . . so cool an iron that it requires at least an hour to press smooth and glossy a medium-sized cloth."

No wonder oilcloth table covers were in popular use.

Most onerous of all was the annual spring housecleaning. The invaluable *Good Housekeeping* tells us how to do it. You prepare by laying in a supply of food, because those three meals a day go on inexorably. Bake a good big ham, two roasting chickens, a loaf cake (store it in an air-tight tin), have some soup stock and a big jar of applesauce.

Now get plenty of laundry soap (dry it carefully ahead of time), a quart of ammonia, a quart of turpentine, two cans of floor wax, a bottle of furniture polish, scouring soap, plenty of chlorides; gather up lots of old heavy flannel rags.

Empty all the closets. (Of course you turned out all the trunks and bureau drawers weeks ago—didn't you?) Hang the winter garments outdoors and brush them. Take down the beds. Beat mattresses and pillows out in the sweet spring air. Carry out all the rugs and beat them, too. Wipe all the walls, oil the floors, dust the books, wash all the dishes, launder the ruffled curtains, wash the blankets. . . .

When finished, rest for two days, except for cooking those three meals a day, and rejoice that fall housecleaning is six months away.

Could the well-advertised frailty of ladies have been a pose?

The new century had its new fashions in houses. Architectural lines became stark. Windows were larger. Inside and out there was a craze for plainness, in reaction against Victorian over-ornamentation. No gingerbread around the front porch. Foursquare, heavy brick pillars supported the porch roof. Plain doors; no panels or carving.

Inside, beamed ceilings. Tall, austere wainscoting in the dining room. Horsehair settees go out, wicker chairs come in. Florid curves of nineteenth-century mahogany are replaced by mission oak in stern, straight lines. Tables and pianos are swept bare of everything except a doily and a brass lamp with a colored glass shade. Away with old-time clutter of china cupids, seashells, hand-carved walnuts, hand-painted pine cones, dear little watercolors of angels. Swagged velvet draperies (dusty! unsanitary!) come down from the mantel. Layers of heavy curtains come down from the windows.

There was a craze for sanitation, too. Brass bedsteads (washable) replaced carved walnut. Hardwood floors were sprinkled (sparsely) with throw rugs in geometric patterns to replace Mama's dusty flowered carpets.

The total effect was spacious, but severe.

Young people flung their bedroom windows wide open at night even in winter, proud to be known as fresh-air fiends. The good housekeeper aired every blanket, pillow, and woolen garment on clotheslines once a week.

Families lived frugally as a matter of course, even those who were reasonably well-to-do. It was usual for mothers to make the clothing for themselves and their daughters; and to raise chickens and plant a garden if there was space. Clothing was handed down from older to younger children, stockings were darned, elbows and knees of garments were patched. Furniture bought by a bride and groom was still in use when the couple celebrated their golden wedding anniversary.

Plates and pictures, sweaters and toys—nothing was thrown away just because it was old; it was used until it wore out or broke. Boxes and wrapping paper were saved; string that the butcher tied around the package of Hamburg steak was unknotted and attached to the ball of string in the top drawer of the Hoosier Maid kitchen cabinet.

Magazine articles repeatedly advised young girls to be cheery, helpful, happy with small blessings. "Make the household pleasant for your brother, so that he shall not be tempted into paths of danger," says a writer in a 1901 *Ladies' Home Journal*, "...[and do]what you can to cheer a hard-working father into forgetfulness of care. ... Do not disturb the one or antagonize the other."

One questions whether young girls were actually so sweet and humble as all that, but certainly every girl had demure "accomplishments": she could sing a little, or play the piano, or do fine embroidery in a winsome style. She cultivated these graces in order to display them before gentlemen callers.

If she was the least bit worldly, she also practiced picking up her long, full skirts swiftly with one hand when stepping off a curb or climbing a flight of stairs. A flourish of the skirt and a certain twist of the lower body (the naughty minx!) would bring a sparkle to a gentleman's eye. And when she performed this slight, elegant flip, she never, never looked down to see if heels and hems were in order; to look down would have been a sure sign of social clumsiness.

This dear little woman did not question the rightness of the status quo, but a few strong-minded females sprang up who challenged the system, and some did so by beating the drum for woman suffrage or temperance.

Mention of these two movements makes a point about crusading women of the decade. Except for the National American Woman Suffrage Association and the Women's Christian Temperance Union, women with causes did not form into platoons, companies, and regiments. Each fought alone. Even the hatchet-swinging Carry Nation was a lone battler, and the WCTU swung into action behind her after her initial attacks.

When Carry Nation Takes Her Hatchet, Demon Rum's A-Going to Catch It!

"Men! I have come to save you from a drunkard's grave!"

Half a dozen silent, brooding men bracing themselves with an early-morning hair of the dog leaned against the bar at Dobson's saloon in Kiowa, Kansas. They looked around vaguely.

In the doorway stood a broad and robust woman dressed in neat black alpaca, white bow at the chin, old-fashioned bonnet on her gray hair.

She strode into the saloon. With a variety of missiles cradled in her left arm, she selected half a brick and balanced it in her hand. "I told you last spring to close up this place, Mr. Dobson."

"Now, Mother Nation," began the barkeeper placatingly.

But the lady squinted at his expensive gilt-framed mirror, took careful aim, and heaved her brick. Smash! The glass spattered into fragments. Another brick, a rock, a bottle flew through the air. Crash! Slam! Bash! Soon shelves and bar held nothing but splinters of glass. A rich smell of whiskey filled the air, and shelves dripped golden liquids.

Carry roared a hymn, "Who hath sorrow? Who hath woe? They who tarry at the wine cup!" *Smash!*

Dobson and customers fled to a corner and huddled there.

Carry was often privileged to see things invisible to lesser folk. Now in a rocking chair she saw President William McKinley, shawl over his shoulders, sneering at her. With a howl of rage, she snatched up a handy brick, hurled it at him, and was gratified to see chair and Republican go down in pieces.

"Now, Mr. Dobson, I have finished. God be with you." She marched out of the saloon.

At the sound of breaking glass, storekeepers and early-morning pedestrians in the small town had rushed toward Dobson's. Carry Nation smiled happily at everyone, stepped into her buggy at the curb, slapped the reins on old Prince, and rattled down the street to a second saloon. Then a third.

Patrons and barkeepers were too paralyzed with surprise to stop her. At each establishment she smashed windows, mirrors, and bottles, overturned tables, broke up chairs, tore down pictures, and strode out with the cheery farewell, "God be with you!"

But outside the third saloon she found the street jammed with citizens, all looking disturbed and puzzled. She marched to the middle of the street and threw up both hands for attention.

"Men of Kiowa," she thundered, "I have destroyed three of your places of business. If I have broken a statute of Kansas, put me in jail!"

She stepped into her buggy, but Kiowa's Mayor Korn rushed to catch Prince's bridle. "Pay me," he shouted, "for the front windows you broke in my building!"

"I won't do anything of the sort!"

Councilmen, town marshal, city attorney, and others present rushed back and forth in the crowd, dithering about what to do. It was a ticklish situation because Kansas was a dry state. They could charge Mrs. Nation with destroying property, but it was property being put to an illegal use. The temperance people, whose votes were as useful as the saloon crowd's, would raise a howl all over Kansas.

At last the marshal slapped Prince's rump and snarled, "Go on home!"

"Peace on earth, good will to men!" Carry shouted, raising her arms in benediction. She rode out of town standing, lustily singing hymns.

This, in June of 1900, was Carry Nation's first raid. A few months later she swooped without notice on the Carey Hotel Annex, the most spectacular saloon in Wichita. Since Kansas was legally dry, saloons in the state capital were called "sample rooms." Their owners turned up in court once a month and paid fines, and no one complained about the system except a few WCTU zealots.

This establishment had a magnificent cherrywood bar, a $1,500 mirror that covered an entire wall, and a hand-painted oil entitled "Cleopatra at the Bath, or the Temptress of the Nile." It showed the lady on a couch, nude, surrounded by voluptuous maidens and eunuchs. A disgrace!

This was Carry's target. When she tramped into the saloon, her generous cape hid an arsenal of stones and an iron rod fastened to a sturdy cane, end-to-end. With no word of warning this time, she hurled her first two rocks at Cleo. Glass over the painting shattered. The bartender was so startled that he dropped the whiskey bottle in his hand. "Stop!" he shouted. "Stop!"

For reply she aimed her next missiles at the immense mirror. It fell in a storm of splinters. "Peace on earth! Good will to men!" she roared. She ran up and down the bar, whipping her rod-and-cane at everything in sight, smashing bottles and glasses, denting the brass rail, splintering chairs, gouging the cherrywood.

The bartender raised a white face above the bar and she flung a beer bottle at him. He ducked out of sight. Whiskey and beer flowed across the floor.

Detective Park Massey stalked into the saloon and took her arm. "Madam," he said with perfect decorum, "I must place you under arrest." He removed the weapons from her hands and led her away from the scene of demolition.

"Am I a soldier of the cross?" she sang as she tramped along beside him toward police headquarters. She was jailed for three weeks, probably the liveliest three weeks that the Sedgwick County Jail had ever known. Groups of women swarmed in and kept the jail ringing with hymns and prayers. "Take hatchets, rocks, brickbats, take anything handy," Carry shouted to the sisters, "and clean out this curse! Smash! Smash! Smash!"

Her fellow prisoners howled and catcalled.

Most of these men were smokers, and knowing that the smoke bothered Carry, the sheriff told them that he would supply them with all the tobacco they needed. He moved four constant smokers into nearby cells and put Dutchman John, a trusty, into an adjacent cell because John used a particularly stout pipe. All the favored prisoners obligingly blew smoke in Carry's direction.

She had her Bible with her. When she had no callers, she knelt beside her cot, read aloud from the book in her commanding voice, prayed forcefully, and shouted joyful hymns while her fellow inmates groaned and tried to drown her out.

But little by little the prisoners began to change their minds about her. The old girl had spunk. Some of them quit tormenting her with smoke.

Letters and telegrams poured into the jail. To pass the time, "the boys" helped to sort it, commenting on this letter and that one. A friendly spirit began to grow between them and the crazy old woman with the Bible. Carry became more convinced than ever that good lurks in every human being, and later she wrote, "I never see a face behind bars that my heart does not pity."

The fact is, Carry Nation disapproved of nearly everybody, but she couldn't dislike anyone.

Many of her admirers sent money to help pay for her defense. She spent it instead on fruit and butter for the boys, because jail meals were so terrible. To the pipe-smoking Trusty John she gave her last four dollars because his wife needed money for food.

At last charges against Carry were dismissed and she was freed. As before, she was an embarrassment to the law. If the silly old woman would only go home and keep quiet!

But meekness was no quality of Carry Nation's. On her next Wichita raids, she was not alone, but led bands of demonstrators armed with stones, iron bars, and hunks of scrap iron. For the first time she herself carried a hatchet, the weapon that became the symbol of her work.

Protest raiding spread like prairie fire. In towns all over Kansas, armed women strode into saloons and demolished them. Then in Illinois, Wisconsin, Minnesota, Arkansas, New Jersey, Kentucky, Massachusetts—in states where the sale of liquor was legal and the courageous smashers faced serious penalties for destroying property. No matter. The smashing went on, a national pandemonium. Carry breezed all over the United States, and became familiar with jails from Los Angeles to Philadelphia.

Saloonkeepers were now prepared for defense. She was, in various battles, given the bum's rush, knocked down, kicked, cuffed, and socked with brass knuckles. "Glory to God!" shouted Carry. "Lord, let me die for the cause!"

Ridiculous? Of course. But she fought so bravely for the thing she believed in that she earns our respect.

The decade progressed with a diminishing sound of crashing glass. Pro-salooners again rested their bellies peacefully against unchopped bars, and violent ladies let their hatchets rust in tool sheds. The anti-liquor passion, however, brought to expression by fearless, bigoted, generous Carry Nation lived on through the second decade until it culminated in passage of the Volstead Act.

The Suffrage Movement

Susan B. Anthony, grand old lady of suffrage, died in 1906. For more than half a century she had stumped the country, lecturing on women's rights and organizing bands of feminists. She cheerfully endured ridicule, insults, and exhaustion for the cause.

She and Elizabeth Cady Stanton were comrades in arms. These stalwarts lived to be eighty-six and eighty-seven. Nineteenth-century feminists were notably long-lived. One of the Grimké sisters died as a girl of seventy-four, but most leaders went on to maturity. A woman had to be healthy, thick-skinned, and zealous to stay the course in those embattled years.

When Susan B. Anthony died, presidency of her National American Woman's Suffrage Association was in the hands of a younger woman, Anna Howard Shaw. Dr. Shaw had two devotions: to "Aunt Susan," and to suffrage.

Anna Howard Shaw was a short, fat woman with piercing eyes, a quick, hearty laugh, no patience at all, and a gift for oratory. Born in 1847, she was reared in the Michigan backwoods, and even as a child she loved to orate. She would stand on a stump and preach to the silent trees around her.

She studied at Albion College in Michigan, and later at Boston University, determined to enter the ministry, though every member of her family by turns commanded and implored her not to humiliate them by appearing on a public platform. But obstacles only spurred her on, as they did Carey Thomas, to greater frenzy of effort. She paid her college fees and supported herself (meagerly—just ahead of starvation) by giving lectures on temperance and by preaching in country churches.

Her own church, the Methodist Episcopal, refused to ordain a woman, but a smaller sect, Methodist Protestant, did so. Even after ordination, however, church doors in many a city were closed to her because of her sex.

Once she was asked to preach at a Michigan lumber camp when the regular minister was away on his honeymoon. She rode a stagecoach toward her destination, but twenty-two miles from the camp she discovered that the rest of the journey was up to her. The road led through dense forest and night was coming on. She found a man with a two-seated wagon who agreed to take her to the camp, and though she did not like the prospect of traveling with such a surly stranger as he was, she engaged him.

It was a slow, jolting ride. Halfway through the night, the driver suddenly stopped his horses, turned toward her, and snarled, "You must think I'm a fool not to know what kind of woman you are—alone with a man in the woods at night."

Anna replied, trying to sound calm, "You know this is the only way I can keep my appointment to preach tomorrow morning."

"I'm damned if I'll take you," he said. "I've got you here and I'm going to keep you here."

Though she was terrified, Anna slipped her hand into her satchel. "I have a revolver," she said. "It is cocked and aimed straight at your back. Now drive on. If you stop again I'll shoot you."

Sullenly, he drove on through the night. Dawn came at last. In all those hours she had not dared relax for a moment, or take her hand from the weapon.

That morning, she preached in the pulpit as she had promised to do, and to her surprise the rough little church was packed to the walls with lumbermen in blue and red shirts with yellow scarves twisted around their waists. They stared at her as she preached, listening intently. When the collection plate was passed, the offering was the largest ever taken up in that settlement.

"Put in fifty cents!" the men yelled to each other across the room. "Go on, give the gal a dollar!"

It was not Anna's spiritual message that appealed to the men. They had all turned out to see the girl preacher who carried a gun.

On another occasion, she preached a one-week series of revival sermons with only faith and a box of crackers to sustain her through her work for the Lord. Her eloquence won a fine crop of converts. But, at the end of the week, the church fathers told her regretfully that they could not afford to pay for her labors. She was saved from starvation, she says, by a grateful lady in the congregation whose rakehell grandson had been converted. She gave Anna $5.

Her life as a pastor on Cape Cod, where she supervised two parishes, reads like a tale of hardship piled upon hardship, but Reverend Shaw feared she was softening up in a life of ease. She determined to become a doctor. After earning a medical degree in her thirties, she practiced in Boston, found herself still seeking fulfillment, and hurled herself into temperance work. No bottle smasher like Carry Nation, she was, all the same, ardent for prohibition. But when she met Susan B. Anthony, she knew what her life's work was meant to be: laboring for women's rights.

Thereafter she and Miss Anthony traveled the country together on speaking tours, often under those hardships that seemed so exhilarating to Dr. Shaw. One year, when the suffrage issue was to be voted on in South Dakota, they went on tour through that state. Some days they rode forty or fifty miles in an uncovered wagon and then spent the night in a one-room cabin with all the members of a family, sometimes sleeping on the floor. Other times they rode all night from one mining town to the next to keep their schedule. It was a year of drought, so that the water was brackish and even when boiled for tea was so salty it left the drinker thirstier than before. A bath was a rare luxury.

"But," reports the rugged doctor, "we had some great meetings."

They lost South Dakota for suffrage, though.

One time she reached a railroad station to learn that the train she was to meet would not run that day. But, while she stood on the desolate platform, frustrated, another train rattled to a stop. She snatched up her grip and sprang aboard.

"Wait," cried her companions, "that's going in the wrong direction."

But Anna only yelled goodbye, settled her dusty hat, and prepared for the next development. As it turned out, farther down the line she was able to transfer to another conveyance that took her, roundabout, to her destination in time for that evening's speaking engagement.

"Which proves," she said triumphantly, "that in a moment of decision it is better to make the wrong move than to make no move at all."

Her life's ambition was gratified when she inherited the presidency of the National American Woman Suffrage Association.

In later years, however, feminists called those first years of the twentieth century the doldrums. Suffrage languished. Congress ignored the issue. State referendums were lost.

The fact is, though Anna Howard Shaw's heart and soul were devoted to the cause, and though she was an inspired orator and a gallant worker, she was a poor president. Blunt and impatient, she alienated her fellow workers so that valuable women resigned from her board. State suffrage organizations became discouraged. Membership fell off. It became clear to everyone, including Dr. Shaw, that the NAWSA needed new leadership, and so at the 1915 convention, she quietly stepped out of office and Carrie Chapman Catt stepped in.

The 1910s

FEMINISTS ON PARADE

The New Broom

One of Carrie Chapman Catt's early memories was of an evening when her father and a group of neighbor men sat in the Wisconsin farm kitchen discussing local politics while her mother briskly prepared supper and listened. Turning from the stove, the mother cut into the talk, saying, "But what I think is . . . ."

The men looked at her in astonishment, she faltered, and they broke into roars of laughter. The idea of a woman having any thoughts about politics! Carrie's mother pressed her lips together and turned back to her stove. Young Carrie watched and listened, and said nothing, but she remembered.

After graduation from Iowa State College, she taught school, worked on a newspaper, and then held a job of stature for a young woman of her time—or even of a later time: she was superintendent of schools in Mason City, Iowa. Married twice and widowed twice, she devoted her middle years to suffrage.

As a young woman she was tactless and unsympathetic, as clear-sighted executive types tend to be; but she was also perceptive, and when she saw that these qualities limited her success, she deliberately set out to assume a gracious manner. It did not detract one bit from her ability to manipulate fellow suffragists, anti-suffragists, and politicians of both persuasions.

She had a genius for organization. As soon as she succeeded Dr. Shaw at the helm of the National Association, she set up headquarters in New York. She drew together a new board of women with special qualifications. They must not only be devoted to the cause of suffrage—that was an easy stipulation—but they must also have sturdy health, independent means, and freedom from family entanglements. Whenever an assistant broke down in one of these areas, she was to be replaced, and never mind sentiment. The day of the amateur reformer was over. The day of the hard-headed organizer dawned.

A tough, prudent general, Mrs. Catt never looked back. When a suffrage amendment in Maine was defeated, she said only, "A battle has been lost. Forget it. Others lie ahead."

She had the good fortune to have a million dollars in her hand, a legacy from Mrs. Frank Leslie. Mrs. Leslie was a beautiful woman with wide, appealing eyes, and a very firm mouth. She married four times, her fourth husband being publisher of *Leslie's Weekly*, the big-circulation magazine of its time. After Frank died in 1880, the widow remained in suitable seclusion for a year, then summoned a photographer and a reporter, and through them announced to the world that her husband (in a private, deathbed scene, presumably) had told her to "go down and rescue the business, pay the creditors, and manage the establishment."

Employees and business associates were naturally dismayed at having to work with a female, but she had the brains and the resourcefulness to hold her own. *Leslie's Weekly* prospered as never before.

Glamorous and eccentric, she was the most photographed and most talked-about woman of her day. Her origins were tactfully lost in a fog, but when she retired from business, after twenty successful years, she took the name of—she said—an ancestor, and called herself the Baroness de Bazus.

She had never been a suffragist, though she sometimes donated small sums to the cause, and why she chose to leave a large bequest to suffrage workers is anybody's guess. Maybe, in spite of her imperious manner and her beauty, she had felt the sting of too many putdowns from gentlemen colleagues.

Half of Mrs. Catt's million was in cash and the other half was contained in a suitcase delivered to her office: the famous Leslie jewels. Carrie poured them into a glittering pile on her desk, and called in her assistants to help her gloat. Necklaces, rings, bracelets, jeweled hatpins—even a diamond tiara. Radical feminists love jewels, as most women do, and they caressed these brilliants, tried them on, held them up to the light, exclaimed and reveled. Then all the pieces were briskly returned to their cases to be sold, and the women went back to work. Incidentally, Mrs. Catt sensibly named a commission of suffrage workers to administer the Leslie funds and to present annual accountings thereof. The funds lasted until 1929.

Money was nice to have, because suffrage had some rich enemies. Brewers' associations and the liquor interests were among the most powerful. With ample funds and a nationwide network of barkeepers to staff their campaigns, they easily kept suffrage squashed in Nebraska, Wisconsin, South Dakota, and Iowa. And why did they fear suffrage? Because the women's vote was sure to be a vote for reform.

A second powerful anti, especially in the East, was big business. Railroad, oil, and manufacturing lobbies all fought suffrage. If women had a chance to vote, they said (to each other, not to the press) they would vote against high tariffs, in favor of railroad regulation, the direct primary, the taxation of war profits, and an investigation of Wall Street. They might even vote to improve the conditions of working women.

In the South, the enemy was racism. If black women got the vote, what would happen to white supremacy? Northerners were just as hysterical in their fear of the female immigrant vote. Those foreign women would become the docile tools of corrupt ward heelers and would double "the ignorant vote."

Professional politicians also ran scared. They knew how to organize and control the men's vote, but those women! What if women disdained the machine?

It may seem odd, but many women feared suffrage too. One of them wrote: "[Women] are to be brought down from their altruistic heights by being released from all obligations of purity, loyalty, self-sacrifice, and made free of the world of passion and self-indulgence, after the model set them by men of low and materialistic ideals."

If this seems highly colored, ponder some of the claims of the suffragists: Woman, being morally and spiritually superior to man, would vote only for the good. After she got the vote, there would be no corruption in government, no injustice in the laws, little crime, and no drunkenness. Schools would be better, and poverty would disappear.

Naturally, not all suffragists expected this utopia right away.

The Returnees

New leaders appeared on the suffrage scene, one of them being the offspring of an old leader. Elizabeth Cady Stanton's daughter Harriot had married an Englishman and lived in Great Britain for twenty years, but after his death she returned to the United States to devote herself to the cause in which she had been, literally, reared.

The suffrage movement in America wasn't lively enough for her taste (Carrie Catt wasn't on the job yet) and Mrs. Blatch therefore shaped up a league of her own; by 1910 it had thousands of members. They organized public meetings. They campaigned against politicians who opposed them. They lobbied for the suffrage bill, and they talked labor unions into taking an interest.

That same year—1910—she organized an unheard-of stunt: a parade of women. Women!—marching right on Fifth Avenue, in front of everybody! Even loyal suffragists drew back. Dr. Shaw, pioneer though she was, shook her head and called it radical.

The parade was scantily attended.

Nevertheless, the following year Mrs. Blatch tried it again, but it was not until 1912 that it really caught on. That year fifteen thousand women marched—factory girls, nurses, college students, typists—and even Anna Howard Shaw. Also philosopher John Dewey, Rabbi Stephen Wise, poet Richard Le Gallienne, and a brigade of men six hundred strong.

This time the crowd cheered. Many a lukewarm observer of the suffrage fad was so stirred by the spirit of the striding women that he said in surprise, "Maybe it's time these women did get the vote."

The ferment over suffrage dramatizes one of the strong impulses of the second decade: a will to change. All across the country, people made up their minds to improve life, to throw out the old and set up the new. It was a vigorous movement, rich in optimism and generosity. It was based on the widespread belief that humanity was growing wiser and better all the time, and with a hearty push from Americans of good will, it could go on climbing right up to perfection.

While Mrs. Blatch was beating on the doors of union halls and organizing parades, another American, even more colorful, returned to the United States from England. She was a Quaker girl. In the 1850s, many suffrage workers had been Quakers. Probably this was because among the Friends women have always been regarded as nearly the equal of men, and that gave them self-confidence. Besides, Quakers were already used to bucking society. For example, they'd never take an oath, and women could be preachers.

This young American Quaker was Alice Paul, in appearance as delicate as a porcelain doll and in spirit as tough as rawhide. While she had done postgraduate work at a London university, she had also turned her hand to the strenuous suffrage work there.

Returned home, she moved on Washington as Sherman had once moved on Atlanta. She found no suffrage organization in the Capital, but within two months she fixed *that*. She decided she would have a little procession. The date? It had to be March 3, because the following day—the year was 1913—was Woodrow Wilson's inauguration day. Washington would be full of people from all over the country on March 3, and the president-elect himself would be in town. In fact, when Mr. Wilson arrived in Washington and found the streets empty, he is said to have asked where all the people were. "Over on Pennsylvania Avenue," he was told, "watching the women march for suffrage."

They were to parade from the Capitol to the White House, and then on to Constitution Hall, about five thousand marchers with banners. One of the handsomest sections was that of nurses in their white uniforms. There was a college section, the girls all in caps and gowns. (Alice Paul marched in that group.) There was the beautiful society girl Inez Milholland, riding a white horse. Inez was so lovely to look at that in all suffrage parades she was placed conspicuously in the lineup. That day she wore a white Cossack suit and long white kid boots, and from her shoulders swung a pale blue cloak adorned with a golden Maltese cross. She rode astride, by the way, but now, in 1913, that was scarcely shocking anymore.

There were a men's section, and a foreign section, and decorated floats, and a section of black women from the National Association of Colored Women—but that caused trouble. Suddenly the southern women refused to march. The leader of the men's section, however (another Quaker), solved that one by offering to have the men march between the southern delegation and the black section, and everybody was satisfied.

At first the procession was orderly enough. But the town was so full of people that they simply poured, or so it seemed to the paraders, onto the streets, a flood of people, all eager to see the astonishing spectacle of marching women. Some cheered, but more catcalled and shouted insults. They pressed from the sidewalks into the streets and harried the paraders into such a close and jumbled crowd that they could hardly move three abreast. The women "fought their way foot by foot up Pennsylvania Avenue," reported the Baltimore *Sun*. Rowdies spat upon some, tripped, pushed, and pelted the women with cigar stubs.

The police were not prepared for this unruly mob—half a million onlookers, reporters estimated. A Massachusetts National Guard unit was asked to help clear the way, but members refused, laughing. A Pennsylvania National Guard regiment agreed to do police duty, and students of the Maryland Agriculture College leaped into the act: they formed in single file on each side of the anxious and bedraggled suffragists, and in front of them a squad locked arms and formed a crowd-breaking vanguard. But it was not until cavalry from Fort Meyer galloped to the rescue that order came to the affair.

Later, there was a congressional investigation into the laxity of the police, and the District chief of police was fired. Congressman Kent of California was one of the first to demand an investigation because he was so enraged at the insults flung at his pretty daughter Elizabeth as she rode on the California float.

For publicity, Alice Paul's "little procession" was a smashing success. But it was only a curtain raiser. She believed that state referendums were too cumbersome to bother with, and that the way to reach suffrage was to crash a federal amendment through Congress. Workers called it the Susan B. Anthony Amendment.

One postscript to the parade: beautiful Inez Milholland, a stirring speaker, went on the lecture circuit, seeking support for the Susan B. Amendment, but she overtaxed her strength. At a mass meeting in Los Angeles she paid a dire price for all that ardor. Dramatically, she cried to the audience, "How long must women wait for liberty?" and then fell fainting onto the platform. Within a month she was dead, both a martyr and a grievous loss to her cause.

Though generally known by her maiden name, she was married to Eugen Boissevain, a Dutch importer, who loyally supported her suffrage work. More later about the excellent Eugen.

Two weeks after Wilson's inauguration, Alice Paul and three other women waited on the president to ask his support for a federal suffrage amendment. Very politely, he declined to give it. The delegation, equally polite, departed. A few days later they sent another delegation to him, and then another, and another, and another, and another, and another, until 1917. After the United States entered World War I, the president declined to admit any more delegations. The suffragists responded that they would provide a perpetual delegation right in front of the White House so that he couldn't forget them.

Then the picketing began. In orderly fashion, a dozen women at a time would march from the headquarters of the Woman's Party, as Alice Paul's company was now called, across Lafayette Square to the White House. Each carried a banner affixed to an eight-foot pole; some banners bore legends and others were the party's colors—purple, white, and gold. Lettered banners carried such slogans as "Mr. President, what will you do for woman suffrage?" or "How long must women wait for liberty?"

The picketers were perfectly orderly. But implacable. There they stood, day after day, working in relays. Each time President Wilson rode through the gates on his daily drive, he gravely took off his silk hat and bowed to the ladies. They bowed in return.

What kind of woman was this Alice Paul who could plan and direct a campaign that continued so relentlessly?

Like Harriot Blatch, she had the strength of an ox. And she was apparently unemotional. Most of all, she was utterly concentrated. Her aim was woman suffrage, and nothing else mattered. No other person mattered much, either, and in consequence she was plainspoken to the point of rudeness. It never occurred to her to thank anyone for a service. Once a volunteer, who had worked all morning on an assignment Miss Paul had given her, returned to headquarters at noon and reported on what she had done. Miss Paul made no comment, but asked her to go downtown at once on another errand. The woman refused, left, and did not return. When Alice asked someone why, a friend explained, "She is offended. You didn't thank her for what she had done."

"But she didn't do it for me! She did it for suffrage!"

Mrs. Oliver Hazard Perry Belmont, another worker in the Woman's Party, had a background unlike that of the other leaders. Before a divorce, she had been Mrs. William K. Vanderbilt, and was the mother of Consuelo, who became the Duchess of Marlborough.

Handsome and impetuous, fond of action and excitement, Mrs. O. H. P. Belmont willingly threw her wealth into women's causes. At one time she hired a train known as the "Golden Special," filled it with eastern suffragists, and directed its way west on a speaking tour in support of the Susan B. Anthony Amendment. Unfortunately westerners, always touchy about what they believe to be eastern arrogance, were goaded to envy by the luxuries of the train and by the sables and emeralds that adorned some socialites. In spite of Mrs. O. H. P. Belmont's good intentions, the Golden Special probably did more harm than good.

Survival Problems

Suffrage wasn't the only issue that involved women.

The decade opened with trouble on the women's labor scene. In two New York shirtwaist factories—Leiserson and Company, and the

Triangle Shirtwaist Company—workers considered conditions so bad that they went on strike. As negotiations dragged along with no prospect of settlement, thousands of aroused workers answered a call for a mass meeting at Cooper Union, and there they adopted a daring plan: they called a general strike. A good guess was that three thousand workers would strike, but in fact many more thousands did. Seventy-five percent of them were women, dissolving the old myth that women could never be organized. The cause was so vigorously supported that from one to five thousand new members joined the unions every day.

The infant Women's Trade Union League—WTUL—took its case to the public. It explained that the shirtwaist shops were housed in filthy old buildings where windows were nailed shut and little light came in through the unwashed glass. Fire hazards were enormous. There were fines for talking, singing, laughing, and for getting oil stains from the sewing machines on the goods. Work hours sometimes ran on until ten o'clock at night, with no overtime pay. Wages were as low as $6 a week for highly skilled work, and pay was often withheld. Young immigrant girls with a shaky knowledge of English and in desperate need of their money had no means of collecting what was owed them.

Mrs. O. H. P. Belmont, Miss Anne Morgan, and Mrs. J. Borden Harriman called a meeting of their friends at the fashionable New York Colony Club, and collected $1,300 for the strikers—no great sum considering the wealth of the group, but the meeting gave the strikers good publicity. The ladies also provided money for bail when girl strikers were arrested on charges of disturbing the peace and similar misdeeds.

Mrs. Belmont, wrapped in furs and wearing an enormous, swanky hat, appeared in court one day to stand bail for four girls. Bail was only $200 for each, but Mrs. Belmont, putting up her Madison Avenue house as security, announced dramatically that it was valued at $400,000, and added, "There is a mortgage of $100,000 which I placed to help the cause of the shirtwaist workers and the woman suffrage movement."

The strike went on for thirteen weeks of bitter cold and hunger, but finally collapsed, in spite of help from society friends and from unions. Settlements were made shop by shop, sometimes with little gain. Conditions at the Triangle Shirtwaist Company were not improved at all.

The next big strike came in Chicago at Hart, Schaffner, and Marx against working conditions. The strike spread until forty-five thousand workers were involved, and it lasted fourteen dreary weeks. Many shops resumed working with no advantages gained, but Hart, Schaffner, and Marx signed a historic agreement with the United Garment Workers, recognizing the principle of arbitration, collective bargaining, and a grievance committee.

As in the shirtwaist strike, the women showed their mettle. Thousands of them were mothers, and during the winter 1,250 babies were born to striking women or to strikers' wives. A visitor from the Chicago WTUL told of visiting a young woman who lay in bed in an unheated room, a newborn infant in bed with her, and three other small children in the room. The mother said, "It is not only bread we give our children. . . . We live by freedom, and I will fight till I die to give it to my children."

The story of the Triangle Shirtwaist Company has another chapter—a disaster so horrible that the whole country was shaken. The factory occupied the eighth, ninth, and tenth floors of the Asch Building at 23 Washington Place, New York City. Electric sewing machines stood in solid rows with the narrowest of aisles between them, and in corners great piles of rags and cuttings were collected, to be held until a ton accumulated so that they could be sold at a profit.

One Saturday afternoon half of the work force, or about five hundred workers, mostly young girls, were doing overtime to catch up on back orders that had piled up during the strike. When the power-off signal sounded at 4:30, the lower seven floors were already empty because companies that occupied them had closed down earlier. Chattering girls left their machines, glad to be free on this sunny afternoon, but within minutes they were trapped in a furnace.

One of the rag piles caught fire. Was it a lighted cigarette? A hot iron, heated by gasoline that was also stored in the workroom? Or was it a spark from worn wiring that caused the rags to ignite?

The fire department arrived promptly, but there was little it could do. The tallest ladders reached only to the sixth floor.

The girls panicked. They ran for the elevator, but it could not carry them all. Girls jumped or were pushed into the shaft, and their bodies, caught between wall and car, jammed the elevator so that it could not run at all. Other girls ran for the stairs and some escaped down the narrow winding staircase. Some found escape doors locked. Other doors opened inward and in the press of struggling, screaming girls, the doors could not be opened. Some victims raced for the fire escape, but it broke under their weight and dropped bodies onto a glass skylight, which crashed and let them fall to the street below.

Other girls, their clothes on fire, rushed to the windows, and with fire licking at their backs, they jumped. Firemen held nets, but so many girls jumped at one time that their weight carried the nets straight to the sidewalk, and men holding the nets were flipped in on top of them.

That fire cost the lives of 146 people, mostly Italian and Russian Jewish girls, some as young as fourteen. They burned to death, fell to the concrete, or were impaled on iron fences as they fell.

Horror swept the city, the nation. Eleven days after the fire, eighty thousand people marched up Fifth Avenue in solemn procession, in a drenching rain, to the beat of muffled drums, between sidewalks filled with a quarter million silent watchers. The procession was led by an empty hearse drawn by six white horses draped in black, and each marcher wore an armband reading, "We mourn our loss."

New York safety laws were reexamined and stiffened, and became models for the country. Owners of the Triangle factory were tried and acquitted of guilt. The cry arose that, if acquittal was the kind of justice that women could expect, then women had better get themselves the vote and straighten out the laws.

Working women had always been hostile toward women of the leisure class. At the same time, these women often looked upon laboring women as subhuman. But in this labor turmoil and the grief over the Triangle fire, working women discovered that college girls, professional women, settlement-house workers, even society ladies, cared about them. Upper-class women discovered that the sullen-faced poor had human needs, even ambitions. The idea dawned and then spread like daylight that the classes could cooperate. They began to mingle in suffrage work, realizing that they all needed the same thing—equality at the ballot box.

It has already been remarked that the decade of the 1910s was remarkable for its spirit of reform. A second generous impulse of the time was this ballooning of empathy among the classes. There had not been such a surge toward democracy since the days of Andrew Jackson.

But there was still a third movement afoot.

The great ladies of the 1900s had nearly all been loners, who pursued their separate ambitions with private zeal. But in the 1910s ladies joined forces.

Of course there had been clubs for years. The General Federation of Women's Clubs was formed as early as 1890. But that group, the WCTU, church societies, literary clubs, all of them involved relatively few of the total female population.

But now! Women in their thousands were rushing out of the house like Ibsen's Nora. They joined civic improvement societies and trade unions and suffrage clubs. Crowds of them applauded lecturers, committees of them badgered politicians, hundreds tramped in parades. They signed petitions. They swirled around a leader and founded a new antiwar society. They even organized their daughters: Girl Scouts and Campfire Girls were founded. Life had never been so stimulating.

Booth Tarkington wrote fondly of the girls of the 1910s: "They had a look of independence and an air of having made this freedom for themselves and intending to make it complete, no matter who didn't happen to like their having it."

Struggles for Peace

Pacifism was the ideal of millions of American women. They believed that the splendid upswing of civilization in this greatest of all centuries rendered warfare obsolete. The humblest housewife with little sons playing in the back yard believed it, and so did intellectual Jane Addams. In 1914, outbreak of a savage war in Europe scared them both, and scared all the millions in between them.

If men insisted on starting wars, it was up to women to stop them. Miss Addams organized a Woman's Peace Party and twenty-five thousand women enthusiastically joined it. Carrie Chapman Catt was one of the distinguished sponsors, but she told Miss Addams that she could play only a small role in the peace action. The shrewd suffragist could not afford to scatter her shot; her one aim was the vote for women.

The Peace Party quickly set up delegations to go to Europe and confer with officials. Jane Addams led one delegation. The great powers on both sides of the conflict received her courteously and then turned to their plans for the next campaign. European neutrals dared not act as referees lest they too be drawn into the war. It was all no use. Peace could not be achieved by reason.

All through 1916 America drifted closer, closer to war. At Chicago's great preparedness parade, thousands cheered and wept as phalanxes of flags passed by, and stern-faced young National Guardsmen, and marching bands led by prancing drum majors in enormous shakos. Members of the Woman's Peace Party stood on the sidelines with a banner of protest, but policemen tore the banner from their hands, telling them fiercely that their sentiments were treason. Two men tried to rescue the peace banner and were arrested, a sample of what would be commonplace after America entered the war, when pacifists were treated as active traitors.

Troublesome crosswinds blew. Some women tailored uniforms for themselves and practiced drilling. Defiant pacifist women on the other hand published a journal called *Four Lights* until the Post Office took away their mailing privileges. Wellesley fired Emily Green Balch for teaching world politics and peace. Thousands of women, less sure of their convictions than Miss Balch, teetered unhappily between love of country and love of peace.

Then war was declared. Instantly, for these women, doubts were resolved. Now they knew: patriotism over all! They began furiously knitting, gardening, canning, writing cheery letters to the boys in uniform, buying Liberty Bonds. They set up canteens in railway stations; they waved flags at every opportunity.

But this was not enough. Organized womanhood demanded a share in the great adventure, and they poured their offers of service into Washington. But-but-but, stuttered the government, what are we to do with all those women? Why can't they stay in their houses and nag their own husbands? In desperation, the Council of National Defense set up a clearinghouse and created a unit that enjoyed many florid titles in its lifetime, but was called, simply, the Woman's Committee. Anna Howard Shaw was its chairman and other members were presidents of august organizations: the National Council of Women, the General Federation of Women's Clubs, the National League for Women's Service, the National American Woman's Suffrage Association, Colonial Dames, International Glove Workers Union, and others. All that talent and ability in one group!

But after they had spun their wheels for a time, members realized that the committee was only a handy sidetrack onto which troublesome women could be shunted and ignored, while the men got on with their war. Anna Howard Shaw, that battle-scarred old combatant, finally forced an arrangement by which her committee would have a voice in national affairs. But then the war ended, and the Council of National Defense gladly saw that the Woman's Committee was disbanded.

But if the committee accomplished nothing, member organizations were "doing their bit," as the phrase went. They collected millions for war bonds, the Red Cross, and the YMCA. The Federation of

Women's Clubs sent one hundred girls overseas to entertain the soldiers. Mrs. Catt's National Association bought and equipped ambulance units, staffed by women doctors, nurses, aides, drivers, and mechanics. The United States Army rejected the units, but the weary and battered French Army accepted them thankfully.

Some women made it to France as Red Cross nurses—the nurse was the Rose of No-Man's Land—and as Salvation Army or YMCA girls, who ran canteens and acted as jolly little sisters to The Boys.

At home, thousands of women busied themselves selling war bonds. Helen Taft, niece of the former president, once sold hers with the help of a ladder—an extension ladder operated by a crew of firemen. A crowd quickly gathered, and each time one of the audience bought a bond, she climbed one rung higher on the ladder, until she was more than ninety feet in the air. She climbed up four times, then offered to dive into a rescue net held by the firemen, if someone would buy a $5,000 bond. She quickly got her subscriber, but he anxiously stipulated that she was *not* to dive.

Anne Morgan, daughter of banker J. Pierpont Morgan, headed the American Committee for Devastated France, a vast enterprise of mercy.

Hundreds of girls swarmed upon Washington to do office work in the swollen Departments of Defense, Interior, Labor, and others. Every hotel and boardinghouse, and private homes too, were jammed with these newcomers, who crowded three and four to a room. Restaurants could hardly cope with the mob.

At quitting time, streets were crammed with federal workers streaming out of office buildings. "Why," panted old gentlemen jostled this way and that by exuberant young femininity, "why have all these young ladies—if they are ladies—run away from home and family? Whatever has become of the old-fashioned girl? *She* stayed at home where she belonged."

The wartime girl was noisy, assertive, and happy. She was out in the real world; she was taking part. There was a spirit of exultation in the air. Music was peppier, dances were faster, traffic was thicker, emotions were nearer the surface. For civilians war can be fun.

It was a time of the heroic gesture. There were many parades and every organization put on patriotic programs. The tableau was in vogue because it could be ever so arty and yet required no acting talent. Often a well-fleshed lady stood grandly, in golden drapery, with torch held

high; she was doing the Statue of Liberty. Without the torch she was
Columbia the Gem of the Ocean. Sometimes a gallant Boy Scout,
lightly rouged, knelt before her, looking up soulfully as he offered her
the nation's sword. No parade ever lacked a Spirit of Seventy-Six
quartette, bandaged and tattered, fifing and drumming to hysterical
cheers of onlookers.

It was a time for eyeing your next-door neighbor if he had a German
name or spoke with an accent. (Doubtless a spy for the Kaiser.)
Sauerkraut was renamed "liberty cabbage."

It was a time of singing: "Over There," "How Ya Gonna Keep 'Em
Down on the Farm After They've Seen Paree?" "Mademoiselle from
Armentières," "It's a Long Way to Tipperary," "My Buddy" (that one
always drew tears), and "The Star-Spangled Banner," which brought
people to their feet in instant unison.

Women joyously went to work on farms, in shops and factories and
war plants. Feminists rejoiced at the new types of jobs they were
allowed to hold, and at their even stepping up, occasionally, to
supervisory posts.

It was a time of feeling noble, glorified, sublime, all this in what was
called "the cleansing influence of war."

Meanwhile, Back at the White House

When President Wilson refused to meet any more suffrage
delegations, Alice Paul's "silent sentinels" remained staunchly at the
gates of the White House. For several months picketing was peaceful.
Many passersby were tolerant of the women as harmless crackpots;
more of them applauded the feminists as crusaders. White House
guards and police were friendly.

Then official sentiment changed. The girls were arrested on charges
of obstructing traffic, or unlawful assembly, or, if they resisted rough
treatment by a policeman, disorderly conduct. Arrests went on day after
day, and day after day new picketers marched up to be arrested in their
turn. Now crowds swirled around the gates to watch the excitement,
and in the mob were rowdies who snatched banners and roughed up the
girls, while the police made no objection. Ninety-seven picketers went
to prison.

The story of the suffragists' treatment in jail is a shocking one. They were thrown into filthy cells, given foul meals, and at any sign of rebellion were popped into solitary on bread and water. They were not allowed to communicate with anyone outside or to consult a lawyer. One woman, flung into a cell, vomited all night with a heart attack, and though her fellow prisoners called to the guards in the halls to bring her aid, they paid no attention.

A number of the prisoners, including Alice Paul, went on hunger strikes in protest at being treated as criminals when they insisted they were political prisoners. The hunger strikes failed. The custom was for five people to hold the prisoner down while she was forcibly fed by means of a tube that led through the nose, and the tubing was not the flexible kind now in use.

Of course members resigned from the Woman's Party in droves when officialdom struck at it; but new members surged in to take their places. The attitude of defiance is expressed by feminist Anne Martin, replying to the judge who tried her case: "So long as you send women to prison for asking for justice, so long will women be ready to go in such a cause."

During all this turmoil in Washington, speakers from the Woman's Party swarmed over the country on a lecture schedule planned by Alice Paul. Their potent argument was that while Our Boys fought for democracy overseas, American women were denied it at home.

Toward the end of 1917, it became clear that the arrests were damaging, not the women's cause, but the government's. All prisoners were released and no more arrests were made.

Barricades were falling. Antis could no longer claim, "Women don't really want the vote." The suffragists produced a showy petition 18,333 feet long signed by 500,000 women. Senators were moving toward suffrage, not, as one of them said, because they saw the light but because they felt the heat. By 1914, twelve states and Alaska already had woman suffrage, and after the 1916 elections, six more gave women the vote in presidential elections. One (Arkansas) cautiously gave them the right to vote in primaries.

Year by year, President Wilson came closer and closer to tolerating suffrage, and finally he was a convert. Shortly before the Armistice, he made a stirring speech calling for the Susan B. Anthony Amendment as a war measure. The following May the House passed the amendment, and in June the Senate passed it too. It was ratified by thirty-six states in time for women to vote in the presidential election of 1920.

Seventy years of effort at last paid off.

"Woman at Work"

In 1912, the Socialist party, abhorred by the right-thinking, well-regulated business community, swept in one million votes, its biggest tally. If women had had the vote then, votes of working women would probably not have changed that figure very much. Working women were always cool toward socialism and its promise of a classless society. Resentful of ladies though they were, they wanted the right, nevertheless, to imitate ladies. They even hoped that with good fortune they could themselves rise to a higher class.

Still less did they care for the theories of that firebrand Emma Goldman. Anarchists never did have much of a following, perhaps because they couldn't abide organizations of any kind and therefore couldn't organize speakers, a platform, or a campaign.

Miss Goldman had her personal problems. In 1916 she was jailed for publicly advocating birth control, jailed again in 1917 for obstructing the draft, and in 1919 was deported to Russia. There, however, she was soon disenchanted with Bolshevism.

It wasn't just socialism and anarchy that working women edged away from. They were cagey about joining unions, too. Only one working woman in twenty belonged. There was a certain stigma in being a union member, and these women were pathetically anxious to protect their dignity. Also, if times were bad, they were afraid of being fired if the bosses knew they were organized.

Besides all that, a girl often reasoned, "Why join a union? I'm not going to work forever. I'm going to get married"—forgetting, in a romantic mist, that she would almost surely marry a laboring man, have a family, and be forced back to the factory to help provide bread for that family.

These women never heard the term "pin money." The pin-money theory, complacently held by the affluent, was that few working women really needed jobs, but only wanted a bit of spare change to indulge in frivolities. Bitter proof that they didn't work for fun was that at the end of their ten-hour day in mill or factory they went home and with the dregs of their strength cleaned house, cared for the children, washed and mended clothes. Men of that time and class naturally never did women's work.

This pin-money theory, which survived even beyond World War II, seemed to be the only thing that could make the even-tempered Mary Anderson sit up, claw the air, and sputter like a wildcat.

At sixteen, Mary Anderson came to the United States by steerage as a Swedish peasant girl who couldn't speak English and had no job training. Her first job was washing dishes in a lumberman's boarding-house in Ludington, Michigan, for two dollars a week plus board and room. At seventy, she retired as head of the Women's Bureau of the Department of Labor.

This woman attended the Paris Peace Conference in 1919, was a delegate at labor conferences all over the world, was given an honorary doctorate by Smith College, and knew that her work was respected by five presidents. Yet, as an old lady dictating her memoirs, she said, "[My] job on the Hart, Schaffner, and Marx agreement (in 1913) was the most important thing I have ever done."

This job of slow and patient negotiation, in which she represented the Women's Trade Union League, lasted for two years. Miss Anderson lived in Chicago then, and had risen from dishwashing and housekeeping (she always did hate housework) into factory jobs paying as much, when she was lucky, as $15 a week. But times were sometimes bad, and she knew how it felt to tramp the streets looking for work, with the sick anxiety of soon being penniless and hungry.

One evening during a working period, the girl went to a meeting of the Boot and Shoe Workers' Union "just to be friendly," joined when she learned that a union might mean better wages and shorter hours, and within a year was president of the Stitchers' Local 94, a local composed entirely of women. In the years that she held that post, she had a lot of practice adjusting grievances and striving for better working conditions for women.

Her autobiography, *Woman at Work*, tells almost nothing about her personal life ("Swedes don't talk much") but deals only with her work. A number of photographs are in the book, showing her round, honest face to be pleasant, but not smiling. Her costumes are neat and have as much style as a pair of overalls. Sturdy, practical hats sit squarely across her head. But if her pictures also make her look stolid, they mislead. She loved her bit of fun. In telling about her early years in a shoe factory, she writes, "Sometimes the machines broke down and we could not work. Then we danced, told jokes, laughed, and made considerable noise. One day when the power was off our foreman was on one of the lower floors and another foreman said, 'You'd better go up on your floor. There's a terrible noise up there.' Our foreman said, 'You mind your own business,' and he wouldn't go up until the power started again. Then he told us about it and said, 'But for heaven's sake, don't do it again! It *was* a terrible noise!' "

In spite of the sore relations between management and labor, workers often liked their supervisors, who usually had risen from the ranks.

As president of the local, Mary's life was devoted to persuasion. She persuaded girls to join the union, and once they were in, she had to persuade them to stay. She explained over and over that they must stick together when they had a grievance, and then she negotiated between the bosses and the girls.

The literary style of her book is as plain as a grocery list, but when she talked to her fellow laborers, this simple idiom was useful. It was more persuasive to them than the elegant prose of a professor.

Mary discovered that to lure girls to union meetings she had to find pleasant places for them to gather in. The men met in dirty rooms, sometimes in halls back of saloons, but the women liked a sociable atmosphere. Therefore, she contrived to find attractive rooms, and also arranged that every second meeting be a social affair, sometimes even with coffee and cakes. This was not an easy thing to manage, because the local had no funds to spare, the organizers were tired after their own day's work at the factory, and clearing up after a party is never fun. But she did it because it helped to keep women interested.

After 1919, when she became chief of the new Women's Bureau, it would be nice to think that her life was a jubilant history of triumph and reward. In truth she spent her twenty-five years in the Labor Department in full battle array: she fought for funds to operate the bureau; to get women admitted to policy-making boards, not as consultants but as voting members (here she usually failed); battling to get equal pay for women; and, when Communist hunting was high fashion in Washington, she had to fight the charge of being subversive herself.

But Mary Anderson was a slugger. Patient, level-headed, she fought her battles year in, year out. Her photographs, progressing through the book, show her turning grayer and broader-faced as the years pass, but always the same old dependable Mary, achieving a bit here and a bit there to make life better for the working woman.

One of her endearing qualities was modesty. Of her retirement she wrote: "The department gave a banquet in my honor at the Mayflower Hotel. The Secretary of Labor [Mrs. Perkins] presided, and everyone made a big fuss over me. But it did not seem very real. I kept feeling that all the fine things they said must be about someone else."

Ardent Reformers

Julia Lathrop, a fellow Chicagoan who had been on the staff of Hull House for years, held a post similar to Mary Anderson's: she was chief of the new Children's Bureau in the Department of Labor from 1912 to 1922. Miss Lathrop has the distinction of having established the first juvenile court in the United States, in 1899.

Helen Keller too, though she never held public office, was in this mainstream of reform. She marched in suffrage parades, supported the Socialist party, and felt that to spread well-being was both feasible and right. This bright spirit in its darkened world had, says William James, a sense of being in a wider life than that of this world's selfish little interests.

Two other women who devoted their lives to reform were Margaret Dreier Robins and Florence Kelley.

Mrs. Robins was a great beauty, tall and dark with magnificent eyes. She had tact and warmth and that rare quality of bringing out the best in everyone she met. All who knew and wrote of her wrote with the tenderest affection.

She came of a well-to-do family and married Raymond Robins, a millionaire who had struck it rich in the Klondike and came home to spend himself and his fortune in trying to reform politics and labor. The idealistic young couple moved to Chicago and rented a fourth-floor tenement flat in the slums of the Bloody Seventeenth, so called because there were always fights in that ward on election day. The Robinses were so much in love that whenever they were separated telegrams and love letters rushed to and fro between them.

Along with beauty and charm, Mrs. Robins had ability as an organizer and leader, which accounts for her having been president of the National WTUL from 1907 to 1922. She also poured her wealth into support of Hull House. Of course she, Jane Addams, Mary Anderson, M. Carey Thomas of Bryn Mawr, Carrie Chapman Catt, and Dr. Shaw of the suffrage movement and other leaders all were acquainted. They met and met again, in the course of their busy, peripatetic lives, each woman intent on her special phase of reform.

Fiery, impatient Florence Kelley was the daughter of Pig-Iron Kelley, a congressman famous in his day as a Radical Republican. She had a thorough grounding in Marxist Socialism, and all her life believed firmly in the long-range program of the Socialist party. Yet she found, to her exasperation, that she could not devote herself to working for a distant revolution. People were in need today. She had to help *now*. This urgency was especially marked after she joined the staff of Hull House and blended into its atmosphere of earnest, day-by-day work with the needy closest to hand. And so, in spite of her convictions, she had to batter away like any bourgeois crusader at getting legislation enacted to protect working children and women.

Unlike most reformers, Charlotte Perkins Gilman was an intellectual whose work was with the pen. She had a curiously deprived childhood. Her father deserted his wife and two infants, and though Mrs. Perkins sturdily presented him to the children as a great and admirable character, Charlotte was always bitter about his defection.

The mother determined that Charlotte should never suffer from loss of love as she had suffered, and therefore denied the child all show of affection, so that Charlotte should never expect love, nor long for it. She rejected all caresses from the girl, and never caressed her unless the child was asleep. When Charlotte discovered this, she used to force herself to stay awake until her mother came to bed, then, pretending to be sound asleep, would rapturously enjoy being gathered up, held close, and kissed.

An imaginative child, Charlotte created a fantasy world, and each night, alone in bed, she went forth into this enchanted world. But, when she was thirteen, she made the mistake of telling an adult friend about it. The friend was so shocked by this abnormality that she reported it to Mrs. Perkins, who commanded Charlotte to stop it at once. All the brightness of life was denied her.

No one could tell whether she obeyed or not, but, "Obedience was Right," she says in her autobiography. "The thing had to be done and I did it. Night after night to shut the door on happiness and hold it shut. . . . just thirteen!"

When she was seventeen, an older cousin invited her to a student concert at Brown University, but her mother automatically declined for her. That same day another cousin twenty years older than Charlotte invited her to a family theater party to see Edwin Booth in *Hamlet*. What rapture! Nothing else could have made Charlotte so happy. But again her mother refused. Why? Because, she explained, having refused Robert she had to refuse Edward also, or Robert's feelings would have been hurt. "But how about my feelings?" cried the girl.

"I have never since that day," she writes, "felt a sharp sense of disappointment, only a numb feeling. . . . It was many years before I learned to accept an offered pleasure naturally."

With this crippling background, it is not remarkable that her marriage and motherhood were disasters. After the birth of her baby, she came close to a nervous breakdown. "Here was a charming home, a loving and devoted husband; an exquisite baby, healthy, intelligent, and good; a highly competent mother to run things; a wholly satisfactory servant—and I lay all day on the lounge and cried."

Her depression was so profound that her husband consented to a divorce to save her reason.

With the practice of rigid self-discipline, she struggled back from the edge of insanity and became a noted lecturer and writer, a truly impressive achievement. Over the years she wrote more than twenty volumes of poetry, fiction, and social criticism. Her books were among the most widely read in America.

The stoic sat down one evening to write out her thoughts on the economic position of women, a subject on which she had been lecturing for years. In seventeen days she had produced the rough draft of a book; in fifty-eight more days she had finished the manuscript of *Women and Economics*, her masterpiece. It is the most influential book ever written by an American feminist, and was a best seller in its day. Even yet it is required reading for students and an international classic.

So self-controlled was this woman that at seventy-five, when cancer was about to prevent her carrying on her work, she put her affairs in order and arranged her own death by chloroform.

Radiant Rebel

"The first right of every child is to be wanted, to be desired, to be planned for with an intensity of love."

This is the opening sentence of a speech by Margaret Sanger that she delivered 119 times during one year.

She was a small, sweet-voiced woman with wide-set gray eyes, thick auburn hair piled on top of her head, and a dainty bit of lace at her throat. Delicate though she looked, Margaret Sanger was an indomitable crusader, a fanatic who blazed at her brightest when the going was tough.

Dissatisfied with suburban housewifery and motherhood—though her marriage to William Sanger was not an unhappy one in its early years, and though she fiercely loved her children, Stuart, Grant, and Peggy—she had felt imprisoned by her small role, and had had to hurl herself into the larger currents of the day.

She was influenced by the books of Charlotte Perkins Gilman on the freedom of women, and was concerned with pacifism, women's rights, and suffrage. After years in the kitchen, she went back to her profession, and her work as a public-health nurse led her into the swarming tenements of New York's Lower East Side. There she found a cause big enough to devote her life to: birth control. Often her cause was blocked by injustice or bigotry; she had to fight the police, because there was a New York law against giving anyone information about birth control; and she also fought the obscenity law, public prejudice, and the Catholic Church. The bigger they came, the more lustily Margaret fought.

Poverty, she found, went hand in hand with large families. In one block where she often worked, more than 3,000 people lived miserably crowded together, and the infant death rate was a horrifying 204 for every 1,000 births. Infant mortality increased proportionally as the number of children in the family increased.

When she took her cause to the suffragists, they said, "First we'll get the vote. Then we'll see about birth control." Their sights were set too low for Mrs. Sanger; the misery of poverty-stricken women with five, eight, twelve children mattered more to her than the right to vote. She appealed to the unions, but their single ambition was shorter hours and higher pay. So she set forth on a lone crusade.

She wrote and edited an eight-page monthly newspaper called *Woman Rebel.* In flaming phrases it described the horrors of abortion, often fatal. It argued that abortion would be unnecessary if contraceptives were available. It pleaded with women not to bring unwanted babies into the world, but to make themselves absolute mistresses of their own bodies.

Next she wrote and distributed a booklet, *Family Limitation,* that freely gave contraceptive information. Later this booklet would be translated into thirteen languages and ten million copies would be printed during the first few years of its life. But that goes ahead of the story.

She knew that distributing this information was illegal, but she did not consider herself lawless. There was a higher law, she avowed, the law of the sacredness of life. But of course she was arrested, both for disseminating forbidden information, and for sending "obscene material" through the mails.

The affair made headlines, and by the time her case came to trial, such a storm of sympathy was aroused that the prosecution, after many delays, dismissed the case. Even though Margaret was denied a victory in court, she had brought birth control versus obscenity out of the dark, splashed the topic across front pages, and made people all over the country argue about it.

Margaret Sanger now set forth on a speaking tour. She spoke in Pittsburgh, Cleveland, Chicago, Minneapolis—right across the country, except where she was thrown into jail, of course, or where she found that the hall or theater that she had engaged was locked up tight. Sometimes the jittery owner of the place, key in his pocket, had left town quickly when he found that if he let that Sanger woman appear and give her filthy talk his building would be boycotted by a righteous public. Except for these instances, she talked to jam-packed halls.

Everywhere there were some who hurled insults at her as an advocate of unbridled sex lust, and who called birth control unnatural and immoral. But everywhere too women crowded around her after lectures and begged her to tell them how to avoid pregnancy.

The need, she saw, was for a chain of clinics across the country. She had to lead the way now by opening a clinic in New York City. She knew that arrest and imprisonment were almost certain. But Margaret Sanger, who looked so mild and defenseless, could never be stopped by obstacles.

In Brownsville, a dilapidated section of Brooklyn, she found two first-floor storerooms that would do. Helped by her sister Ethel, also a nurse, and by a woman friend named Fania Mindell, she furnished the rooms meagerly, advertised the opening by means of handbills—but not one single doctor in the whole state of New York would risk his license by joining the little staff. So the three women opened their clinic without a doctor.

On the day of the opening, they looked out the door at seven o'clock in the morning to find that more than a hundred women were already lined up on the sidewalk, women in shawls and wornout shoes, their red, chapped hands clasping the smaller chapped hands of their children. Many carried babies in their arms. Many looked old and broken at thirty or thirty-five, but just now their faces were beaming with hope.

For nine days the clinic served all comers, accepting a ten-cent fee from each, and gave them freely all the advice and information available—and pitifully little that was in 1916. On the tenth day the expected happened: the three women were arrested and driven away in the police van.

As it started up, there was a scream. A woman wheeling a baby carriage came around the corner, preparing to visit the clinic, but realizing what was happening, she left the baby carriage, rushed through the crowd shouting, "Come back! Come back and save me!" She ran down the street after the moving van, tears pouring down her face, until friends caught her and pulled her to a stop.

The criminal sisters were tried and given thirty days each; Fania was fined fifty dollars. Their attorney appealed the case.

That act of defiance, opening the clinic, was the breakthrough for birth control. By 1918, the case had got up to the Court of Appeals, highest court in the state, and the judge, while upholding the convictions, also wrote a liberal interpretation of the section of the criminal code that dealt with giving birth-control information. By his interpretation, the physician was permitted to leak the vital news to a married patient for her health.

Margaret was jubilant. At last doctors were free to tell women the facts that would set them free. Now clinics could be legally operated in New York, and other states would follow New York's lead. The first battle was won.

The story of Margaret Sanger's achievements and her iron will make her seem a fearsome Amazon. But flip over the coin and there is a very feminine woman pursued by men, adored, cherished. The Englishmen H. G. Wells, Hugh De Selincourt, and Havelock Ellis loved her. American men found her enchanting, too. She was an exciting woman. One man wrote that two weeks they had spent working together were "the happiest, the most inspiring I have ever known. . . . I have loved you beyond my power to understand it."

Margaret Sanger wrote later, "I was hard on men. I didn't have time to waste on people unless they would do something to help forward the movement." In a letter to a friend she once wrote, "Where is the man to give me what the movement gives me in joy and interest and freedom?"

One of her admirers called her "a radiant rebel." She was so highly charged with vitality, sweetness, and ardor that people lived at a faster pace when they were with her.

Early in her crusade she and William Sanger had drifted apart, without any bitterness, and after several years of separation were divorced. She remarried at last, J. Noah H. Slee, wealthy head of the Three-in-One Oil Company. He was as strong-willed and energetic as she, had courted her for three years in the United States, and pursued her halfway around the world as well, on her tornado-like speaking tours.

But she could never give up her independence, and they made a unique marriage pact. She would accept no money from him. By that time her books brought in royalties. They agreed to live in the same house but in separate apartments with separate keys. They communicated by phone, even making dinner engagements instead of taking them for granted. Mr. Slee considered her the most beautiful and fascinating woman alive and once said of her, "Before I met Margaret, nothing important had ever happened to me. She was, and always will be, the greatest adventure of my life."

Artist from the Prairie

"The quality of a second-rate writer can easily be defined, but a first-rate writer can only be experienced. It is just the thing in him which escapes analysis that makes him first-rate."

Willa Cather wrote that in an essay on Katherine Mansfield, but the idea can just as well be applied to her own work. You may speak of the simplicity of her writing, the purity and lucidity of her style, and the compelling reality of her fictional characters; but the grandeur of *My Antonia*, for example, can only be felt, not explained.

In her early years in Nebraska, where the Cathers moved when she was nine, she was a sturdily-built, energetic girl, keenly interested in people. The neighboring farmers—Swedes, Danes, Norwegians, and Bohemians—captured her imagination.

"I particularly liked the old women," she said later. They told her many stories of life in the Old Country. "I have never found any intellectual excitement any more intense than I used to feel when I spent a morning with one of these old women at her baking or butter making. I used to ride home in the most unreasonable state of excitement; I always felt ... as if I had actually got inside another person's skin."

This delight in getting inside the skin of another person was a foreshadowing of her future as a fiction writer, but in childhood her ambition was to be a doctor. It was not until she had studied at the University of Nebraska for a year or two that she knew her life had to be given to literature.

In those college years she was fun-loving and gregarious. She liked to wear mannish straw hats and starchy shirts with four-in-hand ties instead of ruffly shirtwaists. She kept her hair cut short, wore skirts shorter than fashion decreed, spoke in a deep voice, and signed her name "William Cather." After her school days, she dropped this masculine play-acting, except for the tailored look of her costume; that she kept.

For years she earned her living teaching high school English or as a journalist, and from 1906 to 1912 was associate editor of the lively *McClure's Magazine.* Her work at *McClure's* was tempestuous and arduous, and it left little time for her own writing. She was tugged in two directions: pulled by her loyalty to the eccentric, explosive, possessive editor-in-chief, S. S. McClure, whom she loved almost as warmly as she loved her father and brothers; and at the same time she was pulled by her longing to escape the chaotic world of journalism into the quiet of a solitary, creative world.

She fretted and shilly-shallied, unable to make a clear-cut decision for herself. But circumstances made one for her. McClure's flamboyant and irresponsible financial behavior made it necessary for his whole magazine empire to be reorganized. She quickly resigned.

At this time she was a brisk, square woman with a sharp, direct glance, a masculine handshake, and an enthusiastic way of talking.

The job at *McClure's* had paid her well and she had thriftily tucked away a portion of her earnings; besides, she could write a magazine article whenever she had to bring the pot back to the boil. Her imagination seethed with unwritten characters and places that she was eager to put on paper. At this time she wanted to write about Nebraska and those old immigrant women and their families.

Willa Cather could write successfully only about people and places that she loved. Her characters might be queer or foolish or set upon self-destruction, but there had to be something about them that warmed her heart. Further, ideas that had rolled quietly around in her mind for years resulted in fine writing; whereas the vivid transfer of immediate impressions onto paper made, for her, merely journalistic writing.

Now, in 1912, settling down to a quiet desk with her ambition totally bent upon the writing of fiction, she was not a beginner. She was a woman of thirty-six with three dozen short stories and a first novel published—*Alexander's Bridge*, which she always spoke of disparagingly. Years of practice had polished and simplified her style. She believed that the essence of art is simplicity: finding what detail can be omitted while yet preserving the spirit of the whole.

O Pioneers! appeared in 1913, the first of her great writing about the prairie; *The Song of the Lark* in 1915; and *My Antonia* just before the Armistice. The reading public loved them, and the critics approved. H. L. Mencken called *My Antonia* the finest thing of its sort ever written in America.

Later works included *One of Ours* (which won the Pulitzer Prize), *A Lost Lady*, *Death Comes for the Archbishop* (which she considered her best), *The Professor's House*, and *Shadows on the Rock*.

During the writing of *My Antonia*, she was hardly aware of the World War. Her disinterest in all matters political was colossal; it was impenetrable. She was equally opaque to women's rights; social reformers she found very dull people. She cared for only one world, the world of art.

Willa Cather had a lively capacity for hate, but an equally lively affection. Often she made a new friendship based on intuitive liking at first meeting, and such a friendship usually developed into a lifetime devotion. Over the years she wrote thousands of personal letters.

In later life she acquired an obsession for privacy; this earned her many enemies, who considered her irascible. But her door always stood open to old friends. She became a short-tempered, impatient woman whose health was breaking, and to those who saw her only at public gatherings she seemed harsh in personality and awkward in her movements. Hamlin Garland was one who was surprised to see her thus; then he was quick to add, "But she did a noble book!"

Pussy Jones Makes Good

Edith Wharton's work fills forty-two volumes written over a period of forty years, but her two masterpieces appeared in the second decade. *Ethan Frome*, that simple, stark tragedy, came out in 1911, and *The Age of Innocence*, picture of the New York society of her girlhood, appeared in 1920.

Little Edith Jones's mother disliked and resented her. Her father felt a mild affection for her, but seldom bothered to visit her in the schoolroom. Her two brothers, Harry and Freddy, were ten and twelve years older than she; in childhood that is the distance of a whole generation. She had no playmates. She grew up in a long, cold misery of shyness, longing for approval but never knowing how to achieve it.

Fortunately, one person loved her: Doyley, her nurse. Sometimes Doyley took her hand and led her down a long, dark flight of stairs to the basement, where she would have tea with the servants. There the little girl relaxed in a warm, cheerful atmosphere where she could laugh and chatter and feel wanted. All her life "Pussy," as she was called, was comfortable with her servants, and they served her devotedly, usually for many years.

When she was ten, she began to write stories. Too shy to ask anyone to buy copybooks for her, she begged brown-paper wrappings from the kitchen. Flattening them out on the floor, she crawled back and forth across them, writing with stubs of pencils that she found somewhere.

At eleven she wrote her first novel, and when it was finished she took it timidly, but proudly, to her mother. Surely this achievement would win her mother's approval. Frowning a little, Mrs. Jones took the brown sheets in fastidious fingertips and read:

" 'Oh, how do you do, Mrs. Brown?' said Mrs. Tomkins. 'If only I had known you were going to call, I should have tidied up the drawing room.' "

The mother looked at Edith coldly, said, "Drawing rooms are always tidy," and thrust the manuscript back into the child's hands.

Edith was never sent to school, but by a lucky chance the governess who happened to be engaged during her teens, Anna Bahlman, was a scholarly German who introduced the little bluestocking to the exciting world of literature and languages.

After her debut at eighteen, Edith was a dismal flop, socially. Too brainy, too sharp-tongued, she frightened away possible suitors. At debutante parties, she fixed a glassy smile on her lips and sat among the chaperones, hiding the agony of being a wallflower. Guilt gnawed at her because she was failing at a young girl's only business: getting a husband. Fear, too, because there simply was no satisfactory place in society for an old maid; she would be caged forever in the household of a relative, not even mistress of her own money.

Then she fell totally, helplessly in love with Walter Van Rensselaer Berry, a man a few years her senior. She saw him as brilliant, witty, warm-hearted, and adventurous. Other people described him as cold and completely selfish. Unfortunately for her, he was not, to use the Victorian phrase, "a marrying man."

In that tight little social world of theirs, what did people have to do but to watch each other? And, though bashful Pussy Jones was not quite "compromised," still her infatuation became more and more apparent, and the luckless girl "got herself talked about." Walter Berry was never in love; he was only entertained by Edith's quick wit and intelligence; unlike most men of the time, he didn't mind brains in a woman. But when he felt the cold mists of matrimony rising higher and higher about him, he whisked himself away to Washington and pursuit of his legal career.

From the public shame of being a rejected woman, Edith was rescued by the only rescue possible in her class: proposal of marriage from an eligible bachelor. Edward Wharton, twelve years older than Edith, had exactly the qualities that the humiliated girl needed: he was mild, considerate, protective. He lived for huntin', fishin', and trampin' across country, and he had just enough money to be able to live without working. Because of this way of life, he was a copout from Boston society, where a gentleman was expected to devote himself sternly to useful work.

In 1885 he and Edith were married, and she was free. No longer was she a clumsy girl teetering on the social tightrope, but a handsome young matron with a respectable protector and an independent income inherited from her father, who had died a few years earlier.

The bridegroom's family did not attend the wedding, but before the newlyweds set out on their honeymoon, they went to Boston, where Edward introduced the bride to his family. The Whartons of Boston looked coldly upon this nobody from New York. Anyone not from their Boston circle was a nobody. The duty of Edward's mother was of course to place the girl in the family carriage and take her calling upon family friends. Mrs. Wharton did nothing. The girl left Boston, frigidly snubbed.

The young couple had a leisurely European honeymoon (Edith always loved travel) and, at home once more, they rented a little house and settled down in Manhattan. After years of not writing, Edith took up her pen once more. One day she decided to submit three poems to three magazines, one each to *Scribner's*, *Harper's*, and *The Century Magazine*. Time passed and none of the editors replied. The poet gave up hope. Then one morning she found three letters in her mailbox, one from *Scribner's*, one from *Harper's*, one from *The Century*. She took them indoors and with shaking hands slit open the three envelopes. All three poems had been accepted! She ran screaming with happiness up and down the staircase, up and down, wild with joy.

Warmed by the first success of her life, she hurled herself into the writing of short stories, and every one was accepted by a magazine. Next she moved on to the writing of novels. Each day she woke early, was at work by six-thirty, and wrote steadily until noon. Then, stimulated by her morning's work, she sallied downstairs, beautifully dressed, ready to be the charming wife and hostess.

She never talked about her writing to anyone unless it was to her secretary, Anna Bahlman. The scholarly governess had returned when Edith needed her, and stayed to the end of her life. Edith kept the two sections of her life strictly divided: the social part and the literary part.

Some observers find it puzzling that this intellectual woman should have cared so much about being a conspicuously successful hostess. But is it so surprising when one remembers the longing of little Pussy Jones to be loved and approved of? When one thinks of the wallflower agonies of those debutante days? And the icy snubs she took from her Boston mother-in-law?

Wryly, she once observed that in New York she had been considered too intelligent to be fashionable; in Boston she was considered too fashionable to be intelligent. Add to this, at the turn of the century it was not quite respectable to write. In the Jones family, her novels were considered a disgrace, never, never to be mentioned. No, no—one understands why this ambitious woman wanted to be known as a great hostess.

In 1902 she and Edward built The Mount in Lenox, Massachusetts. It was a great, solid, square white house, grandly furnished and set in splendidly landscaped grounds. Here Edward could act the part of country squire, and Edith could entertain with a glitter that no New York hostess could top, and with an imperious finger could beckon distinguished literary guests whose presence the most high-handed Boston hostess might envy. Henry James, that literary giant, had become one of her closest friends.

By the time she was in her forties—and in her generation a woman was middle-aged at thirty-five—she had, at times, a manner that one biographer describes as "polished impudence"; she had a joyous sense of the absurd, a witty tongue, and a laugh of infectious gaiety. Another biographer, Percy Lubbock, says of her air of self-assured grandeur, that she "rustled unhesitatingly into the locked church, the gallery that happened to be closed that day, the palace that wasn't shown to visitors."

In 1913, the Wharton marriage ended in divorce. For years Edith shrank from taking this step, years during which she and Edward were more and more painfully incompatible. In her social circle and at that time, divorce was still a scandalous action; before, during, and after it, she and Edward maintained a stately silence about it.

She was nearing fifty when she had her one love affair, with the journalist Morton Fullerton. Their secret was well kept; only her best, most discreet friends knew about it, and they kept loyally mum.

Two years before her divorce—in 1911—*Ethan Frome* was published. This story presents the tragic spectacle of man pursued by perverse, relentless fate. At that time the American public demanded light, cheerful stories with happy endings, and therefore it should logically have rejected *Ethan Frome* massively. Instead, the critics viewed it coolly, while readers took it to their hearts because they were moved by the stark reality of its three characters, and by the simplicity of the bleak, heartbreaking tale. It is a case of the rank-and-file having keener instincts than the literati, for the book has become a classic.

Edith Wharton's other great book, *The Age of Innocence*, was a different kind of story. In slow and formal steps, like the minuet that was still fashionable in ballrooms at the time of Pussy Jones's debut, it portrays the New York society of her youth. The tragedy moves deliberately from the opening scene to the final one, never ruffling the surface of the protagonists' lives. Edith Wharton tells her story with clarity and flawless precision; her hand never falters nor writes a false scene. This was a book she had to write. Here is material that grew within her mind for years, as Willa Cather's best books slowly matured for years in her thoughts.

The Age of Innocence was published in 1920, and the same year saw publication of *Miss Lulu Bett*, a novel of small-town Wisconsin life, written by that gentle, tiny, withdrawn woman, Zona Gale, herself a Wisconsin small-towner. The book was an instant success, applauded by Henry Seidel Canby, Ida Tarbell, Fannie Hurst, Heywood Broun, and Franklin P. Adams among others. It was made into a Broadway play (which won the Pulitzer Prize), then into a movie starring Lois Wilson. *Miss Lulu Bett* shared best-selling honors for 1920 with Sinclair Lewis's *Main Street*. Go into a bookstore today and you will probably find *The Age of Innocence* on the shelf, and students' editions of *Main Street*, but if you ask for *Miss Lulu Bett*, your response will be a baffled shake of the head.

Probably neither Zona Gale nor Edith Wharton—nor even Willa Cather, though she lived in New York City—were habituées of Mabel

Dodge's salon at 23 Fifth Avenue. Hundreds of people dropped in, with or without invitation, not for the food and drink, but for the intoxicating conversation. Poets, newsmen, trade unionists, anarchists, clergymen and lawyers, suffragists and anti-suffragists, artists, murderers, clubwomen, birth-control advocates, and just plain people met there to argue, to shock and be shocked, and to go away euphorically drunk on new ideas. Mabel Dodge's evenings were among the most exciting in the city.

Fashion and Frivolity

In 1911 women's coats were long, baggy, and drab in color; the jackets of their dark suits were also long—to the knee—and hats were elephantine. Many hats were shaped like the vast boxes they'd come out of, were balanced squarely on the head, and heaped with all the products of field and forest.

Then, having achieved the ultimate in clumsiness, fashion about-faced and the decade went blithely back to chic in a variety of styles. Skirts could now be peg-topped, panniered, tiered, hobbled at the ankle, or they could be tube-straight. A bodice might be slung about with drapery, or skin-tight, or softened with a fichu. One item of dress, however, was *de rigueur* in every wardrobe: the plain, high-waisted skirt worn with a white shirtwaist, which might be plain or elaborate, according to taste, but usually fitted very tight and had an upstanding, boned collar. With this a lady might wear a prim cameo under the chin, or she might pin a little gold watch at her bosom.

The vasty hats toppled off, to be replaced by tall, wrapped toques, or cocky little pillboxes, or, for the dreamy mood, by picture hats with wide, drooping brims and wreaths of pink rosebuds. The ultra-fashionable might wear a cartwheel tipped to the side of the head. There was something new in hat trimming: long, narrow feathers or foot-long sprays, curled at the tips, stood up erect from the center front of the hat. Worn with an air, the effect was theatrical.

Enormous fur muffs were stylish in winter; in summer every lady sauntered with parasol in hand, a long-handled, elegant parasol, carried with a flourish.

Variety was so great that a fashion commentator in *Woman's*

Home Companion wrote petulantly, "It would almost seem as if individual preference in selecting one's clothes might in the near future become quite the proper thing."

Along with this new permissiveness in fashion came new patterns in behavior. Girls took up golf and tennis, though they had to scamper over the courts in long, heavy skirts, and of course they wore hats—little sailor hats. Some girls learned to drive cars.

And there was the dance craze. It began in 1912, swept the country like an epidemic, and didn't begin to taper off until the depression of the thirties. This new dancing was not that of the waltz or the two-step, either, with the partners holding each other respectfully at arm's length, but the one-step, the difficult tango, the bunny hug, the Castle walk, and, most enduring, the foxtrot, in all of which the partners danced in close embrace.

Irene and Vernon Castle—that beautiful, well-bred couple whose dancing was described as a breeze made visible—began the dance craze. Their performance was decidedly low-key. When performing at a restaurant, for example, instead of whirling onto a platform in exotic costume, they would rise from a table among the diners, wearing evening dress, and with exquisite grace would perform on the dance floor.

Irene Castle became the rage. She had a charming, simple manner and walked with long strides, free and athletic. At ease, she stood with pelvis thrust forward and body leaning back, one leg placed to the rear for balance, and one shoulder raised. Only the young and supple were able to imitate that. The fashion photographer Cecil Beaton described her as having put the backbone to femininity, showing its vertebrae instead of its dimples, and thus typifying emancipated woman. With her unique boyishness, Irene Castle had, paradoxically, a fragile look of girlishness; she usually wore soft, flowing dresses of simple cut.

It was Irene Castle who began the fashion for bobbed hair, but it is not true that millions of women promptly took to the shears. When your crowning glory has been the very symbol of womanhood your whole life long, and when your family rises up ranting, and threatens you with the whole clan's damnation if you dare to cut those beautiful tresses, well, you don't take up the shears without anguish. Nonetheless, year by year, more and more women discovered the light-headed freedom of short hair until, by the mid-twenties, only the old or dowdy or the nonconformist, had need of hairpins.

America's Sweetheart

Why was Mary Pickford the darling of millions? It could only be because something basic in the emotions of all those people responded strongly to her projection of sweetness and mischief, her pathetic vulnerability combined with the will to fight back, and her utter femininity. She was the girl everyone wanted to protect and be loved by.

The public thought of her (and still does) as one who always played little-girl roles: in *Rebecca of Sunnybrook Farm, Daddy Long Legs, Little Annie Rooney*. In reality, this talented actress could perform quite as well in serious drama, such as *Tess of the Storm Country, Stella Maris,* and *The Taming of the Shrew*. Like most performers, she enjoyed breaking out of the mold and doing a variety of parts, and was more successful than lesser stars at escaping the rigid type-casting of that early movie period. Even so, the public liked her best as the innocent young thing who would never grow up, the child with shining curls spilling down her back.

Mary Pickford escaped something that has plagued many an American favorite, notably Jacqueline Kennedy Onassis and Elizabeth Taylor. Having raised their darling to dizzy heights, the public may grow bored, or jealous, or disillusioned, and rudely knock down the pedestal, leaving the former idol to pick herself up, bruised and bewildered, and shake off the plaster dust. This charmer, on the other hand, gracefully retired to private life while she was still "Our Mary."

The divorce from her first husband, Owen Moore, presented a test. In that era, stars usually concealed their marriages because fans were believed to want their heroes and heroines forever single, forever thrilling to chaste romance. Nevertheless, Little Mary wed, then divorced, and her popularity survived both shocks. But more was to come: in 1920 she married Douglas Fairbanks, himself recently divorced. The two must have held their breaths. Would the fans put up with this? They did; the king and queen of Hollywood could do no wrong.

Their honeymoon trip abroad was like the triumphal journey of heads of state. There were such crushes of admirers wherever they appeared that they were in danger of being injured. To escape the mobs, they fled from England to Germany, incognito. How refreshing it would be, they told each other, to walk on the streets and not be jostled by adorers. How delightful to be quietly together, composed and civilized, like any private tourists. They had one day of it—shopping, sightseeing, dining—without a flicker of recognition on any face.

At the day's end Douglas asked, "Do you really like being left alone?" She replied that she had had enough obscurity to last her lifetime. They quickly left Germany and went back to those pleasant scenes of mobbery.

In the 1910s, Marguerite Clark was one of the few movie actresses who approached America's Sweetheart in popularity. But there were others who filled special niches and had their own fans.

Theda Bara, she of the heavily painted eyes, was publicized as "the wickedest woman in the world." She was a vampire, a richly under-dressed maneater. She, like Mary Pickford, wanted a change of role now and then, and tried nice-girl parts. The fans would have none of that; they wanted their soulless siren back.

Pearl White was queen of the serials, starring in *The Perils of Pauline, The Exploits of Elaine,* and other cliff-hangers. A former trapeze performer in the circus, she did all those hazardous stunts herself.

Other stars were the talented Clara Kimball Young; Bebe Daniels; lovely Norma Talmadge; Elsie Janis, who entertained the troops overseas and was dubbed Sweetheart of the AEF; brilliant and steel-willed Gloria Swanson; Lillian Gish with the tender, emotional mouth; Russian-born Nazimova; gifted Pola Negri; and a host of others.

Ziegfeld Follies starred Anna Held, Mae Murray, Ruth Etting, Marilyn Miller (who was married for a time to Mary Pickford's brother Jack), Ina Claire, Lilyan Tashman, Nora Bayes, and of course that marvelously funny woman Fanny Brice.

A few Broadway stars of the time were Jane Cowl, famous for her portrayal of Juliet; Ruth Chatterton, who sprang to stardom in 1914 in *Daddy Long Legs;* Mrs. Patrick Campbell, who played *Pygmalion* (George Bernard Shaw wrote it for her on a dare); Ethel Barrymore, starring in a 1919 version of *Déclassée;* and Eva Le Gallienne, making her first American hit in *Not So Long Ago.*

Voice of Velvet

Rosa Ponselle's singing career really began when, as a child of twelve, she sang in restaurants. Later she toured in vaudeville, but she was twenty before she decided that she must have professional voice lessons. Her excellent teacher one day invited a friend of his named Enrico Caruso to drop in at his studio as if for a casual visit, and then he had Rosa sing arias in which he had carefully coached her. Singing away, the girl suddenly realized that the visitor was singing along with her—the great tenor himself.

When they finished, Caruso seized her hands and spoke to her in her parents' native Neapolitan dialect, calling her Schugnizza: little street urchin. "You, little girl, are going to sing with me at the Metropolitan," he said. And within a few days she was indeed invited to sing the part of Leonora in Verdi's opera, *La Forza del Destino*.

In her first interview with Gatti-Casazza, director of the Met, he asked her to learn "Pace, pace, mio dio," from *La Forza* and "Casta diva" from the opera *Norma*. Not knowing that these are two of the most difficult arias in the whole operatic repertoire, Rosa replied airily that she would do it, and for a week she worked day and night, forgetting to eat, forgetting to sleep. When she went back for her audition, Rosa got through the formidable "Pace," Leonora's emotional outburst in the last act of *La Forza*, when she learns that her lover has mortally wounded her brother. But, when she began to sing the even more trying "Casta diva," her breath stopped in the middle of the allegro and she fainted.

With a less perceptive director than Gatti-Casazza, that faint might have ended her career before it began, but he saw beyond the faint to the girl's courage and to her wonderful voice. He once said that it was a voice like Caruso's. "It is like velvet. It is without holes. Most voices are like a garment, thick in one place, thin in another. Hers is strong and even."

When Rosa left his office that very day, she had a contract to debut at the Met in *La Forza del Destino*. But, before she left him, Gatti-Casazza looked at her severely and said, "You will be the first American to appear at the Metropolitan without having been to Europe first. If you make good, I will open the door to all American talent as long as I am here. If you fail, the doors are closed forever. The future of the others depends on you."

What a dread responsibility for a young girl! But Rosa studied industriously under a new teacher, the famous Romano Romani. When rehearsals began at the opera house itself, she said that on the great stage she felt "like a bird trying to fly for the first time."

On opening night she was in such a panic that she thought she might die. Drenched with perspiration, she ran for comfort to Caruso. She found him behind the flats glug-glugging a salt-water gargle and nervously muttering, "Never again! It is too much to ask of a man. I will never sing again."

In the wings she saw her mother, rosary clutched in hand, and her sister Carmela, smelling salts in her hand, lest Rosa faint again.

She could not let her family down.

With no one to lean on, and all those unknown Americans of the future leaning on her, she went onstage and not for a moment did she let herself get out of control. She restrained each gesture, each phrase, to its proper level.

She had a second difficulty that evening. The voice range of Leonora in *Forza* is pitched unusually high, and as she sang, Rosa had constantly to tell herself, "Up, up—top, top, top!" In later years, whenever she faced difficulties in a part, she would remember that first night. Having survived that, she could survive anything.

Next day, the critics unanimously praised the sweetness of her voice, its evenness, its luscious tones. Rosa Ponselle went on to star triumphantly at the Metropolitan for twenty years.

CALL IT A SPADE

The It Girls

Movie star Clara Bow personified the girl of the 1920s. She was impudent, flirtatious, gay, and independent, and she loved to upset tradition. Her lively and sensual beauty suited the times as the elegant beauty of the young Ethel Barrymore had suited the 1900s. Clara Bow's little dancing feet were never still; her mobile face and expressive body were in constant motion. The playful toss of the head, the defiant shrug, the mischievous wink, the fingers caressing a man's lapel—these quick gestures were those of the active, eager girl idealized in the 1920s.

It was English novelist Elinor Glyn (who preferred to be called Madame Glyn) who invented the new meaning for the old pronoun "It": sex appeal. It was the thing for the girl of the decade to cultivate It.

Clara Bow, publicized as having more It than anyone else around, lived on the screen in a world of ceaseless action and fun. Her real life was different. She became involved in a number of minor scandals which finally alienated her public, because fans of the twenties wanted their stars to be a little bit naughty, but not too naughty.

Every week 77 million people attended the movies, and a girl without strong behavioral patterns at home did her best to follow the style set by movie stars. Movies, however, did not try to deal with reality. Their version of life showed razzle-dazzle gaiety, romance, and opulence, with a strong accent on youth. The heroine might be flamboyantly risqué, or a gold digger, or a bossy executive (of whom there were almost none in real life), or a sexpot—all this in a never-never land of the director's imagination. But here is the paradox of 1920s movies: however the star might be idolized in the course of the plot, at the end she was always put down: immodesty, gold digging, and assertiveness had to be chastened.

So many movies ended with the following scene that it became a weary cliché: the male, tired of the female's screeching that she is independent, or equal, or self-sufficient, sweeps her into his arms and kisses her diligently. She fights him with blows of her pretty little fists, but the blows grow less and less positive ... her arms grow limp ... and at last she sags in his embrace, the happy victim of desire. Of course all audiences knew that the heroine, whatever her perverse behavior, had really wanted nothing but love anyhow—and furthermore she wanted it with marriage.

Women had come a long way since Carrie Chapman Catt's mother was laughed at for having political ideas; but the stigma of being an old maid still haunted the average girl. Few of them were Jane Addamses or Carey Thomases, caring more for achievement than for the respectable wedding ring.

It was still usual for women to say—not argumentatively because there was only one side to this proposition—that of course the best musicians, poets, ballet dancers, even chefs, were men. This, they said, would be true forevermore.

But, though they had a low opinion of themselves as people, the girls of the 1920s reveled in the new freedoms, which they considered gigantic steps upward. The most remarkable change since the previous decade was the obvious one of fashion. In 1923 hems began to rise and skirts went higher and higher until they reached the knees. Girls cast off their corsets and their high-buttoned shoes, those layers of petticoats and all that thick underwear, rolled their stockings below the knee, and strode about more comfortably than women had since togas went out of style.

Heretofore, styles had been set by mature women, and the girls followed. Now youth was the thing, and older women tried to appear girlish. Fashions for age nineteen, thirty-nine, and fifty-nine were all alike.

Girls imitated the masculine figure. Narrow hips were admired, no one minded having a big waist, and breasts were flattened. (Pity the self-conscious girl with the swelling bosom that was impossible to conceal!) More and more women wore their hair short, and by mid-decade the smart style was a mannish cut, worn close to the head, and sleek.

Hats came in different colors and fabrics, but all were shaped the same: they were like helmets of ancient days, drawn down to the eyebrows. No well-dressed woman went out-of-doors hatless; a young girl might carry her hat in her hand (this signified a limited rebellion against convention) but she still wouldn't be seen without it.

The costume of the 1920s had a sexless look. Jewelry was permitted, and evening gowns were cut very low in back, almost to the waist, but there was a severity of line and a looseness of fit that made dress curiously unfeminine. Women seemed to be saying to men, "We are your playfellows, your pals. Let's do things together."

This directness of approach was evident in manners too. Formality was crumbling like sugar cookies. Girls painted their faces and combed their hair in public. Sometimes a young girl boldly telephoned a boy and proposed a date instead of waiting to be asked. She smoked in public, often with a cigarette holder, the longer the smarter. She visited speakeasies. Dancing was her favorite sport. Dance floors were jammed; music screeched and blared, dominated by the saxophone. The Charleston with its swinging arms and kicking feet expressed the hilarity and freedom that everybody wanted to feel. The girl added "Hell!" and "Damn!" to her vocabulary, though perhaps not in the presence of her mother and father. Her whole effort was to seem as mannish as possible, while giving to men an unspoken promise of feminine surrender.

She spoke of unladylike topics such as pregnancy, birth control, homosexuality, and venereal disease, which she disdained to call by the euphemism "social disease." She called a spade a spade. One of the jokes of the decade was that the girls looked everywhere for a spade so they could call it that.

Never were young people so battered, so pummeled in press and pulpit as the youth of the 1920s. Disrespectful, they were called, undisciplined, decadent, debauched, dissolute, depraved. Their loose sex morals in particular were irritating to the elders.

It is handy to blame any puzzling variance in human behavior on the Industrial Revolution or the latest war. Nevertheless, World War I can't be brushed off as an influence on the altered moral standards, sometimes called the sexual revolution of the 1920s.

In those hectic, emotion-filled days before the troops went overseas, there was a desperate, now-or-never feeling among lovers. The Boys were about to fight and die, and in consequence many hasty marriages and equally hasty illicit affairs were entered into. Overseas, the soldiers experienced European wartime sexual freedom, and returned, moreover, in a mood of bitter disillusionment; they were unfitted for a return to the prim Edwardian restrictions of their boyhood. "How ya gonna keep 'em down on the farm after they've seen Paree?" asked the catchy song.

Among serious-minded youth, there was a mood of despondency after the war. An angry young man expressed his generation's disillusionment in an *Atlantic Monthly* article: "The older generation had pretty well ruined this world before passing it on to us. . . . They gave us this thing knocked to pieces, leaky, red-hot, threatening to blow up; and then they are surprised that we don't accept it with the same attitude of pretty, decorous enthusiasm with which they received it 'way back in 1880."

Segments of the Society

There were at least three major components in the makeup of the 1920s. One was disenchantment, a lost and lonely feeling that something good had gone out of life. Young people blamed their elders and vowed bitterly to hand on a better world to their children: a world without war or hypocrisy. Their elders blamed the young for lacking the moral fiber of past generations of Americans.

The second component, a direct opposite of the first, was a glorious love of life. There were exciting new novelists—Faulkner and Hemingway and Dos Passos, for example. There were painters and composers who discovered new patterns in shapes and sounds. Newsmen and dancers and architects and playwrights met in ardent groups to beat out plans for their brave new world.

But the third aspect of the 1920s was the most conspicuous and the longest remembered: the new sexual freedom and the postwar concentration on superficial pleasures—dancing, joyriding, spectator sports, movies.

Young women were romping on longer leashes than their mothers had been permitted. It was popular to say, especially when the theory fitted your desires, that repressed sexual drives led to disasters of personality. Books appeared that taught the techniques of love-making. They were circulated surreptitiously, and were much discussed. A most important innovation was the automobile; it whirled young people away from parents and chaperones into the privacy of a million lovers' lanes.

One lady who had been young at the turn of the century said, "When I was a girl, everyone knew that a certain amount of spooning went on in buggies, but the girls didn't talk about it—and we hoped the boy didn't, for mercy's sake! But today's children"— she laughed helplessly—"they 'neck,' as they call it, two and three couples in one car—right in front of each other!"

That was the crux of the matter: the new openness. The free talk. Everywhere, it seemed that sex was Topic One, no longer laughed over among men only, and whispered about among girls only. Necking was the national recreation, and the unkissed girl felt, not virtuous, but unblessed.

Illegitimacy, however, was only a little bit less shameful for the unhappy mother than it had been a generation earlier; but, in all except the strictest communities, the child himself could now grow up with less stigma than before.

There was a sorry lack of understanding between mothers and daughters, and it was the trivial things that chafed the most: flimsy dress, plucked eyebrows, painted cheeks, late hours, the girl's insistence on "being dressed up all the time," instead of frugally wearing her old things at home and saving "her good clothes" for important events.

Mothers and daughers were more alike than they knew. Both looked upon marriage as a woman's best career; both believed that chastity was a girl's greatest asset in the market. In a movie of the late 1920s, a young man said plaintively to his girl, "Listen, why don't we get married or something?" And she replied sharply, "We'll get married or *nothing.*" What bewildered Mother was the *way* Daughter pursued the business of being a woman. The girl marched right out into the world to select her own mate instead of waiting like a rose on the bush to be plucked by the right man; or at least, with genteel modesty, appearing to wait.

The modern girl's boldness alarmed men, too. There was considerable tension between male and female in these early days of girls' self-conscious freedom. Woman was changing her role from passive to active, he thought, and he felt threatened, not only sexually, but as a political figure and as a wage earner too. Anger was one weapon, but derision was better. And so in cartoons, in night-club jokes, in magazine stories, in newspaper columns, the "brassy" female was made much fun of.

Men needn't have felt such consternation. The girls' boldness was as much a surface application as the bright rouge they applied to their cheeks.

Patterns for the Period

Successor to the Gibson Girl of the 1900s was the John Held, Jr., girl. Charles Dana Gibson's young lady had been haughty, graceful, composed, and upper-crust. The girl in John Held's cartoons was middle-class, and always a little bit ridiculous. Long-legged, short-skirted, shingled, she was as awkward as a colt. Sometimes she was insolently self-confident, but more often was caught, as in a snapshot, in a moment of comic dismay. Every sketch was full of life and action. The girl has an endearing, angular look of adolescence.

Another version of the 1920s girl is Iris March, heroine of *The Green Hat* by Michael Arlen, a favorite novel of the decade.

Respectable wives and mothers reveled in the book and kept it hidden in a drawer underneath the chemises, where daughters wouldn't discover it, while high-school girls were passing copies from hand to hand. Reviewers praised its sophistication and its gaiety of style without quite coming out and mentioning that it was excitingly sexy. For its time, it was. There were no clinical details of anatomy or performance, but tawny Iris March—the chic, the gallant Iris March—was a heroine to be adored and imitated.

The thing is, on Iris's wedding night her bridegroom, "Boy" Fenwick, flings himself out of the bedroom window because he has syphilis and decides he really oughtn't to inflict it on this pure girl, whom he loves madly. The reader isn't told his noble motive for suicide until the end of the story. Meanwhile, Iris, rather than tell the simple truth and do the world out of a good plot, announces cryptically (she is a master of the cryptic), "He died for purity." This implies that he died in shock from learning that she was no virgin—though of course she really *was* all the time.

Iris then sets out on the nymphomaniac trail in order to make herself a scandal, thereby proving that Boy was a true Galahad.

Readers of *The Green Hat* didn't wish to imitate the tawny Iris's record as a tramp. It was her gallantry that they loved; also, to a lesser extent, they loved the urbane Mayfair set in which she moved, and the sleek yellow Hispano-Suiza that she drove.

The fact that the superb Greta Garbo played tawny Iris on the screen and Katharine Cornell had the part on the stage didn't make Iris's image any less alluring. No one complained that all this self-sacrifice of Iris's was for a fairly silly reason.

In the final scene, wearing a green hat, Iris dies gallantly in a dramatic auto crash. (Too bad about that yellow Hispano.)

When this classic was at its height of popularity, if one saw a teen-age girl pacing the street with long-legged stride, eyes turned inward and mouth tragic, one might guess that she was doing Greta Garbo as gallant Iris.

The Sheik was popular with the same readers, but it was the hero who made that book. The thrilling Rudolf Valentino played the lead on the screen.

Yet another pace setter for the era was Zelda Sayre, witty, capricious, reckless society girl of Montgomery, Alabama, who married novelist F. Scott Fitzgerald in 1920 and suffered her first emotional collapse in 1930, after a flamboyant career in the literary and social world of New York, Paris, and the Riviera.

The beautiful, talented, extravagant Fitzgeralds personified the Jazz Age, of which Scott wrote so brilliantly in *This Side of Paradise, The Great Gatsby,* and *Tender Is the Night.*

Zelda allowed herself no inhibitions. She turned cartwheels around a ballroom floor if the impulse seized her; she and Scott rode up and down Fifth Avenue on the roof of a taxicab; they jumped into the Plaza fountain; raced around and around in the revolving door of a hotel entrance. They were drunk every day by teatime, sometimes by lunchtime, and continued to drink all night. If they drove home (both of them with cavalier disregard for traffic laws, and at top speed) they were apt to fall asleep in each other's arms on their own front lawn. They were obsessively in love, but had ugly quarrels that usually began during hangovers and might rage along for days.

They dressed with magnificence, drove a secondhand Rolls-Royce, and traveled to and from Europe on a whim. They gave parties that might last for a week and were attended by socialites, artists, publishers, and fashionable wits, because the madcap Fitzgeralds were the style. They had a compulsion to live like millionaires. They were always in debt.

In truth, Zelda was a deeply troubled young woman, tormented by anxiety and unfulfillment; but the golden legend is that of devil-may-care gaiety.

The French have a saying that all sweeping generalizations are false, including this one. Of course it is a generality to say that "all young women" of the 1920s lived or tried to live like Zelda, Iris, or the It girl. Many ladies now in their seventies must say wonderingly, "But where was I when all this fun was going on?"

There were girls who lived obediently at home, wore a modest touch of lipstick, and went with "the crowd" to Saturday-night parties at friends' houses, where the raciest drink was lemonade. There were girls who never saw a hip flask nor ever said "Hell!" Plenty of young married couples worked hard, lived frugally, and for a big time they took the children to the park on Sunday afternoon.

The war years were followed by a turbulent two-year period of strikes accompanied by violence, race riots, religious intolerance, the rise of the Ku Klux Klan, and finally by the great Red Scare, that led to an orgy of illegal arrests and brutal imprisonments. Slowly, these explosions quieted down to a sullen rumble. People wanted to forget them.

As for feminism, it had not died, but it was taking a long nap. Girls so young that they had not taken part in the suffrage movement laughed when their elders tried to explain how idealistically the suffragists had worked together to achieve the vote for women. The girls were willing to have the vote; they deserved it, didn't they? "But don't be so earnest!" they said, and the elders were silenced by this baffling flippancy.

The fashionable young laughed at reform. They refused to think of it as an effort to make life better for the unfortunate, and pictured reformers as skinny, black-dressed women with grim mouths, trying to take all the fun out of living. Furthermore, young people didn't want to hear about that old-time patriotism, or about the ills of society. They wanted to dance! They wanted the accent to be on self.

Where was that "moral vote" whose menace had made machine bosses and liquor magnates chew the bedclothes at night? Time proved that women didn't vote in a bloc. They were as individualistic as men, they were motivated as selfishly, and when opportunity came their way, no less corrupt. Woman suffrage corrected a political injustice, but it did not remake the nation. Women, after all, were only people.

Housework was much eased by the new mechanical gadgets. By 1925 nearly every middle-class house had an electric iron, toaster, vacuum cleaner, and washing machine; many had electric refrigerators, and half of them had telephones. But in 1925 only half as many families had paid help as had it in 1900. Of course the pay was higher. In 1900 a full-time "girl" had to be paid only $3 a week; by 1925 her wages were $10 to $15.

The new morality—or immorality, as some called it—was reflected in the divorce rate. The rate was 50 percent higher than it had been in the 1910s and two-thirds of the decrees were granted to women.

By 1920, only 800,000 more women were in the work force than had been in 1910, because many workers had retired to their homes when The Boys came back from the war. But some changes had been wrought: women were admitted permanently to a few new categories; they could be elevator operators now, and theater ushers. Many more women than formerly were now librarians, social workers, and college teachers.

More and more girls went to college. By the end of the decade, 40 percent of all master's degrees went to women, and 15 percent of all Ph.D.s were awarded to women.

Few women went into politics. At last they had the legal right to run for office, but social pressure was against it. Precinct committeemen laughed them away, and women's whole training had taught them they weren't really the equals of men, however they might pretend to be. You know—the best musicians, poets, ballet dancers, even chefs . . . .

Fifty years later, Mrs. Dwight D. Eisenhower, when asked if she thought there would ever be a woman president, replied in a startled tone, "Good heavens! I should hope not!"

There was, however, one woman who entered politics on a high level during the 1920s under unusual circumstances.

Two Governors for the Price of One

Governor "Farmer Jim" Ferguson was impeached in 1917 by a Texas State Senate that had twenty-one grievances against him. The most spectacular charge was that he had accepted a gift of $156,000 from unknown friends (actually six Texas breweries). The senators were also provoked by his vetoing most of the University of Texas budget after the Board of Regents declined to fire five professors whom he didn't like. And there was a matter of $100,000 in fire insurance from a state college fire; the governor had deposited the money in his own bank, where it drew no interest. Exasperated with the fellow, the senators voted twenty-five to three to remove him from office.

But "Pa" Ferguson had a wife more loyal than those backbiters, and in 1924 "Ma" (her name was Miriam and she hated the nickname) threw her sunbonnet into the ring. She was a woman of culture, really, who deftly ran a household staffed with servants, but the image of a simple country woman had more appeal, so she engaged in a few homespun skits, such as inviting the press in to watch her make peach preserves.

On the credit side, let it be recorded that the Fergusons were enemies of the Ku Klux Klan, then riding high in Texas as in many other states.

It was no secret that Ma did not expect to sit in the governor's chair. Pa openly announced in his weekly, *The Ferguson Forum*, that if she was elected he intended to run the state. They campaigned hard. "Our motto," they said, "is never say 'die.' Say 'damn.' " They won, and Mrs. Ferguson became the first woman elected to a full two-year term as governor of any state, though Mrs. Nellie Tayloe Ross of Nevada had been named to fill the unexpired term of her late husband.

A popular joke in Texas became: "How does it feel to have a woman governor?" And the reply, "I don't know. We haven't got one."

But Miriam Ferguson was not a humble kitchen drudge whose proudest skill was preserving peaches. She could be as salty as any politician when she chose. At one time there were rumors of a second Ferguson impeachment and one hundred legislators petitioned for a special session. "Let them assemble," she said. "Let them start something. I'll still be here at the finish. . . . They'll soon find out how dumb I am."

Unfortunately for the record of women in politics, during her brief governorship, there were charges that splendidly profitable highway construction contracts were awarded without competitive bidding to contractors who chanced to be faithful advertisers in *The Ferguson Forum*; and charges that the governor's husband earned his spending money by selling pardons to prisoners.

Meanwhile, far from the broad and windswept plains of Texas, a new coterie was shaping up in crowded, clamorous Manhattan.

Wittiest Woman in New York

In 1919 six bright young people began to meet every day in New York's Algonquin Hotel for luncheon. Alexander Woollcott, humor columnist Franklin Pierce Adams (later to be known simply as F.P.A.), and Harold Ross (soon to establish *The New Yorker*) had worked together in France on the army's newspaper, *Stars and Stripes.* The other three were Robert Sherwood, Robert Benchley, and Dorothy Parker, new staff members of the sophisticated *Vanity Fair.*

More and more New York wits joined the clique: Heywood Broun, artist Neysa McMein, Charles MacArthur, Donald Ogden Stewart, novelist Alice Duer Miller, to name a few. All were authors, editors, artists, drama critics, playwrights, or columnists. Through their writing, they helped set the taste of a nation. Broun, for example, reached millions of readers with his syndicated column "It Seems to Me," and what he wrote was the Algonquin Round Table view of life.

Dorothy Parker was the darling of this quick-witted group. Less than five feet tall, a girl in her twenties, she had a spritelike charm that instantly drew people to her—women as well as men; a quick, wild play of the mind; and a singular gift for listening, so that people found themselves telling her about their private lives, often to their dismay when they discovered later that she was repeating some of their shyest confidences—with comic Parkerisms added. Clever, adorable Mrs. Parker! She had to play to an audience; she hated herself for doing it, but it was a compulsion.

She and the rest of the inner circle met not only for luncheon; after work they met at speakeasies, which served as informal clubs, went on to dinner and to the theater afterward; and sat up all night together. The whole purpose of their lives was to have fun, to know the latest catchwords and the newest fads and the best bartenders; to pretend that they never worked; and to be clever.

The great thing for the Round Tablers was the one-liner. At a Halloween party hosted by Herbert Bayard Swope, the newspaper editor, Dorothy Parker saw a group clustered around a washtub. When she asked what they were doing, someone told her, "We're ducking for apples." She sighed. "There," she murmured, "but for a typographical error, is the story of my life."

At another time she said, "I was the toast of two continents: Greenland and Australia." She also remarked that she didn't need a big apartment, only a place large enough to lay a hat and a few friends. When her dog came down with mange, she said in her soft, deprecating voice, "He must have caught it from a lamppost."

People hovered around and leaned close to hear the things she muttered as if to herself. ("A girl's best friend is her mutter.") Less funny is the fact that she made poisonous remarks about people, even her best friends, behind their backs. Kindness was not one of Dorothy Parker's weaknesses.

There were always men in her life because she was an alluring young woman—gentle, helpless-looking (as helpless as a nest of hornets, someone said) with a sad mouth and enormous dark eyes that pleaded for understanding and love. She had two husbands: the first was Edwin Pond Parker II; after their divorce in the early 1920s, she kept his name because she hated her Jewish one, Rothschild. She had, in addition, a number of lovers. Every love affair began in glory, went through vicious quarrels, and ended in disaster. Either she dismissed the man in sick boredom, or was thrown over to recover by herself from grief and loneliness.

She was a complicated woman. She cared deeply about her writing and longed to write more, but suffered writer's block so severe that often for weeks at a time she was unable to put a line on paper. She said that when she did sit at the typewriter, she wrote five words and erased seven. She was paralyzed by fear of failure. At the same time, in every area of her life she sought out failure, she flung herself at failure. She was witty, the life of the party, the one who wanted never to stop the merry-go-round; and she attempted suicide at least twice. She loved her friends and clung to them, yet told scandalous lies about them. She thrived nowhere except in Manhattan, but longed for a vine-covered cottage. Again and again she fell in love, yet always held back from total commitment to anyone. Finally, her view of life was that from birth, man is pointed toward suffering, despair, and death.

She had lived with unhappiness as long as she could remember. She kept the story of her early years locked in a bitter silence, but the facts are that she was half Scottish and half Jewish, and that her affluent father and stepmother totally rejected her. She repaid them in full with hatred. Sent to a Catholic school, she was rejected there too as a minority of one.

Then and in later life, she was a sharp observer and a sharp listener. Her short stories are enriched by pure colloquial speech. For example, in "The Standard of Living," her two stenographers, Annabel and Midge, do not seem at all like characters in a piece of fiction; the reader recognizes them with their first words as two girls he knows but had never quite noticed—grave, humorless, obsessed by the trivialities of their monotonous lives. All her stories have this reality. People sometimes comment that they read a story of hers—the superb "Big Blonde," perhaps—when it first appeared in the twenties, and remember it still in all its flat, tragic reality.

All of her work is tragic. Even the funniest stories and poems are, under the humor, written in sorrow for man's wretched plight. Her plots are slight, many of them more slice-of-life than genuine stories; but she, like Ernest Hemingway, was plowing a new field, with her realism and her terseness of style.

The 1920s, that time of laughter and irresponsibility for the Round Table crew, began closing down, and so did the least unhappy part of Dorothy Parker's melancholy life. In the early 1930s she married again. With her second husband, Alan Campbell, she moved to Hollywood (which she hated); collaborated with him on movie scripts (which stunned her with boredom); earned enormous sums of money (which she spent as fast as it touched her fingers); became politically conscious (perhaps in shame for having all that money in a time of national poverty) and crusaded for the Anti-Nazi League. She and Alan quarreled without cease. She wrote less and less, drank more and more, and faced life with increasing despair.

For this tormented woman, it was now downhill all the way. She spent the final lonely years in a squalid room of a rundown New York hotel. With Alan dead, her friends looked after her as well as they could, and kept her bills paid, though sometimes her mind was so cobwebbed with alcohol that she might shout, when they called on her, "Get out, you Jew-hating Fascist son of a bitch." She died alone when she was seventy-three, escaping at last from a world in which she had never been at home.

Fabulous Ferber

Unlike Dorothy Parker, Edna Ferber grew up untouched by anti-Semitism. Edna was poorer in worldly goods, but happy in a warm and loving family. She felt no need to be on the defensive about Judaism; she was comfortable with it—at least she was until Nazism loomed dark and ugly on the horizon.

Edna was short and plump, with frizzy black hair; she was full of fun, outgoing, competitive, and popular, and she had a wonderful time at school. Her great ambition was to train for the stage, but her family forbade it. Therefore, a few days after graduating from Ryan High

School in Appleton, Wisconsin (class of 1904), she began her career as a reporter. She worked on the Appleton *Daily Crescent* at a salary of $3 a week. From the *Crescent* she moved on to the Milwaukee *Journal*. She had the greatest zest for newspaper work. Every new assignment was a new challenge, and every stranger to be interviewed was a fascinating personality to explore.

After five years of zealous work, no vacations, and neglected health, however, she collapsed into illness. During the long, tedious convalescence at home, she tottered downtown one day, bought a secondhand typewriter for $17, and began to write fiction as an invalid's idle pastime. And so an author was born. Unlike many reporters, she had never been interested in fiction writing. Even yet, her frustrated ambition was to go on the stage.

When her father died, the mother—a gay, shrewd, courageous woman ("astringent as grapefruit," Edna said)—moved to Chicago with her two daughters, Fannie and Edna. They took a three-room apartment on the South Side, and Edna at once applied to the Chicago *Tribune* for a job. The *Trib* turned her down; they never hired women reporters. So back she went to her secondhand typewriter.

Her stories caught on at once, especially a series about an aggressive traveling saleswoman named Emma McChesney (the name floated out of the air onto paper when the first story was on page one). Edna wrote thirty McChesney stories, most of them appearing in the *American Magazine*.

On and on she wrote with a well-inked magic wand. Everything she wrote promptly saw print. Most of her novels became best sellers. They weren't great art, but they made great reading; the stuff of life was in them. Her characters caught at the real world with both strong hands, as forthright and ardent as Edna Ferber herself.

By now a young woman in her twenties, she had a work pattern laid out, and she was still following it when she died at eighty-two. She rose early, took a brisk morning walk no matter what the weather, then sat at her desk, relentless and disciplined, from nine o'clock until four, when she lurched out of her room, wild-haired and exhausted.

She tried to write one thousand words a day. Sometimes she achieved only fifty words, sometimes in a spurt she'd get three thousand on paper; but always there was the grim target: one thousand words today.

She wrote the last page of a novel first; then she felt that the story had inevitability; she would reach her destination. First draft . . . second draft ... day after day, month after month ... and by the end of the book she was sick of the whole project, drained, listless.

Families, she once observed, never take their authors seriously. Mrs. Ferber always referred to her daughter's creative work as "Edna's typewriting."

Her novels, she felt, were strong on character and weak in plot. Plot never interested her especially. In that rich imagination of hers, ideas for short stories and novels sprang up as thick as dandelions in a meadow.

Though she was pleased to have so many enthusiastic readers, she did have one wistful thought: everybody seemed to regard her as an assertive, insensitive, best-selling workhorse. She saw herself, on the other hand, as an artist with a Message. Each novel, she said, had a serious sociological theme—and nobody ever noticed.

The 1920s were the time of her great successes. In that decade she wrote *So Big, Show Boat,* and *Cimarron.* In mid-decade she moved to New York and became a sometime member of the Algonquin group, though she couldn't lunch at the Round Table when in the grip of a novel: nothing short of murder or fire within three feet of her typewriter was permitted to interfere with the day's job. But she hobnobbed with Alex Woollcott, F.P.A., Neysa McMein, Harold Ross, and the Kaufmans, George and Beatrice.

Probably some of Miss Ferber's happiest hours were spent collaborating with George Kaufman in writing *The Royal Family, Dinner at Eight,* and *Stage Door,* sophisticated comedies all, and all of them Broadway successes. She watched every rehearsal, attended opening nights, and sat up all night with the cast and producer, waiting haggardly for the reviews in the morning papers.

At forty, she was still the stage-struck Ferber kid.

Her lifetime triumph, though, was *Show Boat.* It was a best-selling novel, was made four times into movies, used for six years as a radio program, and, most important, was a Broadway musical.

It was the musical *Show Boat* that made Helen Morgan famous through her touching portrayal of the octoroon Julie LaVerne in Ziegfeld's production. She immortalized Jerome Kern's "Bill" and "Can't Help Lovin' That Man."

Offstage, Helen operated the nightclub known as House of Morgan, where she was not only manager but her own star performer. Sitting atop the grand piano (this perch became her trademark), she crooned her torch songs. Loneliness and melancholy were not only her posture, they were part of her personality. She was called the composite of all the ruined women of the world. Before the 1920s ended, she disappeared from the nightclub scene, in a condition close to physical and mental exhaustion. The unhappy woman, who died soon after she was forty, spent her last years in an almost unbroken alcoholic haze.

Helen Morgan's spectacular rival in the speakeasy world was Texas Guinan, she who greeted arrivals at her club with the happy shout, "Hello, Sucker!" Texas had big blue eyes, brilliant yellow hair, a brassy laugh, and (allegedly) a million dollars in nightclub profits. It was she who invented the term "big butter-and-egg man" as label for the large spender from out of town.

She was a native of Texas, who at fourteen could (allegedly) round up a hundred head of cattle singlehanded, and had six uncles who (she claimed) were priests. She loved noisy crowds, bright colors, pets, and poker; never drank; and lived in a thirty-two-room house in Greenwich Village, decorated in lavish Oriental style.

The customers loved her. They crowded into her club to pay the exorbitant prices she charged, and to laugh uproariously as she insulted them with the special Guinan gusto.

She Played It Cool

A novelist as different as possible from the passionate, vehement Edna Ferber was unemotional and coldly ambitious Gertrude Atherton. This woman manipulated her talent as she manipulated people: with calculated shrewdness. Her autobiography, *Adventures of a Novelist*, reveals her as an unmoved observer of life, never a participant. She declined responsibility; she even left her little daughter in San Francisco in the care of the child's two grandmothers, while she, a widow before thirty, spent her life as a roving socialite and author.

Moving from one cosmopolitan city to another, carefully armed with letters of introduction to the best people, she occupied herself by attending dinners, teas, balls, and theater parties, but she controlled her social engagements and selected her companions so that no shadow of a shadow of scandal could ever fall upon her impeccably groomed, correctly behaved self.

She liked to collect life stories of the people she met, especially the unlikely, melodramatic tales, and thriftily saved them to be used in future plots; but she cared nothing for the storytellers as fellow human beings.

When she chose the subject of her next novel, she always moved on to a city where she would not be interrupted by acquaintances, and in her disciplined fashion she researched the novel's background, for many of her books were historical novels; and then, in solitude, she wrote steadily until the job was done.

There was usually a space of from fifteen to twenty months between books, and if one accepts her own claims, she never wrote a failure. If she ever experienced gaiety or pity, or knew remorse or sorrow, or if she ever had a lover, she does not mention it.

In 1923 her sensational *Black Oxen* appeared. It is the story of an aging woman who regains her youth through a series of rejuvenation treatments, and what a stir that caused! Preachers rose up in their pulpits to denounce her, readers called her immoral, and some effort was made to have *Black Oxen* banned. For just once Mrs. Atherton's cold intelligence blazed into retaliatory reply.

"The world, and the great and free United States in particular," she wrote in *Adventures*, "is full of narrow-minded, ignorant, moronic, bigoted, cowardly, self-righteous, anemic, pig-headed, stupid, puritanical, hypocritical, prejudiced, fanatical, cocoa-blooded atavists who soothe their inferiority complex by barking their hatred of anything new. The very word Science is abhorrent to them, and, if they ruled the world, progress would cease."

Adventures uses 578 pages to prove that the author is an intellectual of cool and lofty unconcern, but in a single paragraph the delighted reader discovers that when Mrs. Atherton's own oxen are gored, she too has passions.

Other talented women were on the scene in the 1920s. Mary Roberts Rinehart, author of mystery stories and novels, creator of the delightful "Tish" stories in the *Saturday Evening Post*, and a wartime correspondent in France, collaborated with Avery Hopwood to turn her book *The Circular Staircase* into a successful stage thriller, renamed *The Bat*.

Playwright Rachel Crothers wrote *Let Us Be Gay*, in which Norma Shearer starred on the screen.

Poet Amy Lowell brought out a two-volume biography of her idol, John Keats, and the lyrical Sara Teasdale produced a collection of poems, *Flame and Shadow*. Julia Peterkin wrote the splendid *Scarlet Sister Mary*, and Martha Ostenso her tale of the far North, *Wild Geese*.

Anne Parrish, with her light, bright style, earned the spotlight briefly with her novel, *The Perennial Bachelor.*

Amelita Galli-Curci starred at the Met, and Mary Garden was the darling of the Chicago Opera Company.

Meanwhile, two indomitable businesswomen, Elizabeth Arden and Helena Rubenstein, were building their empires in the world of beauty culture.

And in 1925 two British imports added their unique talents to Broadway: Beatrice Lillie, who was wildly funny while giving the impression of doing all that wonderful clowning on the spur of the moment; and witty, sophisticated Gertrude Lawrence, so full of energy that a critic once said of her, "Vitamins should take Gertrude Lawrence."

Anita Loos, so tiny that she was nicknamed Bug, was still a girl in her twenties when she wrote *Gentlemen Prefer Blondes.* Her protagonist, the sexy, witless gold digger Lorelei Lee, was born of Anita's jealousy. One night Anita was on a date with H. L. Mencken, for whom she "carried a torch," to use the slang of the period, when George Jean Nathan joined them, bringing with him a chorus girl so full of hilariously stupid comments and withal so beautiful that Mencken was delighted with her. The brunette Anita, every bit as attractive, and smart besides, went home seething, and began to write her little masterpiece to work off her malice.

If the Lorelei Lee of Anita Loos's book represents the frivolous aspect of the 1920s, a New England poet and her work represent the idealism and the love of life that were also typical of the youth of the twenties.

Golden Vessel of Great Song (from Sonnet xiii)

Edna St. Vincent Millay, known within her family as Vincent, had an extraordinarily happy childhood. She was one of three girls, Norma and Kathleen being the younger sisters, and when Vincent was eight, her father left the family. His defection did not seem to scar the high-spirited, affectionate girls, though his absence may have been the cause of the poet's steadfast belief in the impermanence of love, expressed again and again in her work.

Now required to support her daughters, Cora Millay earned a meager living as a practical nurse, but she presided over poverty with originality and grace. A musician and a would-be writer, she encouraged all the girls in whatever talents they expressed, and always managed to provide the important things—books and magazines, paints, music lessons, pretty dresses—even if there was a shortage of mere necessities, such as food. In the small Maine towns where the family lived, finally settling in Camden, the neighbors must have looked doubtfully at the Millays' priorities, but Mrs. Millay taught the girls that when they believed they were right they must act upon their convictions, however unpopular those might be.

Besides independence, she taught them self-reliance. Her work often kept her away from home for several days or weeks at a time, and the girls, with Vincent as their chief, managed the household by themselves. Their dinner menus might be a bit whimsical—such as stale doughnuts and pickles—depending on what chanced to be on hand; and the dishes piled up higher and higher in the sink until it was time for Cora Millay's return home. Then the girls ripped into an orgy of dishwashing, scrubbing, and dusting, not to escape a scolding, but to prepare a shining welcome for their mother.

Of the three sisters, Vincent was the most gifted. For three years she trained to be a concert pianist, but had to give up that ambition because her hands never grew large enough. Later she showed talent for acting and playwriting, but poetry was her true métier. She was only eighteen when she began to write her famous long poem, *Renascence*, which could have been the work of a mature poet both because of its technical skill and for its wide view of life. It brought her instant fame, and brought her as well a patron who saw to it that she enrolled at Vassar and had the money for a four-year course, though she was already twenty-one when she entered as a freshman in 1913.

Vincent, now beginning to be known as Edna, was very small, with a slight, almost boyish figure. She had red hair, delicate features, and a long, slender throat. At times she seemed quite plain; but the moment she was stirred by an idea, her features became animated, she moved with quick, darting motions, her eyes sparkled, and she was transformed into a radiantly lovely woman.

Her personality was as changeable as her mobile face. Now she was sweet, tender, and gentle; now irritable or absentminded; or hilarious and full of mischief. But underneath these volatile moods was New England bedrock. She always knew what she believed and what she believed in.

Unlike that other artist Willa Cather, Edna cared deeply about politics, about feminism, about human justice. She campaigned hotly for release of the condemned Sacco and Vanzetti. Unlike many other feminists, however, she could never have been charged with lesbianism; in fact, she once said thoughtfully that she wondered if she was a nymphomaniac. Forever falling in love, she even went so far as to become engaged several times, but always broke free before taking the final step of marriage. She was such an exciting woman that one man after another courted her ardently. Literary critic Edmund Wilson, one of her suitors, grumbled that there were so many of them that they ought to form an alumni association.

Her arguments against marriage were chiefly two: that love never lasts, and that she wanted to be free—no, she had to be free!—to live for poetry.

She became a literary idol in her generation. *A Few Figs from Thistles,* which appeared in 1920, was one of her most popular books, containing light, flippant poems that people laughed over and quoted as gleefully as they quoted Dorothy Parker's verses.

Millay's important works, however, are her sonnets and lyrics, dozens and dozens of them, for she was very prolific. One of her lifetime themes is the conflict between the will to live and the will to die, and nearly always she celebrates the triumph of life. She wrote thrilling poems of ecstasy, love, and grief. Often she wrote the first draft of a poem in "fever and excitement," but then she worked it over and over in what she called "a painful kind of sculpture." She chipped away at it until there was not a superfluous syllable in it. She might work for years on the same poem, putting it away time after time to achieve a fresh viewpoint; then she chiseled and smoothed again, and yet again, until it satisfied her rigorous standards.

So versatile was she that besides poetry she wrote six plays and an opera, *The King's Henchman,* for which Deems Taylor wrote the music. It was performed by the Metropolitan Opera Company fourteen times during the twenties. In early years, to earn enough money for survival (young poets are not very pecunious) she also wrote witty prose under the pen name of Nancy Boyd, writing chiefly for the magazine *Vanity Fair.*

At thirty-one, she astonished her friends by marrying. Her husband was Eugen Boissevain, who had been married to the beautiful suffragist Inez Milholland. Eugen was a big, handsome, jovial man, imaginative, sensitive, and warmhearted. He was the ideal husband for Edna Millay, because he believed in the independence and equality of women. His idea was that if one partner in a marriage is doing more important work than the other partner, that first person's work should take first place in the marriage arrangement.

"Anyone can buy and sell coffee," he said, "but not anyone can write poetry." And so he gave up his prosperous business as an importer and devoted himself to taking care of the poet, whose health became very frail, and promoting her work. He looked after the business details of publishing her books, handled her correspondence, operated the farm they bought, called Steepletop, at Austerlitz, New York, and ran the household.

Usually Steepletop had four servants, but if all were absent, he alone did the housework and the cooking. He took the same robust pleasure in preparing a fine meal that he took in everything else he did, leaving Edna free of domestic bothers.. Did ever an artist have it so good? And Eugen did it all graciously, with never a moment's loss of dignity.

This idyllic arrangement operated until his death in 1949, which was followed only a year later by her own death. Edna Millay, who wrote again and again of the impermanence of love, had twenty-six years of happiness with one man.

Though she was an important spokesman for the twenties, she was going out of fashion by the end of the decade. T. S. Eliot inaugurated a new era in American poetry. Millay poured emotion into her poems; Eliot and his followers believed that poetry should be an escape from emotion. Poetry became obscure, the meaning only suggested by symbols and images. The new poets accused Millay of remaining on the surface of life instead of probing to deep reality. They experimented, they created fluid forms and a new conception of flexibility. Also, many of them saw the world as devoid of meaning: bleak, sterile, and despairing.

But Cora Millay's daughter went on to the end of her life expressing in her own style her faith in man and his future as she saw it.

The Achievers

As The Boys came home, victory parades were held and after that patriotism languished. The age of debunking came in. The public discovered that the Puritans were hypocrites and the Founding Fathers were cynical slave owners, that Lincoln had played crafty politics, and the World War was fought only to enrich the munitions makers. Anyone who had an ideal left kept it concealed. Who wants to be known as a backwoods innocent?

The spirit of reform was dead, that spirit which had uplifted women in the 1910s and had brought them charging out of the kitchen into the ranks of suffragists, pacifists, and finally Liberty Bond girls. Reformers now were jeered at as do-gooders and bleeding hearts. Pleasure seemed to be the national target, and yet, when an American achieved a high goal, the public cheered.

Swimmer Gertrude Ederle, muscular nineteen-year-old daughter of a New York City butcher, battled her way across the English Channel against tricky tides in fourteen hours, thirty-one minutes, bettering the men's record by more than two hours.

Returning to New York, her ship was met by circling planes, an official yacht, fifteen thousand cheering fans, and a fire department band. In a welcoming speech Mayor Jimmy Walker likened her feat to Moses' crossing of the Red Sea, Caesar's crossing of the Rubicon, and Washington's crossing of the Delaware.

Trivial things seemed exaggerated, as in a fever dream. By mid-decade the nation was in a period of prosperity, and families that had never before been so well-off seemed to be racing to possess more things, bigger and better things. Installment buying became the custom. Materialism became the target, and spiritual values—what had become of them? More and more Americans felt a sense of confusion, a wish to return to something—but what?

Then an unknown young man set out alone to cross the Atlantic in a flimsy airplane. The nation waited for news of his safe arrival in Paris, paralyzed by fear and by hope. And he made it. Hundreds of thousands of people sat by their radios and heard the news with an almost religious sense of thankfulness, heard a jubilant soprano swing into "The Star-Spangled Banner" over the air, and heard her voice break with emotion for a moment, then sing on.

The nationwide adulation of Charles Lindbergh proved how many millions had needed a hero as a symbol of stability and idealism in those confused times.

Also there was Helen Wills, or "Little Poker-Face," as the newsmen dubbed her, greatest tennis player of the decade. Again and again she won the U.S. singles crown, British women's singles title, and championships in Holland and France. Americans love champions, but they loved Helen Wills for more than that. There was something about her, something as refreshing as a pine forest; something clean as laundry whipping on the line in wind and sun. She always wore white: middy blouse, pleated skirt, and (in the early days) silk stockings. During competition matches, she never smiled. Her severe profile was that of a young Greek boy. You could picture her pacing the groves of Athens beside Socrates—stern, thoughtful, silent.

Another heroine was Grace Goodhue Coolidge, most winsome first lady since Dolley Madison. Visitors to the White House were bewitched by the warmth and poise of this former schoolteacher. During her husband's term of office, she had to endure in public the loss of the younger Coolidge son, sixteen-year-old Calvin, Jr. A tennis game gave him a blister on one foot; for some reason the blister became infected, and the fatal infection spread quickly through the bloodstream. Even this shattering grief she bore with outward composure and grace.

"Behind a Veil of Silver Chiffon"

In a grim World War I story, *Company K,* author William March has a soldier in the muck and misery of the trenches draw a framed magazine picture of Lillian Gish from a pocket every night and every morning to study the sweet pictured face. Knowing that something pure and good still existed in the world was the talisman that preserved his sanity through the war.

Lillian Gish had a similar effect on millions who saw her in the movies. She was not only talented, she had a unique quality: pure, ethereal, elusive. As if she acted in whispers. As if in her hands, the definite blurred into the indefinite. It was drama critic George Jean Nathan who described her as being "behind a veil of silver chiffon." He courted Lillian for years, but she eluded marriage.

She had two great loves: her sister Dorothy and her mother. Her father had deserted his family when the girls were babies. Mrs. Gish, a loving, gentle, sympathetic woman, was not the stereotype mother of actresses; she did not storm her way into producers' offices or manage her children as if they were properties. She was simply there, warmhearted and protective.

The bond between Lillian and Dorothy Gish never weakened. How different they were! Dorothy was mischievous, fun-loving, and irresponsible. She never reached such heights of stardom as Lillian, but she had her followers, who delighted in her gift of comedy. At the same time, she suffered agonies of self-doubt. "Miss Apprehension," her sister and mother called her. Again and again she played major roles in successful plays, and at rehearsals was always her rowdy self, and the cast never guessed her hidden fears; but by each opening night her conviction of failure was so acute that she was nearly ill.

Lillian, who never had Dorothy's skylarking, slapstick moods, was always grave and dignified. Fans often wrote asking why she smiled so seldom in her movies; yet she had a serenity denied the mercurial Dorothy. In early years, the three Gishes lived together whenever the girls' engagements were in the same city; but in later life they gave up this practice. Dorothy was too riotously untidy for the fastidious Lillian.

Miriam Cooper, an actress who later married director Raoul Walsh, tells the story of an evening when she, Dorothy Gish, Mae Marsh, and other young members of a "Hens' Club" held a meeting in Dorothy's room. Lillian was not one of the group. Aloof and studious, she was considered too standoffish. On this evening, as the party became more and more high-spirited, the Hens acted on an impulse, ran across the hall to Lillian's room, and threw open the door shouting, "Surprise!"

Then they stopped, abashed. Lillian lay on her bed in a filmy negligee, golden hair outspread on a pillow. She looked up from the Shakespeare she was reading, and annoyance flashed across her face. But with instant good manners she stood up, welcomed her guests, and talked cordially as long as they stayed—which wasn't long. They backed out, discomforted by the difference between this room, which only Dorothy had seen before, and her sister's room.

Dorothy's room contained only three or four pieces of shabby Mission oak furniture, but Lillian's had velvet draperies, gilt-framed mirrors, and lace-trimmed pillows. They were astonished too at the difference between this seductive woman and the sexless girl who walked around the studio with a book under her arm and was ignored by the men on the set.

Lillian was known as "Mr. Griffith's girl," because they often had dinner together—in public, of course. But as Mr. G. had prim, Victorian standards of behavior; and as his young ladies were strictly supervised; and as everyone on the lot watched everyone else closely, there was no chance for hanky-panky, and no evidence that the Gish-Griffith affair was other than platonic.

Like Maude Adams and other fine actresses, she was sternly

disciplined, and no amount of rehearsal was too much to achieve perfection. She never spared herself hardships, be they heat, desert wind, or around-the-clock labor.

One of her early movies, made under D. W. Griffith's direction, was the melodrama *Way Down East*. The height of the action comes when Lillian's inconsiderate employer, believing her to be a fallen woman, orders her out of the house into a blizzard. The silly girl doesn't stop for hat or coat, but heads for the nearest river and begins walking the ice floes. By and by she faints and is carried downriver toward the neighborhood waterfall. Richard Barthelmess, the farmer's son, likes the girl better than the old man does, and thinks it would be well to rescue her.

This was a genuine Vermont blizzard, for which the cast waited a month or more, because no flimsy studio snowstorm would satisfy Griffith. Rehearsing and shooting the river scene took three weeks.

Nobody had it easy. Mr. Griffith's face froze. Several cameramen came down with pneumonia. To keep the camera upright during the gale, three men had to lie flat in the snow, gripping the tripod legs, and a small fire was kept going directly under the camera to keep its oil from freezing.

For her scene lying on the ice, Lillian Gish had thought up a piece of business that she was foolish enough to suggest to the director and then had to act upon. She let a few locks of hair and one hand trail through the water as she rocked her way downstream. It certainly added to the woe of the scene, but it also froze her hand, which forever after ached in cold weather. She lay on the ice about twenty times a day for those three weeks of rehearsal before the job was finished.

In the final take of the rescue scene, Richard Barthelmess got his. He wore a heavy raccoon coat, and in his cavorting from one ice floe to another he floundered onto one that was too small and tipped him into the water. He clambered out and that soggy coat must have weighed a ton, give or take a few pounds, but there was no time for a retake because now the rescue was for real. While he had fooled around under water, Lillian's ice floe had jogged on, dangerously near the edge of that too-genuine waterfall. But he slogged on, scooped her up, and wrestled to shore with the poor girl pressed to that icy fur bosom.

Among the many fine movies that Lillian Gish made during the twenties was *Orphans of the Storm*, in which Dorothy Gish played the blind sister. To heighten the drama, Griffith had transposed a well-tried old plot to the time of the French Revolution. When the film was shown in France, it raised storms of fury. French pride was outraged because an American producer dared portray French history without its best dress on.

Next Lillian played in *The White Sister*. The whole cast went to Italy to film the story, the first American company ever to do so. Opposite Lillian Gish was a handsome new actor, Ronald Colman. When her lover is believed killed, the heroine becomes a nun, but after she has taken her solemn vows he returns, and a love scene of great power follows. An unhappy ending is arranged, however, that solves the girl's dilemma, as he presently drowns in a flood. *The White Sister* was one of the great successes of the twenties.

After that Lillian Gish played in *Romola*, also filmed in Italy; in *La Bohème*, opposite John Gilbert, and in *The Scarlet Letter*. To speak again of France, audiences there were mystified by all that fuss over the birth of an illegitimate baby.

In 1930 Lillian left Hollywood for Broadway and later appeared on TV. In that medium she played with Helen Hayes in the wonderfully funny *Arsenic and Old Lace*.

Even in old age, Lillian Gish never lost her special quality, that elusive enchantment of being afloat behind a veil of silver chiffon.

Other Charmers

A Broadway star of very different style was Lynn Fontanne, the tall, serene, aristocratic beauty whose stage presence was so great that she could command an audience simply by turning slowly toward it and lifting her chin. In every generation there are half a dozen actresses who have that indefinable allure, the power that transforms each person in the playhouse from a mere human being into a quietly joyful worshiper of illusion. Lynn Fontanne was one of them.

She entered so utterly into every role that while she was onstage she was that person—a cockney hoyden, a stupid, good-hearted meddler, a society belle. She played comic roles with a delicate sense of the grotesque, and played grandly tragic characters with equal conviction.

But romantic America loved her as much for the legend of her married life as for her roles. She and Alfred Lunt were like two pieces of a single coin that by some rare miracle had been joined together. Never separated day or night if they could help it, they were never for a minute bored with each other. In nearly every snapshot of them, you will see them with arms linked. They always refused engagements that would take them to separate cities, and whenever possible they acted in the same play.

They rehearsed and performed at the theater all day, then went home to rehearse again and to talk theater: how to sharpen a line, how well a scene had gone that evening, why the third act entrance wasn't quite right, how to get a laugh at the end of act one. When they went to bed (they slept in the same bed, of course) each took a script to study until they put out the lights.

In social life they refused to be separated. Lady Juliet Duff once invited Lynn to have luncheon with her and Lady Cynthia Asquith, but Lynn replied that she couldn't unless Alfred was invited too.

There was a famous scene in O Mistress Mine, a play by Terence Rattigan, in which they played a love scene so torrid that audiences were sometimes embarrassed, as if they were indecently present at a too-intimate *affaire d'amour*. One day at a matinee, a lady rose to stalk out of the theater in protest against all that passion, but her companion pulled her back into her seat. "It's all right," she hissed, and explained that in private life those two were legally married.

During their long career, the Lunts played in the works of Shakespeare, Shaw, Giraudoux, O'Neill, and other serious playwrights. But in the 1920s they delighted the public with their sparkling, graceful performances in the high comedies of Noel Coward, Robert Sherwood, George Kaufman, and other playwrights of the time.

Fanny Brice was another who had the power to command an audience. She was one of the great clowns of all time, yet her most memorable performance was a profoundly sad one. As everyone knows, she had given her heart to Nick Arnstein, her glib, faithless, handsome husband, who was incapable of loving, though if there was profit in it he might make the gesture.

When Fanny sang "My Man," she seemed always to be singing it to Nick. Each time, she waited until the theater was utterly silent. She stood without moving. She held her bare left arm with her right hand. Then she sang it straight—no frills, no tricks; and there wasn't a dry eye in the house.

Fanny Brice and Lynn Fontanne and Lillian Gish and half a dozen others—they had the magic. Ethel Barrymore had it, and Maude Adams. Bea Lillie had it too, and later Helen Hayes and Katharine Cornell.

The Power, the Glory, and the Hoax

In this same period, there was another performer who had her own special following. This was Aimee Semple McPherson, who enthralled thousands at her Temple in Los Angeles with her simple message of conversion, faith healing, and the second coming of Christ.

Sister Aimee, joyous and triumphant, paces down the flight of stairs to the platform of her Angelus Temple. Spotlights focus on the white-robed figure. Thousands rise to their feet, roaring their love and loyalty. It is the moment for which Sister Aimee lives, the moment when she savors power. She can sway these people. They cheer, shout, "Hallelujah!" They sob, they feel the spirit of the Lord within them, all these at her bidding. She asks them for money and they heap it into the collection plates. She thunders about the Devil, and with ecstatic dread in their hearts they vow never to play cards, attend the theater, or otherwise submit to the blandishments of wily Satan. "Jesus saves!" she calls out in her magnificent voice, and lifts her arms like the wings of a commanding angel. "Repent!"

Undoubtedly Aimee believed in her "Foursquare Gospel" message. She was an excellent actress, with a brisk flair for publicity, and she was a gifted manipulator of mobs; she who had grown up in poverty took a childish delight in luxury when the love offerings of the congregations made her rich. But she did not deceive her followers. She was a sincere fundamentalist who happened to make a fortune by adding showmanship to religion, and she gave her people a good time. She put color, drama, excitement, and emotion into their drab lives.

Her supple imagination made it seem reasonable to her that contributions made to Aimee Semple McPherson were also gifts to the Almighty, but there was no paranoia in her makeup.

Her sanity was as sound as her splendidly healthy body. She always clearly knew that she was not a deity, but Aimee Semple McPherson, putting on a good show and earning a living.

Aimee's genius was for dealing with crowds, but when they poured money into her hands, it would all have poured right out again if she had not been blessed with a business manager, her mother. "Mother Kennedy," as she was known to the flock, was a sharp-tongued, domineering woman, tactless and charmless and a sharp bargainer, who scrutinized every bill with suspicion. She doled out spending money to her daughter. Aimee might be the tyrant of Angelus Temple in matters spiritual, but in lesser affairs she had a sweetness of temper that made her choose obedience to her mother rather than quarreling.

In 1917, when she was twenty-six, penniless, and with two children to support, Aimee had set forth as a wandering evangelist. She developed her talents. She discovered the orgasmic delight of controlling the emotions of the multitude, and she acquired her craving for power. She worked as hard at her trade as any circus trouper, and as astutely as any salesman.

By 1926 she had it all: the power, the money that goes with it, the glory of publicity, physical beauty (she learned later than most women how to make the most of her looks), an intimate circle of adorers; but she was discovering for herself what a certain Samuel Johnson knew two centuries earlier: that it is more fun to travel than to arrive. What now? she must have asked herself, tasting the ashes of success.

Then she fell in love—she who for years had suppressed one side of her ardent nature for the sake of ambition. With all the strength of her emotional, undisciplined makeup, she fell in love with a pleasant, courtly man named Kenneth G. Ormiston, a radio operator who worked at the Temple but was not a member of the flock.

Aimee could not marry and yet remain the Foursquare leader. She was a divorcee, and she had always preached against the remarriage of the divorced. Always one to take the bold, dramatic step, she determined to seize all the money she could get her strong hands upon, and disappear into a romantic void, renouncing religion for love.

Disappear she did, carefully leaving the impression that she had drowned while swimming off the coast of Venice, California. But very soon she must have realized that her ruse would never succeed. She was too well known; and the search for her body went on relentlessly. She must have realized too that for her, love was no substitute for power. She had to reappear, but, being Aimee McPherson, she would not turn up at her own front door one morning and simply confess that she had been having fun and games in a seaside hideaway. No, she had to stage a performance.

Thirty-six days after her suppposed drowning, she staggered out of the California desert with a lurid tale of having been held for ransom in a two-room shack by two men and a woman. She had escaped, she said, and then had run and stumbled and crawled across empty desert for thirteen hours. True, her hair was neatly marcelled, her shoes were in good order, but worse than that was a thing she forgot: a matter of thirst.

After only a few hours of desert heat, one's craving for water amounts to lust, and Aimee had been jaunting about, allegedly, for thirteen hours; but she didn't ask for a drink.

Her worshipers, however, ignored details. They were hysterical with thankfulness just to learn that Sister was alive. When she returned to Los Angeles, she was met at the railroad station by joyful throngs, placed in a wicker chair bedecked with flowers, carried on the shoulders of four firemen through a lane of adorers dressed all in white, transferred to an automobile covered with roses, and driven in triumphal procession, led by the Temple band, followed by cowboys and a squad of motorcycle policemen, through city streets where 100,000 cheered—the greatest multitude ever gathered to welcome a public personage.

Appearing before the grand jury later, she told her fantastic kidnap tale, under oath, and thereby started the grinding of ponderous processes of the law. For months thereafter, the ribald, irreverent public of the whole United States enjoyed a daily circus in the newspapers. They laughed hugely as lies, denials, and contradictions in testimony were heaped upon evasions, perjury, and bribery.

The kidnap shack of course was never found. Ormiston, gentleman first and last, was so elusive that subpoenas could not be served upon him. He dematerialized.

After six months of the most sensational news story of the decade, the prosecution wearily dropped the whole tangled web, with Aimee never convicted of perjury, or cleared either. Thousands of the flock faded away; their Foursquare Gospel, brightest star in their heaven, was devalued from purest silver to tin. But other thousands remained fanatically loyal to Sister.

The evangelist herself emerged from a legal ordeal that could have broken a lesser woman. She went on whooping it up at the Temple and on radio, fighting the Devil and creating dramatic spectacles, her air of triumph undiminished. When her career ended in 1944 (from an overdose of sleeping pills) she was still such a mighty figure that six hundred cars rolled in her funeral procession.

THE DESPERATE DECADE

New Designs for Living

In the 1920s, the girls strode forth, bold and joyous, and played at being men. Then came hard times and they stepped back hastily, timidly, into protective femininity—into the ingratiation that has marked the average girl's behavior ever since Eve, an average girl if there ever was one, offered the apple with, no doubt, a provocative sidewise glance and a swing of the hips.

Eve's daughter of the 1930s let her boyish bob grow longer and arranged it more softly. She rediscovered ruffles and flounces and flowered prints, lengthened her skirts, marked her natural waistline with a ribbon, and, taking off the flattening brassière, let her breasts curve out pleasantly.

She threw away those severe candle-snuffer hats and, in 1933, wore an Empress Eugenie. These debonair little felt hats came in every color, but they were all shaped exactly alike: the narrow brim tilted down on the right side, tipped up on the left—never, never the other way around—and each flaunted a back-swept ostrich feather. Such a flirtatious little hat had not been seen since 1910. Moving swiftly from high style, through the mass market, and down to the back streets, it disappeared forever, but for the remainder of the decade hats had a refreshing variety, though most of them were small and practical. Late in the 1930s they were made still more feminine with flowers, snoods, and veils.

The Old Boys no longer had to wail, "Where, oh, where is the old-fashioned girl?" She was there among them, demure, deferential, and feminine.

Fortunate women had fur coats, the most awe-inspiring being full-length mink. Mink was a status symbol. The less fortunate did well just to have a good, warm coat, and if it was threadbare, it had plenty of company. Least fortunate women hurried through the cold with runover shoes, bare legs, a cotton housedress, and a man's suit coat. The suit coat was either too large or too small, and it was always in need of cleaning. She jammed gloveless hands into the pockets, or crossed her arms and tucked her hands under her armpits.

Eleanor Roosevelt tried to popularize the slogan "It's smart to be thrifty." But the little woman in Kansas City, grimly altering and dyeing her old dress, taking her scuffed shoes to be half-soled at the cut-rate shoe-repair shop, and darning her pair of silk stockings (nylons didn't come in until 1938), recognized this for propaganda. She knew her thrift wasn't smart. It was necessary.

Mrs. Roosevelt was only preaching what she practiced. Every year, even after she became first lady, she bought two or three evening dresses and used them until they wore out. If ambassadors' wives saw her time and again in the same dress, she couldn't have cared less.

She had concerns beyond fashion. She, and millions of others, cared that every week hundreds of families were evicted from their apartments; they were simply moved out to the sidewalk with all their furniture. Families "doubled up," two families crowding into one dwelling. City people who had parents or a brother on a farm moved back to "the home place." Houses and apartments by the thousand were occupied only by mice, spiders, and silence.

About 100,000 meals a day were served in breadlines in New York City alone, usually outdoors, no matter how cold the weather. About 4,500 men stood on New York street corners selling apples at five cents apiece. Competition was so fierce that one businessman sold them at two for a nickel. One-third of the nation was ill-clothed, ill-housed, ill-fed, and one-quarter of the work force was unable to find jobs.

At the beginning of 1930, about ten million women were employed, but by the end of the year about two million of them were out of work. Women were first to be fired, even though they were paid less than men for doing the same jobs. Unthinking prejudice operated against them, and most women meekly accepted the status quo.

"We want every family to have a wage earner," said employers piously. "That wage earner should be the man"—turning a blind eye on the facts that not every working woman was married and that in one of every six urban families the only wage earner was a woman.

Some states passed laws that barred a married woman from any job if her husband earned more than $100 a month. In about half the nation's school systems, married women could not be hired as teachers. If a teacher secretly married, she was dismissed as soon as the guilty secret leaked out. Many young people by-passed marriage and lived quietly in sin—no easy accomplishment in a small town. In 1930 the marriage rate began to drop and by 1932 was the lowest ever recorded in the country. Young people also postponed parenthood.

Working women became fenced into special "women's fields": teaching, nursing, and clerical work. Doors into other occupations began closing against them, even if they were trained. In pharmacy, advertising, accounting, management, and so on, if there was an opening or a promotion, the feeling was that it should go to a man with a family to support; or if the male applicant was young and single, the employer assumed that he would eventually have a family to support.

In those days of many questions and few answers, the pollsters were busy and the public read all the results anxiously. Maybe the newest survey could explain what had happened to us. Or what to do about it. One of the polls studied the use Americans made of their new leisure. Surprisingly, the favorite occupation proved to be reading. Listening to the radio came in second, and going to the movies, third.

Public libraries had never been so busy. In big cities, the newspaper rooms were always filled with quiet, shabby men, poring hour after hour over newsprint, especially the sports and the help-wanted sections. Reading rooms were not only free, they were warm in winter and pleasantly drafty in summer; and the lofty rooms were dignified. They gave a fellow a self-respecting retreat from the woman with her shrill nagging, demanding to know why you never try to bring home any money. Or escape from the gloomy silence of accusation. Escape from failure.

But books were popular too, especially the ones that offered hope: *Life Begins at Forty, Wake Up and Live, How to Win Friends and Influence People,* and all the religious books. As for fiction, reading taste was a good deal more sophisticated than it had been in the *Graustark* days. F. Scott Fitzgerald, John Dos Passos, and Ernest Hemingway had made McCutcheon and Grace Livingston Hill too insipid for most tastes. But the general reader swooped with pleasure on a book by an almost unknown woman named Pearl Buck.

China Observer

She was the daughter and wife of missionaries in China. Working in the attic of her Nanking house, she spent only three months writing the book that was to be called *The Good Earth;* but it was a story whose people she had lived with and whose philosophy and background she had been absorbing for forty years.

Appearing in 1931, *The Good Earth* leaped to the top of the best-seller list and stayed there longer than any book had ever done before. It is still in print and has earned more than a million dollars. Americans loved it not only because it was their introduction to the unknown East, but also for the grave, poetic beauty of its style: a Biblical style, people said, but it really was a Chinese style, familiar to this woman who knew Chinese literature so well. But, most of all, *The Good Earth* caught the imagination of Americans trapped in the confusion and poverty of their own society, because it told of the confusion and poverty of fellow beings on the other side of the world. The comforting message of the story seemed to be that poor is better because rich brings harder problems. Wang Lung, the hero, is happy as a poor, hard-working peasant with no prospects, but melancholy when, at the end of the book, he is a rich landowner suffering the ailments of wealth.

Not long after the book's appearance, Pearl Buck went to New York and there attended a banquet in her honor. The literary world was curious about the woman who had written this moving and powerful novel. They gazed at her inquisitively, these well-groomed, self-assured people, and saw a large, big-boned woman in an unfashionable dress. (It had sleeves!—unheard of for evening wear that year. It looked home-made.) She wore no makeup and her hair was pinned into an undistinguished bun at the back of her neck. She also had exquisite skin and ice-blue eyes. She looked exactly what she was, an unpretentious countrywoman.

Too shy to make a speech, she read aloud instead her preface to a Chinese classic which she had spent many months translating into English, the ancient *All Men Are Brothers.* The audience recognized her scholarship and never knew that she stood before them quaking with fear.

When she went to Sweden, however, to receive the 1938 Nobel Prize for literature from the hand of King Gustav, her fashionably waved hair, her evening dress, and her composed smile were of the most elegant. By that time she had written *Sons, The Mother, A House Divided,* and the two biographies of her mother and her father. By her eightieth birthday she had written nearly eighty books, and the mass of her articles and speeches probably equals that amount in wordage.

Divorced from her first husband, John Buck—the marriage had

never been a companionable one—she married her publisher, Richard Walsh. The couple adopted nine children. In addition to writing and mothering, she crusaded for the rights of women and for racial equality, and worked to aid American-Asian waifs in Japan, the Philippines, Korea, Vietnam—wherever servicemen have left piteous souvenirs of American occupation.

Hers was a busy, fruitful life. Yet she lived isolated, as if a transparent wall of ice separated her from humanity. "I don't think I ever shared anything of my inner self with anyone," she once told a friend. "In both my marriages I had the feeling that I was hardly fair to the man. . . . Life is sad, and I have always, even as a child . . . accepted that fact."

Chicago Prodigy

Many a woman in her forties, shelling peas in her farmhouse kitchen or trudging home through the rain after being on her feet all day in the lingerie department, has dreamed of writing a splendid novel and being acclaimed an instant celebrity. If she had any sense, she knew this for what it was: a fantasy. But there was a woman in Illinois who turned this dream to reality. She wrote a first novel and became that instant celebrity. Her name was Margaret Ayer Barnes.

In early life she had no literary ambitions, though her sister, Janet Ayer Fairbank, was a minor novelist. Margaret grew up in a cultured family, attended Bryn Mawr, married a lawyer, had three sons, and led the busy life of an energetic, prosperous woman of wide interests. She acted in amateur dramatics, worked hard for the Bryn Mawr Alumnae Association, and went on speaking tours to address civic groups on the role of college women in America. (Bryn Mawr's dynamic president, M. Carey Thomas, was one of the people she admired most.)

But in 1925 her literary career began with a crash. On a family vacation in France, the chauffeur-driven limousine ran head-on into another car, leaving Margaret Barnes with fractured ribs, spine, and skull.

During the long months of convalescence, she would not surrender to depression or idleness. Lying flat on her back, holding paper and pencil above the cast that enclosed her chest, she began to write short stories. The magazine *Pictorial Review* printed them. Then, encouraged by a childhood friend, playwright Edward Sheldon, she dramatized Edith Wharton's *Age of Innocence.* Katharine Cornell read the first draft and liked it so well that she agreed to play the lead even before the final version was written.

Barnes and Sheldon then collaborated on two plays. Jane Cowl starred in the first one, *Jenny,* and Katharine Cornell in the second, *Dishonored Lady.* Stories like this one of Margaret Ayer Barnes simply don't happen in every hospital room, but there is more to come. Even before *Dishonored Lady* opened on Broadway, Margaret's first novel was finished: *Years of Grace.*

After all these decades, *Years of Grace* gathers dust on library shelves, but take it down someday, dip into the lives of those upper-middle-class Chicagoans, and you will be as enthralled today as readers of the early thirties were. With sympathy and satire, the author covers events from the turn of the century to the beginning of the depression. She was essentially a social historian; by way of fiction she captured the spirit of her own time and place and social class through sharply observed detail and characterizations as discerning and clear as any in literature.

Mrs. Barnes is remarkable not only for turning out a good novel on her first try, but also because she had the wrong personality for a creative writer. Most imaginative writers are introspective, vague, not quite comfortable in the world of flesh-and-blood people. Not Margaret Barnes. She had a dandy time. A college classmate remembered her at "freshman rush night," outpushing and outshouting everyone around her, in ebullient high spirits. She was fun-loving, witty, and dramatic. Crowds exhilarated her. She could stand up and deliver an impromptu speech at the drop of a hint. But make no mistake—this fast-talking, breezy extrovert was highly organized. In *Years of Grace* she had the life stories of her twenty or more chief characters neatly under her control at all times.

After *Years of Grace* she wrote four more novels, none of which had the impact of her opener; then she disappeared from public view.

At the same time that Pearl Buck and Margaret Ayer Barnes were writing their excellent works of fiction, another remarkable woman was at work on her first book, a very different piece of literature.

Such Good Company!

"It is just *rapturous* out there!" Or "Isn't this day a *joy!*"
So Edith Hamilton would speak about a strenuous walk in the

Maine woods, or about a storm raging on the coast. She loved nature, but only in its wilder aspects.

This Edith Hamilton: she was not a country girl, but an elderly schoolmarm, retired from a prestigious job as headmistress of the Bryn Mawr School for Girls in Baltimore. She was slim, white-haired, and vigorous, with a sharp glance and a quick grin.

An editor coaxed her (bullied her, she said) into writing a book about ancient Greece. She protested that she was no writer and no scholar, but because she loved the subject, she did settle down to write. Titled *The Greek Way*, her book appeared in 1930. An inspiring account of the greatness of the human spirit, it was instantly popular and now it is a classic.

Her style is one of the most beautiful of the twentieth century: clear, uncluttered, concise. Her noble, majestic view of life is that of the great thinkers of the Periclean age. Like the Greeks themselves, she was thrillingly aware of the wonder and the beauty of life. And, like Socrates, she had a gay spirit.

One day a group of friends sat around Miss Hamilton's tea table, and one of them asked her to tell them something about the Greek tragedies. Miss Hamilton began talking enthusiastically about Aeschylus, her favorite tragedian, but suddenly she stopped and said, almost forlornly, "I am so afraid you don't like Aeschylus!" Everyone burst out laughing and one said, "She talks about Aeschylus as if he were her eldest son!" Another added, "She made me feel she must just have had lunch with him."

Another time a friend called on Miss Hamilton, who had been reading. She jumped up from her chair and exclaimed, "Oh, I have been in such good company!" Enviously, the caller asked who the company had been, and her hostess replied, "Plato."

This intense and vivid woman wrote her first book when she was past sixty. After *The Greek Way* she wrote six other books about the culture of the ancient world. She was over eighty when she began making speeches, and this in spite of deafness. At ninety she went, as the guest of the Greek government, to Athens, where a performance of her own translation of *Prometheus Bound* was given, and in a dramatic ceremony in a huge open-air amphitheater she was presented with a scroll that made her a citizen of Athens. This she considered the grandest of all the many honors heaped upon her. Until her death at ninety-five, she continued to travel, write, and lustily enjoy her friends.

One of her former pupils said that Miss Hamilton "brought with her the air of having come from some high center of civilization, where skies were loftier, the views more spacious, the atmosphere more free and open than with us."

South of Mason-Dixon

Before she wrote *The Good Earth*, Pearl Buck taught American and British literature at the University of Nanking. One of the novelists whose work she admired and used in her classes was Ellen Glasgow.

Miss Glasgow was a Virginia woman, all of whose stories were set in the South; yet they were not merely local-color fictions, and emphatically they were not in the magnolia-and-old-lace tradition, which she scorned. She was an ironic realist and her books are peopled with strong but complex men and women who might have lived anywhere but who, as chance would have it, were acted upon by the forces that existed in an area known as Virginia.

Her nineteen novels could be called a social history of the state from 1850 to 1940. The 1930s saw two of her admirable works published, *Vein of Iron* and *The Sheltered Life*. Ellen Glasgow's works reveal that for years she had found compelling the idea of a "vein of iron" in some characters, a stern quality that never permits defeat, no matter how life may invade and batter. These two novels both deal with heroic endurance and ponder what it is that survives in the destructive storms of a lifetime.

Like many creative writers, Ellen Glasgow lived in her imagination even as a child, and she wrote her first short story, called "Only a Daisy," when she was seven. She always felt herself lonely, "odd," and set apart from other people. In her teens she began to suffer from deafness, a sad affliction that made a still higher barrier between her and the world.

She was not an easy woman to get along with. She was domineering, possessive, and quick to anger. She turned her malice instantly upon reviewers who wrote critically of her books. On the other hand, she could be charming, witty, and hospitable when she was in the mood.

In her mansion at One West Main Street, she loved to entertain the socially elect of Richmond and also visiting celebrities. Magnificently dressed (she delighted in beautiful clothes) and sometimes swishing a purple ostrich-feather fan, she waited until her guests were assembled, then swept gorgeously down her staircase to greet them. It is said that people she did not like were entertained in the parlor in the southeast corner of the house. Those she liked and wished to honor were entertained in the grander drawing room across the hall.

She had a barbed tongue and often dominated conversations, but perhaps she did this because of her partial deafness, to save herself the embarrassment of straining and perhaps failing to hear others.

In any case, whether she was malicious or all southern grace, no one so fortunate as to receive an invitation to one of Miss Ellen's lavish parties ever failed to appear; she was the grand lady of Richmond.

Long historical novels, such as *Anthony Adverse,* had a vogue in the 1930s, as did fantasy like *Shangri-La.* Each was an escape from painful today, one into the past and the other into another world. Of all in the historical genre, none was so popular as *Gone with the Wind.*

Serious literary critics never include this work in their list of greats, or at the most they give it a benevolent pat on the binding; but Adela Rogers St. John, whose calmest judgments are usually based on ecstasy or fury, calls it the greatest American novel ever written, and plenty of readers line up behind her.

Gone with the Wind was Margaret Mitchell's only book. She did not, however, simply take up a pencil one day and begin to jot down a thousand-page yarn. Like most authors, she caught the incurable virus young. A friend of hers from Atlanta high school days remembers seeing the teen-age Margaret drifting to and from classes, dreamy and solitary, always with an armful of manuscript and notes.

From childhood, listening to the old folks in parlors and on front porches on hot afternoons in Atlanta, she was bedazzled by tales about the fighting in Virginia and Georgia, the horrors of Sherman's march to the sea, the escape of the refugees, and memories of Reconstruction days. Her writing evolved naturally out of this storytelling.

She spent eleven years writing her book, not chronologically, but forward and then back again, as different episodes captured her imagination. The heroine was named Dorothy O'Hara, but halfway through the writing a friend suggested the name Scarlett; the suggestion was so perfect that Margaret immediately began rewriting the first half of the book. Would Dorothy O'Hara have marched down in American folklore with Ichabod Crane, Tom Sawyer, and Paul Bunyan if she had not been renamed Scarlett?

Margaret Mitchell was not surging toward publication. It is even possible that she would not have submitted the manuscript to a publisher at all had a New York editor named Latham not visited Atlanta. At first Margaret insisted to friends who wanted her to meet him that she had nothing to show him, but a few hours before he left town, she phoned his hotel room from the lobby. He went downstairs and there found a small young woman, looking very scared, sitting on a sofa and surrounded by the tallest stacks of manuscript he had ever seen. She stammered that she had a story he might read if he wanted to, though it wasn't finished, it wasn't revised, and it had no first chapter—and she looked as if she might change her mind any minute and run away. Latham bought a suitcase to hold the manuscript, started reading it on the train back to New York, and became more enthusiastic with every mile.

The book appeared in 1936 and sold nearly half a million copies in three months. Choosing an actress to play Scarlett O'Hara became the great game of 1937. Colleen Moore, Katharine Hepburn, Bette Davis, and many others had their cheering sections; but finally MGM named an unknown English girl named Vivien Leigh for the part. Clark Gable, Olivia de Havilland, and Leslie Howard took the other chief roles, and *Gone with the Wind* became Hollywood's biggest money-maker. When *Daily Variety* years later polled Hollywood for choice of the all-time "best" movie, *GWTW* came in first.

The "One-Woman Team"

Feminists of the 1910s marched for social causes. Flappers of the 1920s danced for pleasure. Women of the 1930s stepped softly in their offices, schoolrooms, and factories lest they be fired; or stood in quiet, desperate lines outside employment offices.

By one of the fascinating paradoxes of history, the decade that saw women in their millions at their most submissive was also the decade that threw up, like exploding rockets, some of the most spectacular women of the century. In sports, in the White House, the theater, the news media, there they blazed: Babe Didrikson, Eleanor Roosevelt, Katharine Cornell, Marian Anderson, Dorothy Thompson—these geniuses superbly giving the lie, or so it seemed, to the generality that the 1930s were a low mark for women.

Phenomenon of the decade was Babe Didrikson. Probably Babe, living in Beaumont, Texas, hardly noticed that a depression was on. The Didriksons, a large, active, loving family, had never known much prosperity anyhow, and the girl herself was too busy playing football with the neighborhood boys, and swimming, and foot racing, and hurdling the neighbors' hedges for practice in jumping, and working out with the boys' basketball team, and starring in girls' high school basketball, to notice a little thing like economics. That Babe! A one-woman team, they called her.

The girl was fanatically competitive. She hurled herself obsessively into practice for anything that challenged her—and in the sports world, what didn't? The day before a contest, she'd stride up to her opponent and cheerfully announce, "Ah'm gonna lick yuh tomorrah."

On her way to the 1932 Olympics by railway, she was the only athlete who never quit training. She did exercises in the aisle, and ran up and down the length of the train, up and down, again and again. Passengers laughed at her, but Babe only grinned back at them and kept on training.

Add to that single-minded zeal a God-given coordination and a wonderfully healthy body, and to all that add whatever her mysterious genius was. A genius for physical action? Like a genius for music or for painting?

At any rate, in the National AAU track and field championships when she was nineteen, she won five events, and tied for first in another one. Two weeks later, at the Olympic games in Los Angeles, she won two gold medals and a silver. She broke the world's record in the eighty-meter hurdle, and also broke the Olympic record in the javelin throw by about fourteen feet; she would have done really well but her hand slipped on the javelin. When she got home, Beaumont, Texas, had a "Babe Didrikson Day."

But, just before going home from the Olympics, Babe played a game of golf with three sports writers including Grantland Rice, one of her ardent fans. She won the game and a new obsession. From then on, she spent all her free time on the golf course. She won the U.S. Golf Association amateur competition and the year after that she won fifteen tournaments. Next she won the British amateur title, then turned pro and won thirty-three more tournaments. The girl was unbeatable.

But Babe had a soft and feminine side, too. Out of her meager teens and into her prosperous twenties, she luxuriated in lipstick and lace handkerchiefs and delicate underwear. Speaking of the last to novelist Paul Gallico, she announced, "It's silk, and Ah like it."

Fighter for the Underdog

After three years of fear and confusion, Americans, especially the young, responded to the new leadership in Washington with delirious joy. There was a surge of excitement and hope. Society would change!—for the better, of course. There would be jobs for everyone! Political reform! Social justice! A new sun had risen!

Eleanor Roosevelt stepped into the national spotlight in 1933 and it became evident at once that she was going to behave as no president's wife before her had ever behaved. All of them had stood modestly in the shadow of their husbands. Millions of people supposed that Mrs. Roosevelt would make a comic spectacle of herself, and were distressed or entertained according to their political bias; but by the end of the decade people took her seriously—with enmity or with admiration, again according to their bias, but she was no longer funny.

When Franklin Delano Roosevelt was governor of New York, citizens of Albany had got used to seeing their tall first lady—she was five feet eleven—loping through the streets bent slightly forward in her hurry, wearing a white dress, tennis shoes, a velvet hair band, and no makeup. Her schedule always listed more activities than she could cram into twenty-four hours.

As the president's wife, she stepped up the pace. People around her worked in relays because no individual could compete in her marathon. She once pressed into political service the attractive former governor of Wyoming, Nellie Tayloe Ross, and required her to shake every female hand within reach, and smile while she did it. During one reception, the star of the show disappeared. Mrs. Roosevelt sent out a search party. It found Mrs. Ross flat on her back on the floor of the ladies' room, exhausted.

One of Eleanor's devices for getting things done was her simple directness. At the White House, when she wanted to go from one floor to another, she took the elevator and ran it herself. "Mrs. Roosevelt!" protested Ike Hoover, veteran chief usher. "The Family doesn't operate the elevator! It just isn't done!"

She smiled sunnily. "It is now," she said, and reached for the controls.

When in New York, she hurried from one appointment to another on the subway, standing when the car was SRO and holding on to a strap. She never allowed Secret Service men to trail after her except when she was with the president.

Her manner was easy and informal; she could talk as comfortably with royalty as with the deprived. When the king and queen of England made a state visit to Washington, she was late in meeting them at Union Station because she had found a family of sharecroppers stranded on a Midwestern highway and had brought them to Washington to help them. She became so engrossed in talking to them at the White House that she lost track of time until reminded that the gold-and-silver-trimmed royal train was awaiting her presence.

But Eleanor was no featherbrain. Before the reelection campaign of 1936—Alf Landon of Kansas was Roosevelt's Republican opponent that time—she sent Democratic National Chairman Jim Farley a detailed analysis of how she thought the campaign should be run, a survey so detailed that it required a twenty-page reply from Farley. Not a man to be tender toward women who got in his way, Farley nevertheless called her "the most practical woman I ever met in politics."

She was practical and she was shrewd, but it was her direct, simple style that baffled politicians. She saw a lot of things in society that needed changing and so she set about changing them. When she found that the colored Home for the Aged in Washington was giving its inmates inadequate food, that the building was ready to collapse and was shelter to a throng of rats, she exclaimed to a congressional committee, "We should be ashamed! If this is the way we care for people who are not able to care for themselves, we are at a pretty low ebb of civilization!"

Congress corrected the situation.

When a lower minimum wage was established for women than for men, she invited National Recovery Act (NRA) director General Hugh Johnson to lunch at the White House and asked him why.

"Because that's always been the American pattern," he said.

"Then," she said, "it's time to change the pattern."

He did.

In Birmingham, Alabama, she once attended a meeting of blacks and whites in a church. Negroes sat on one side of the aisle, whites on the other side. When she sat down on the black side, the chief of police told her he would have to arrest her if she stayed there, because she was breaking the segregation law. Calling for a folding chair, she set it in the aisle between the two sections, then moved it a little closer to the black side.

She took wives of cabinet officers through the Washington slums, which had been a civic disgrace for decades. She badgered Congress until it passed an act to clean up the area.

At first naïve, she soon realized to her chagrin that Congress was not responding zealously to the sensible criticisms of a citizen. It was hopping to her commands in order to keep out of trouble with the White House. Nevertheless, she kept slugging away at social reform, and became the most controversial figure in American life. Traditionalists were outraged at her tramping in where women had no business even tiptoeing. But there was no stopping her.

To spare her husband as much physical effort as possible, she was his stand-in at countless dedication ceremonies and wreath-laying rituals and was state greeter of VIPs. (In spite of the royal family incident, she wasn't usually late.) She traveled the nation on errands for him, logging forty thousand miles a year, most of it by air. Commercial flying was new in the early thirties, and grateful airlines called her their best advertisement. On the evening of her return to Washington, she and her husband always dined alone, so she could report to him on the temper of the nation as she had seen it.

Whatever the truth of FDR's bedroom adventures and whatever her reaction in rage or heartbreak, these two worked together as a loyal team.

To "bring the people to him," she visited slums and tent cities, ate in bread lines, toured the Dust Bowl. Everywhere she went she listened to people's stories and to their ideas. She went down coal mines, inspected prisons, visited hospitals.

All this leaping from coast to coast became a national joke, a mother lode to cartoonists and comedians. One of the stories was of a father who told his little son the story of Robinson Crusoe. "And there on the sand Robinson found a pair of footprints," said the father dramatically. "Whose do you suppose they were?" The boy answered confidently, "Mrs. Roosevelt's."

Plenty of the jokes and cartoons were rancorous, because FDR, Eleanor, and the New Deal were bitterly unpopular with many. All presidents and their wives have their critics, but none ever had such an impassioned congregation of haters as these two. Forty years later there would still be people whose hands would twitch and cheeks turn pale with fury at the murmured word "Roosevelt."

FDR could not take ridicule, and he never forgot a grudge. But Eleanor accepted criticism cheerfully. She often read her critical letters aloud at the breakfast table, laughing at many, like the one from the man who wanted to know where in the hell she bought her hats.

During the 1940 reelection campaign, she laughed heartily at the buttons Republicans wore, reading, "And We Don't Want Eleanor, Either." But her good humor ended quickly when slings and arrows were directed at her children. She was not amused by the buttons that read, "Make Me a Captain Too," a reference to the fact that son Elliott had been commissioned as an Air Corps captain.

In spite of all the ire that she aroused, Mrs. Roosevelt had more admirers than enemies. A Gallup poll at the end of the decade showed that 67 percent of Americans approved of her, while only 58 percent approved of FDR. As Theodore Roosevelt had been the dominant figure on the American scene in the first decade, so his niece Eleanor was the most influential woman of the thirties.

First Ladies of the Theater

Nineteen-thirty was a bad year for Broadway, 1931 was worse, and 1932 was a calamity. Shows folded faster than new ones could open. Theatrical hotels were empty and broke. *Variety* estimated that twenty-five thousand actors were idle. The Actors' Free Dinner Club was established in Union Church on West Forth-eighth Street, and as some stars came to eat and some came to wait on tables, no one knew who was there on the cuff. To liven the scene, star waiters clowned it up, on the theory that lettuce with a laugh is better than T-bone with a moan.

But even in these hard years, there were hits on Broadway. Katharine Cornell and Helen Hayes, who shared the title "First Lady of the Theater," starred in many of them.

Late one evening, in a New York restaurant, a young man of the 1930s saw Katharine Cornell and a party of friends sweep into the restaurant after the theater. Instantly, in his eyes, the wattage of everyone else in the room—diners, waiters, the actress's own friends—was suddenly reduced to a dim glow. Such was Katharine Cornell's brilliance.

This special quality—call it radiance or call it glamour—projected across the footlights in the same way. In the 1920s she had to play a good many silly parts, but she endowed even those characters with vibrant life. Her appearance had such distinction that onstage she always looked like Katharine Cornell, whether she was Jo in *Little Women* (her first rich part, when she was a girl not much more than twenty), Iris March in *The Green Hat*, Juliet, or Joan of Arc. But each time the audience saw a different character of striking individuality.

She was not a pretty girl in the Hollywood-starlet sense, but she had beauty, with a broad, heart-shaped face, heavy-lidded eyes, and generous lips. The first time that producer Guthrie McClintic met her in a group of stock-company actors, he was fascinated; he couldn't take his eyes away from the young woman with the warm smile who walked with that slow, easy grace. Suddenly he thought: That's the girl I'm going to marry. It wasn't that he fell in love with her at that moment; his intuition was simply reporting a future event. Two years later they were married. By that time he had indeed fallen helplessly and permanently in love.

After their marriage he became her director, and the actress went into management. This change of status permitted her to choose only plays that seemed worthwhile to her. The first she put on as manager was *The Barretts of Wimpole Street* by Rudolf Besier. For a year it played in New York with a splendid cast. Brian Aherne was the ebullient Robert Browning, and Charles Waldron the despotic, cruel, mid-Victorian father, Moulton-Barrett.

The part of the invalid Elizabeth Barrett was Katharine Cornell's, and it was an exhausting part. The star was onstage continuously except for the final three minutes, and she half lay on a couch with her side to the audience, so that she projected all her lines toward the side wall of the set. Her costumes were heavy and stiff, and she was further weighted down by an afghan spread over her from feet to waist.

But she never tired of the role. After more than seven hundred performances, she felt that she more nearly approached the author's vision of Elizabeth Barrett than she did the first hundred times. She strove to give an illusion of freshness as if she were speaking her lines for the first time. Fellow players said that, during a performance, when anyone spoke directly to Elizabeth, she always turned up her face toward that actor with an expression of eager expectancy, as if she were hearing those words for the first time.

In 1933–34, the Cornell company pioneered: they went on a long, transcontinental tour. At that time "the road" was dead. But, believing that the country was ready for good plays, well produced, it got theaters to open that had been closed for years, and persuaded movie-house operators to admit a legitimate show.

Audiences packed the houses, audiences that had never seen any drama except on the screen. Altogether 500,000 people saw the Cornell plays, and many of them traveled hundreds of miles to see them. Katharine loved the road audiences; their response to a play was always so warm and spontaneous.

The company, consisting of forty players, fifteen other specialists, and three dogs, traveled seventeen-thousand miles by train—four carloads, including scenery—and they put on 225 performances with a repertory of three plays, *The Barretts, Candida,* and *Romeo and Juliet.*

On Saturday morning before Christmas, the company left Duluth for the long trip west to Seattle, where they were due at eight A.M. on the 25th to open at eight o'clock that night. But there had been a washout between Duluth and Seattle. The train crept. And it rained. And rained. By eight o'clock Christmas morning they were many miles from Seattle. Maybe they'd arrive by late afternoon. . . . Well, maybe by eight in the evening. But when the train crawled into the station at Seattle, it was 11:15 Christmas night, and the tired company prepared drearily to go to bed.

Then they had electrifying news: their audience was still at the theater—still waiting for them. Could anybody fail such an audience as that? The players raced for the theater. The crew tore for the baggage car. Arrived onstage, Katharine said, "Pull up the curtain. Let them watch us set up."

In full view of the audience, stagehands set up backdrops and props. They carried trunks onstage and the wardrobe mistress unpacked there, with every player going to her for his or her costume as she shook it out. Elizabeth Barrett's delightful blond cocker spaniel, Flush, was introduced. McClintic and the stage manager described everything: This is Miss Barrett's sofa—that window opens on Wimpole Street—these small spotlights are called babies. . . .

At one o'clock all was ready and the curtain went down. The house was darkened. Five minutes later the curtain went up again and act one began. When the curtain went down for the last time, it was four A.M. The audience cheered and applauded for curtain call after curtain call. It was a night to remember.

It was not alone this memorable show but the whole strenuous tour that made theater buffs give Katharine Cornell credit for bringing the road back to life.

Helen the Queen

Helen Hayes Brown and her mother played the Geraldine Farrar story all over again: talented daughter and charming, iron-willed mother whose own ambition had been thwarted. Whether the talent or the iron was more responsible, young Helen Hayes (she soon dropped the name Brown) made it onto the stage as Little Lord Fauntleroy, as that glad, glad, *glad* girl Pollyanna, and at fourteen with John Drew in *The Prodigal Husband*. Full-grown, Helen is only five feet tall, and at fourteen she looked no more than ten. The great actor was tenderly protective of his little juvenile, and always called her—it hardly bears thinking of—he called her "Childy."

Her real entrance into stardom came in 1918 when she played opposite William Gillette in *Dear Brutus*. She almost missed the boat on that role, because when the Brutus part was offered her she was playing in *Penrod*, and the manager refused to release her. But the hand of God, as Mrs. Brown happily related, intervened for Helen. He sent a flu epidemic into New York at the appropriate time and caused the shutting down of all theaters apt to be attended by children. *Penrod* closed and Helen was free for *Brutus*.

From then on, she was seldom out of work.

For years the public liked to think of their little Helen as all sunshine and ruffles, but she showed them. On the screen she played Madelon Claudet (in *The Sin Of*, in the early thirties), and opposite Gary Cooper she played the nurse in *A Farewell to Arms*, both of them tragic, emotional roles. On the stage she charmed audiences as the wise and tender little Scottish wife in Barrie's *What Every Woman Knows*, just as Maude Adams had charmed audiences a generation earlier in the same part. In *Mary of Scotland* she played a strong, dramatic role. After seeing that show, William Lyon Phelps went backstage and asked her how she contrived to give such a majestic effect of height, because Mary the Queen was really six feet tall. Helen showed him the platform shoes she wore for the part but added, "I *think* myself tall."

Her greatest role was in *Victoria Regina*, which ran for three years. In act one Victoria is a young girl and by the last act she is eighty. The drama of *Victoria* was enthralling, but the public was obsessed with curiosity about makeup. How did Helen manage to portray great age, with those fat cheeks and the stout body? (As for the rounded face, now it can be told: she did it with wads of cotton stuck in her cheeks.)

Everywhere, people marveled at her growing old before their eyes, but tables turn. One time a Russian countess, new to America, attended *Victoria* and after the performance went to the star's dressing room to meet her. Helen had tossed off jet bonnet and wig, and was receiving friends, still in her eighty-year-old face. The countess entered, curtsied, and said, "But, dear Miss Hayes, how did you make yourself so girlish in the earlier scenes?"

In private life, Miss Hayes was known as one of the ten worst-dressed women of the stage. Her wardrobe was the despair of fashionable Lynn Fontanne, but Helen laughed. Twice she was shanghaied into Hattie Carnegie's salon. Commanded by ruthless friends to bend her mind to fashion, she ordered a dress by pointing to the one Miss Carnegie had on and saying, "I'll take that one." Offstage, she felt most peaceful in an old sweater and skirt.

Helen's critics always said that she wasn't beautiful and she wasn't glamorous; yet the public loved her. Conventional people liked it because she married for love and stayed married, though all the world knew that the extravagant, perverse, witty Charles MacArthur wasn't the easiest or the most faithful husband on Broadway. Millions grieved with the parents when their vivid, talented daughter, Mary, died before she was twenty. But Helen Hayes was loved for more than these things. The spirited walk, the quick grin with teeth edge-to-edge, the sprightly eyebrow, the shrewd and humorous glance—they gave her that human touch.

Eva the Dynamo

Eva Le Gallienne, an actress with a lacy name but steely self-discipline, lived for the theater. (She was, by the way, daughter of the poet Richard Le Gallienne, who had marched for woman suffrage.) Miss Le Gallienne had friends, and an old Connecticut house that she loved, and she read and traveled—but her favorite sport was work. To study and rehearse for eighteen hours was her idea of a good, bracing day.

She was not only a fine performer but a dynamic executive. Impatient with the necessity on Broadway of having high-priced smash hits or nothing, she organized, during the 1920s, the Civic Repertory Theater on New York's Fourteenth Street, and ran it for seven years. At popular prices—tickets cost from 35 cents to $1.50—people could see the classics of the theater with a constant change of billing. Employing about one hundred people, she chose her scripts, selected the casts, designed her sets, supervised the costume department, directed the plays, and acted the major roles. She was business manager and money raiser, too. And she was never tired. As the depression tottered on, however, more and more subscribers had to cut the Civic off their lists of charities, until in 1934 her theater was obliged to bow to hard times.

Miss Le Gallienne is famous for her Hamlet. Her argument for its being played by a woman was that she believed Hamlet was not a man of forty but a youth of about nineteen. His melancholy, the hero worship of his father, his thoughts of suicide, and his jealousy of his mother when she remarried, all are convincing and touching in a boy, she argued, but in a mature man they would indicate a weak and wavering nature. Bernhardt, she pointed out, had often played Hamlet, and played it well.

But one suspects that more than cool logic was at stake here. Hamlet is the supreme role in all the theater, the Everest of roles. Of course Eva Le Gallienne had to play Hamlet.

Escape from the Big, Bad Wolf

If a historian of the future were to judge the 1930s only by the most popular radio shows and movies of the period, he would conclude that this was a prosperous and fun-filled decade. Americans didn't switch on the radio to learn depressing facts about the national plight. They wanted to laugh at Amos 'n' Andy, at Edgar Bergen and Charlie McCarthy, at Bob Hope, Jack Benny, and Ed Wynn, the Texaco fire chief. By the way, only one family in five had a radio in 1925, but by 1935 one half of all homes had them.

A second evidence of escapism was a fever of fads. For a season, miniature golf was such a craze that movie houses actually stood half empty while patrons waited in line for their turn on the toy greens. Monopoly so caught the public's fancy that adults sometimes kept games under way for days at a time. Auction bridge players were converted to Culbertson and became contract zealots. Bicycling and roller skating had a boom. Jigsaw puzzles exercised an obsessive fascination. In 1934 chain-letter hysteria spread through offices, factories, and neighborhoods, whipped high by rumors of riches won by the lucky few. The candid camera had its addicts. People entered trials to see who could sit on ice the longest, or survive longest atop a flagpole, or swallow the most live goldfish. Cruel marathon dances lured the penniless to damage their health in endurance contests.

Driven by their anxieties, people crowded into movie houses. The fee was low—from 20 cents to 75—and for two or three hours the woman who didn't know where Betsy's next pair of shoes was coming from, and the man who couldn't afford to go to the dentist with his aching teeth, could sit shoulder to shoulder in the dark and relax in the fabulous wealth of Jean Harlow in *Platinum Blonde*. They could blend into the wonderfully monied world of Joan Crawford, society playgirl, or weep tenderly at Shirley Temple's little problems, well knowing that she would end up rich and well loved; or laugh at scruffy old Apple Annie becoming a society queen in *Lady for a Day*. They could be lifted to joy by the rhythm of Ginger Rogers and Fred Astaire in *Flying Down to Rio*. Norma Shearer was a favorite, too, in upper-class plays such as the witty *Private Lives* and *Let Us Be Gay*; or *The Divorcée*, for which Norma won an Oscar.

Always there were the light-hearted Disney cartoons to laugh at. The famous old short, *Three Little Pigs*, was rerun constantly; the big, bad wolf became a symbol for the depression.

Most movie plots were vanilla puddings: sweet, smooth, and bland. Boy met girl, and after a few delays, boy married girl. Morals on the screen were incredibly pure. However members of the audience and the actors might behave in private life, it was assumed that the girl on the silver screen had never heard of the birds and the bees.

Nevertheless, some excellent films were made in the 1930s. Among them were *All Quiet on the Western Front*, *Journey's End*, *A Farewell to Arms*, *The Animal Kingdom*, *Anna Christie*, *Strange Interlude*, *Of Human Bondage*. Historical films, like historical novels, were popular too: *A Tale of Two Cities*, *Mutiny on the Bounty*, *Cimarron*, *Drums Along the Mohawk*, *Northwest Passage*, and the English film, *Henry VIII*.

These were all serious stories, but none of them tried to cope with the terrible realities of its own time. Only Charlie Chaplin in *Modern Times* and *City Lights* had the temerity for that; these two were a shrewd mixture of hilarity and satire. John Steinbeck's *Grapes of Wrath*, which depicted the grim predicament of Dust Bowl victims, didn't appear until 1939, when prosperity had turned that corner at last. In its own time, the early thirties, audiences could not have endured to see the miseries of their real life reflected on the screen.

One movie did deal with the depression, but did so with such wit, such polish, that audiences returned to see it again and again: *You Can't Take It with You,* by Moss Hart and George S. Kaufman. Everybody in the zany Vanderhof household faced his depression problems nonchalantly and gave free rein to his creative urges—tap dancing, novel writing, the manufacture of fireworks. No one did his thing very well, but they all did it so cheerfully! There wasn't enough money, but there were much hope and good will—and such marvelously funny lines! Moviegoers could pretend for a light-hearted hour or so that they too were laughing off their dilemmas as Lionel Barrymore, Jean Arthur, Spring Byington, James Stewart, and all the other members of the brilliant cast laughed off theirs.

This decade was the era of the great stars, and Greta Garbo topped the list. She was superbly beautiful. Her beauty resembled no one else's unless it was that of the ravishing Egyptian Queen Nefertiti of thirty-five hundred years ago. No one could anguish before the camera as Garbo could. It was the same in all her roles in all twenty-four of her films: suffer, suffer, suffer. In *Anna Karenina* (the silent version was retitled *Love,* because what did an amateur like Tolstoy know about titles?), in *Mysterious Lady, A Woman of Affairs, The Kiss, Anna Christie, Mata Hari, Grand Hotel, Camille,* and all the rest. The magnificent face would slowly lift, the mouth go slack, the eyelids droop, the tiniest muscles under that flawless skin would stir, and Garbo's emotion would pierce the audience with its intensity. In all her roles, her tragedy was based on a single factor: loss of a man's love.

Women outnumbered men as her fans, and no one can say exactly why. Maybe women enjoyed identifying with Garbo's high emotion and her strong sexuality. Maybe they were unconsciously drawn by her paradoxical masculinity. The story is told of a young man who swore to his bride-to-be on the eve of their wedding that he would be faithful to her until death—unless he had the opportunity to make love to Garbo. The girl nodded agreeably and said, "Me too."

Garbo's efforts to be private only increased her fascination. After her retirement in 1941, she told a friend that she had never, never said, "I vant to be alone." She had only vanted to be *let* alone.

In her movie roles, Garbo was woman incarnate. So was voluptuous Marlene Dietrich, who won fame in *The Blue Angel,* but she added a quality of her own: deadly, sinister danger, and contempt for men. Those veiled eyes, angular cheekbones, and arched brows added up to sultry allure, further accented by masculine attire. She often wore men's suits, sleek and tailored, and oftener still a top hat, tail coat, black tights, and shining stockings on the spectacular legs.

But, scornful of men though she seemed, and possessed of a catlike self-containment, in the famous closing scene of the movie *Morocco* she threw all this aside and revealed herself, after all that posturing, as a true woman. Dowagers of 1900 would have applauded. In this scene the strong-willed, independent woman takes off her high-heeled shoes and trudges, humble and patient, into the desert in pursuit of Woman's eternal prize, Man.

These few feet of film perfectly symbolize Hollywood's conception of women: ultimately, the submissive love object.

A unique movie queen of the thirties was the sluggish but provocative Mae West. She played the archetype of a traditional figure of literature: the voluptuary with the heart of gold. She was feathered, furred, glittering with jewels, and so tightly corseted that she could hardly walk. Sex dripped from her caressing fingers, glowed in the sliding glance of those painted eyes, in the cynical half smile; it rolled in the swaggering turns of fleshy shoulders. Sex spoke enticingly in the nasal voice that drawled, with both humor and disdain, "I used to be Snow White, but I drifted." Or the much-quoted, "Why don't you come up and see me sometime?"

Mae West promised sex but delivered nothing. There were few kisses and no passionate embraces. Nevertheless, her seductive promises outraged the proper, they antagonized the censors, and brought coins rattling into the box office.

Musicals were popular in the thirties, and in addition to Deanna Durbin, Judy Garland, and Jeanette MacDonald, stars of the Met trekked to Hollywood. Grace Moore made *One Night of Love*, Lily Pons played in *I Dream Too Much*, Gladys Swarthout in *Rose of the Rancho*, and Kirsten Flagstad appeared in *The Big Broadcast of 1938*.

But while frivolity filled idle hours for many, a small but angry and articulate group of actors, authors, and artists raged against society. The *Daily Worker*, a Communist paper, and *New Masses*, its Socialist counterpart, battered against the horrendous status quo, and at some time during the thirties nearly all intellectuals favored Communism. At the peak of its popularity, the party had 75,000 members, with three times as many sympathizers.

But the bulk of America was immovably conservative. Although there was widespread rapture when Roosevelt took office in 1933, this euphoria soon wore off, and many Americans considered even the mild reforms of the New Deal suspiciously radical. What they longed for was a return to 1928, and never mind all this experimentation.

Off-Broadway audiences, however, cheered experimental plays, especially those with a message of protest. The International Ladies' Garment Workers' Union, for a weekend of fun, put on a musical revue entitled *Pins and Needles.* Members of the cast were cutters, pressers, and sewing-machine operators. The show lampooned society ladies, industrialists, financiers, politicians, and even their own union. Gem of the show was the number "Sing Me a Song with Social Significance." Also there was "Doing the Reactionary" and "It's Better with a Union Man." *Pins and Needles* was such a delight that it ran for four years. Society ladies, industrialists, financiers, and politicans went in droves to laugh at themselves.

Woman with a Pencil

There was a good deal of "isn't-it-wonderful" hoopla about all those women in government positions under the New Deal. Frances Perkins became first woman cabinet member as secretary of labor. Ruth Bryan Owen was minister to Denmark, our first woman minister. Later Mrs. J. Borden Harriman was named minister to Norway. FDR appointed the capable Judge Florence Allen to the federal judiciary. Nellie Tayloe Ross became first woman director of the United States Mint, and Josephine Roche assistant secretary of the treasury. Marian Banister was assistant treasurer of the United States. Stella Akin special assistant to the attorney general. Rose Schneiderman, that veteran of many a hassle to get working women organized into unions, was a member of the NRA Labor Advisory Board. On second thought, is that really so many?

On a lower level, of the 1,600,000 workers in government projects, only 142,000 were women, or about one in eleven.

Except in teaching and nursing, women were thinly represented in the professions, too. At the beginning of the 1930s, there were fifteen thousand women reporters in the country. Some of these were laid off, and by 1940 only one thousand others had entered the field. In journalism as in other professions, a woman not only had to be good to succeed, she had to be better than her male colleagues. One female correspondent was just that: Dorothy Thompson.

Dorothy Thompson's political columns flamed with emotion. She denounced anti-Semitism. She raged against Fascism. She was the angriest and most eloquent enemy that Hitler had in the world's press. In 1934, Hitler threw her out of Germany in revenge for a piece she had written about him before he climbed to power. "He is inconsequent and voluble," she wrote after her first meeting with Hitler. "[He is] ill-poised, insecure. He is the very prototype of the Little Man."

But if Hitler hated her for that so much that he ordered her out of the country, she was a favorite with the American and British correspondents there. Nearly the entire corps went to the railway station to see her off, to shout their good wishes and give her an armful of American Beauty roses. Almost hidden by the mass of flowers, she leaned out the carriage window to wave goodbye, half weeping at such a show of affection.

Dorothy Thompson was a strikingly handsome woman. She was tall and erect, with even, classic features, blue eyes, and a rosy, baby-fine skin. She took such a lusty delight in food that she gained weight easily and from time to time she had to go on crash diets.

As a correspondent, she seemed always to be on the spot when something exciting happened. A street riot in Vienna? An attempt of King Charles to seize the Hungarian throne? Joseph Pilsudski's military coup in Warsaw? Dorothy was there. She fired her stories to the United States—vivid, fast-paced, breathtaking.

In matters of importance, her stories were accurate, too. The reporter's own picture of the reporter, however, edged toward the picturesque. Part of the Thompson legend was a tale that once, wearing evening dress and satin slippers, she slogged all alone for miles through Polish mud to report a military crisis. In truth, she wore a tailored suit and walking shoes and was one of a group of correspondents traveling together, part of the way by bus; but the kernel of the story is true: Dorothy Thompson was a keen and indomitable reporter.

Of course a woman as vital as she loved often and deeply. In 1922, in Budapest, when she was twenty-nine and a newcomer to European journalism, she married Josef Bard, a handsome and intellectual Jewish Hungarian. Though trained as a lawyer, he was at work writing a long philosophical book to be entitled *The Mind of Europe*. Dorothy pictured herself as a devoted handmaiden of a creative genius, with her life equally divided between her profound love and her exciting job. But inevitably Josef, with his European standards of family life, felt humiliated by his wife's greater earnings, by the more conspicuous figure she cut among their friends, and by her frequent dashes around the continent to cover news events.

Dorothy had friends in for drinks and conversation whenever she wasn't on duty, and maybe Josef tired also of this continuous party giving. "You are drunken with life," he once grumbled. One evening in the midst of a conversation with guests Dorothy suddenly jumped up and said, "Excuse me for a few minutes. I've got to get an article done." In her bedroom-study, she typed rapidly for half an hour, then came back and reentered the conversation as if she hadn't been away. "She was a great talker," said one of her friends. "Josef was a witty fellow, but she dominated the room when she was there. It wasn't comfortable."

After five years of hectic married life, Josef, who had fallen in love with a more peaceful woman, asked for a divorce. Dorothy pleaded with him, she reasoned, she had moods of suicidal depression, she grieved, but at last she had to give him his freedom.

It was during the grief-stricken time after the divorce that she met Sinclair Lewis, himself just then undergoing divorce from his first wife. He proposed to her after the first evening they spent together. She was astonished—and of course flattered—because Lewis was the most spectacular figure just then in the American literary world. He courted her rapturously and publicly, and at last, a little dubious, she agreed to marry him.

"I am not nearly so much 'in love,'" she wrote to a friend, comparing Lewis to Josef. "But he pleases me. He is a superb comrade . . . he heightens my sense of life. . . . For the first time in years I dream of tomorrow as well as enjoy today. Thus he gives me back the gift of youth."

And so in 1928 these two people, both sparkling in the world's limelight, embarked on a strenuous marriage that was to last for fourteen years. They had some joyous times together, and more times that were murky with anger, jealousy, and resentment.

Dorothy talked too much about politics, which bored Hal (as she called him, though to most of his friends he was Red). Often he refused to join the friends she invited to their home. "Dorothy's cabinet," he called them. But if Dorothy talked too much, Lewis drank too much. Humorous and companionable when sober, drunk he was bad-tempered and quarrelsome. An entry in Dorothy's journal reads, "It was a nice day. Hal didn't lose his temper with me once."

Late in their tempestuous marriage, Dorothy wrote to a friend, "Work with me has always been a by-product and a secondary interest; I'd throw the state of the nation into the ashcan for anyone I loved."

What romantic nonsense! Again and again she rushed away from husband (and later, son) to lecture or to witness the fireworks in Europe.

There was tragic tension between her life as a woman and her life as a journalist. Jane Addams, Alice Paul, Edna Ferber, and countless others who were ardent for a career solved the puzzle by forgoing marriage. But Dorothy Thompson wanted both worlds.

The Lewises' son, Michael, was born in 1930. They loved him and they arranged scrupulously for his welfare—a trained nurse to care for him, the best medical attention—but when he was an infant they were bored if he had to be with them for long at a time.

Dorothy had her devotees and her critics. One reporter tells the story of an evening when, on a quick trip to England just before World War II, she met with a group of London journalists to be briefed on current politics. But she did most of the talking. When she asked a question, she answered it herself instead of listening. Also she drank more than her share of the Scotch, unaware that it was a "collector's item." Even among her hard-drinking colleagues, Dorothy's drinking, no doubt stepped up by her unhappy private life, caused some comment.

The years of the Thompson-Lewis marriage were the years when her career skyrocketed to its height. Her syndicated column, "On the Record," appeared three times a week. Beginning in 1937, she broadcast once a week over the radio, with five million Americans listening. She wrote seven books, most of them on European politics. She was a tireless lecturer, delighting audiences with her vividness and exuberance. She wrote an essay every month for the *Ladies' Home Journal*. One year in the late thirties, her income was $103,000.

Her divorce from Sinclair Lewis gave her as much anguish as her first divorce had, and her friends were relieved when, in 1943, she married Maxim Kopf, an artist and a native of Prague. This was a friendly, tolerant marriage that ended only with his death fifteen years later.

A touching quality of Dorothy Thompson's, and a surprising one in a woman of such flamboyant personality, was her absolute lack of vindictiveness. She always spoke generously of the two men who divorced her, and she came to be on the friendliest terms with Eileen Agar, the woman who had won Josef Bard's love from her. She was equally amiable toward Grace Hegger, first wife of Sinclair Lewis. Some of her tenderest affection was devoted to Grace and Sinclair's son Wells, and she grieved to despair when he was killed in World War II.

Margaret Bourke-White

A gifted artist rose to prominence in the 1930s whose instrument was not a sculptor's chisel, nor a paintbrush, nor a violin, but a camera. Margaret Bourke-White had the eye of an artist for composition, she had the imagination of a playwright for seeing human drama, and she had indomitable will.

When, pursuing a degree in biology, she entered Cornell for her senior year, she had to earn part of her expenses; but not one single student job remained unclaimed. However, she owned a secondhand reflex camera and a resourceful wit. She took pictures of the magnificent scenery of the Ithaca campus and arranged with a commercial photographer in the town to use his darkroom at night to work up enlargements. Fellow students bought her prints, and the biologist turned to photography.

That turning-point anecdote has more than one significant facet. She was not only resourceful; she was alert. She profited by technical advice from that commercial photographer in Ithaca, and from then on she learned from every specialist that she met.

Undoubtedly her attractiveness made more than one teacher quick to offer help and advice. She was a graceful, slender girl with lovely, regular features and a glowing smile. Whether she wore skirts, slacks, parka or (after Pearl Harbor) a war correspondent's uniform, she was always delightfully feminine. She loved beautiful clothes. She used her femininity whenever it helped her career, but she never used it to avoid hard work or danger.

After graduation, she scraped out a living in her home town of Cleveland by photographing gardens and public buildings by day and developing her work in her kitchen by night. But her obsession just then was shooting pattern pictures in the "Flats," a cluttered industrial area called Cleveland's backyard. How she loved the vitality, the hugeness, the turbulence of industry! Often, against a skyful of luminous clouds, she photographed the abstract pattern of a trestle, the traffic span of a bridge, rooftops, towering smokestacks in a majestic row.

Week by week she learned. From failures. From tireless practice. From other photographers. Nothing was too hard. When at last she won the privilege of admission to the Otis Steel Mill of Cleveland, where women had never been permitted before, she worked every night for five months. During the day she kept the wolf a few doors down the street by free-lancing. Nights she prowled through the steel mill with her cameras, learning what equipment and what lighting to use, what timing. At the end of her five months, she had only a dozen good pictures, but a know-how possessed then by no other photographer.

Moving on to New York, Margaret Bourke-White spent many months and earned a lot of money doing work she came to hate: advertising photography. She free-lanced for news agencies, and was also on the staffs of Henry Luce's two new magazines, *Fortune* (born 1930) and *Life* (1936). In these two jobs she was free to do what she liked best: to take pictures in series; to tell a story without words. It was an entirely original approach to reporting, a contribution as inventive in its medium as the work of the new poets in theirs.

She did a photo story on shoemaking at Lynn, Massachusetts, on glass making, on orchid raising, then made an industrial cross-section of an entire city (South Bend, Indiana), and next she was given a plum that young foreign correspondents dream of: she was sent to Russia on a picture assignment. In 1934 she traveled west to do a Dust Bowl story. She covered Roosevelt's second inauguration for *Life*.

At about that time, Erskine Caldwell's *Tobacco Road* was a controversial novel and an equally controversial play, then in the midst of its three thousand-performance run in New York. He was ruffled by the fact that hosts of people refused to believe that the ignorance, misery, and poverty dramatized in his story were genuine. He determined to find a cameraman to go south with him to prove the truth of his fiction. Margaret at the same time was searching for an author with free time, to go south with her to collaborate on a book about back-country people. The two discovered each other, immersed themselves in their job, and came up with a splendid book of photographs-with-text entitled *You Have Seen Their Faces*.

In the course of their work they fell in love. Caldwell was a brilliant, gentle, quiet man, given to unreasonable jealousies and unexpected frozen silences that usually ended in an emotional tempest. Margaret was apprehensive about marriage to him, but after a long courtship she agreed to try it. On board the plane that carried them to Nevada, where they were to have the ceremony, she drew up a marriage contract. Erskine must agree that if a difficulty arose between them they would talk it out before midnight; that he would treat her friends courteously; that he would try to control his moods; that he would not try to hold her back from photographic assignments. He signed this curious document and they entered into a marriage that lasted nearly five years.

It was the war that separated them. Erskine had a Hollywood offer that he wanted to accept, but adventure lured Margaret. She had to get into the war. They parted, she said, "with affection and respect," but each was too strong-willed to subordinate career to the other's demands.

She photographed German air raids in Moscow. She was aboard a ship that was torpedoed off North Africa. She took pictures of Gandhi, of Nazi murder camps, of mines in South Africa. She reported the war in Korea. Surely no professional woman, not even Dorothy Thompson, ever had a more adventurous life than did Margaret Bourke-White.

The Lady Who Would Be Queen

A very different career was that of Wallis Warfield Simpson. If Thompson and Bourke-White represent the aggressive woman achievers of the present, Mrs. Simpson equally personifies the woman of history: a fashionable woman whose wish was to be admired and loved, and to play a paramount role in her social circle.

At a hairdresser's one day in London, Wallis Simpson discovered an old friend from her home town of Baltimore under the hair dryer beside her. Lifting up her own hood she leaned forward and confided, "Guess what! I'm in the Prince of Wales' set!"

As the prince singled her out more and more conspicuously at parties, she was photographed, gossiped about, and envied. She became a popular hostess. Invitations to Ernest and Wallis Simpson's parties were prized because the prince would be there. Her drawing room became a fragrant flower garden, and everyone knew who sent the flowers. There were gifts of jewelry; Wallis delighted in jewels and Edward delighted in heaping gifts upon her. There was an ecstatic round of dances and theater parties and cocktail parties and dinner parties—and most of all there was the glamour of royalty. The most eligible bachelor in the world wanted her company.

"But what does he see in her?" people marveled. "She isn't young and she isn't beautiful." As if only youth and beauty could entrance royalty. Those who knew the prince well were not surprised. She made him laugh—right out loud. Laughing out loud was not done in strict society; but at her dinner parties he would lean forward, watching Wallis, waiting for one of her witty remarks so that he could roar with laughter.

He had always felt inadequate and shy, but she built up his ego. No one before had given him tenderness, but she mothered him. ("It's too cold to wear that light coat, sir. You must borrow a fur coat.") And she cared about his work. ("Tell me about your next trip" and, sitting very close beside him, she listened intently to his reply, those large violet eyes fixed upon him.)

More than that, Wallis Simpson was so natural and informal that, when they were together, the prince, accustomed as he was to stiff protocol, happily relaxed into informality, too. And how he treasured her gift of laughter!

They had much in common. Both loved games and puzzles and dancing; sometimes they danced until dawn. Both liked popular music (but not opera), they enjoyed people more than books, and both loved dogs (but not cats).

Wallis was a small woman, so small that Edward stood taller than she, and that was nice for him. She walked and stood with elegance. She had that trim, bandbox look: sleek hair parted in the middle and never a hair out of place. Narrow skirts, small hats. Tailored.

The romance continued after the death of George V, when Edward was no longer a prince but the king; and he was determined to marry Wallis. He convinced her that she would be queen, no matter what the prime minister thought, no matter what the archbishop of Canterbury said, no matter how the royal family and the old aristocracy hated it; and Wallis agreed to a divorce.

Ernest Simpson played the gentleman's part and, acting out the customary charade, allowed himself to be discovered by a hotel chambermaid in bed one morning with a lady other than his wife; then Wallis sued for divorce on grounds of adultery.

The king loved Wallis obsessively. In a roomful of people, his eyes followed her wherever she moved. Away from her, he kept the telephone wires humming. Reporters noticed how contented he looked these days, and how little he drank and smoked. Winston Churchill, one of the few of the upper class who favored this alliance, said of the king, "I saw him when she'd gone away for a fortnight. He was miserable, haggard, dejected, not knowing what to do. Then I saw him when she'd been back for a day or two, and he was a different man—gay, debonair, self-confident. Make no mistake—he can't live without her."

A friend walked into the king's bedroom late one morning, supposing the king was ready to receive him, but discovered the man sound asleep; and all around the bed, facing him, were picture after picture of Wallis, propped up on tables and chairs.

Wallis, on the other hand, loved the king fondly, but she was not *in* love. She liked the fact that he needed her. She liked being the most famous hostess in England.

Until the time of the divorce, the British public knew nothing about the Simpson affair. Newspapers suppressed the story, and magazines imported from America were all meticulously clipped before going on sale: every article, every reference to the king's love affair was snipped out.

But now the news leaked out. To the king's surprise, and to Wallis's consternation, his popularity was not enough to outweigh the people's shock and disapproval. It was all very well for a prince to have his fun, but when he became king he had to act like one.

Curiously, the upper classes didn't object to Wallis because she was divorced, but because she was American. The lower classes didn't mind her being American, but their respectability was outraged by her being twice a divorcee, and by the blatant, cynical style of the second divorce; because no one doubted that the real adultery was in the other bed.

Wallis's mail was full of hate letters. Some even threatened violence. Her laughter was silenced. She seemed to be the most hated woman in the Western world. Now she saw that for her to be queen of England would be to carry a crushing burden.

"Let us have a morganatic marriage," she pleaded. As the king's wife—not the queen—she would be socially the most powerful woman in the Empire, without having a searchlight played on her, pitilessly, every hour of the day. But the government was absolutely opposed to the marriage on any terms.

And so the king abdicated and delivered that famous speech of December 11, 1936. Probably no message in history has ever been heard by so many millions. There was the immortal sentence "I have found it impossible . . . to discharge my duties as king, as I wish to do, without the help and support of the woman I love."

For nearly forty years after their marriage, the Duke and Duchess of Windsor lived, never quite out of the public eye, and always with gallantry and gaiety. If the duchess never gratified her ambition, she occupied a unique place in the history of romance as the only woman for whose love a king gave up his throne.

All in One Year...

George VI and Elizabeth were crowned in majestic ceremony in Westminster Abbey in May, 1937. Princesses Elizabeth and Margaret Rose were eleven and six years old.

America's depression began to show signs of tapering off. The unemployment rate dropped. Steel neared its peak of production, with U.S. Steel's plant at Gary, Indiana, turning out 85,000 tons a week. Steelworkers earned their top wages, $5 a day for a forty-hour week.

The Ohio and Mississippi rivers went on a rampage and flooded city and country from Pittsburgh to New Orleans. Margaret Bourke-White flew to Louisville to record the disaster on film.

FDR tried to pack the Supreme Court by increasing its number from nine to fifteen. Congress quarreled over how many millions should be spent on relief projects. Strikers discovered a new and potent weapon, the sitdown strike.

In 1937 the Dionne quintuplets celebrated their third birthday.

College girls reversed their cardigan sweaters and buttoned them up the back. Toeless shoes and wedge soles appeared for the first time. Ankle socks became universal wear, worn over either bare legs or silk stockings. People danced the Big Apple. They sang "Sweet Leilani" and "Red Sails in the Sunset."

The Hindenburg burst into flames over Lakehurst, New Jersey.

Airlines began to hire hostesses. They had to be not only young, poised, and attractive, but also R.N.s. They performed a few tasks unknown to stewardesses today. They were required to swat flies in the cabin after takeoff, and to persuade passengers not to throw still-burning cigar stubs out the windows.

Sonja Henie, ice-skating ace turned pro, made the movie *Once in a Million*. Pearl Buck's *Good Earth* appeared on the screen, Paul Muni playing Wang Lung, the peasant hero, and Luise Rainer, O-Lan, his slave-girl wife. Without a change of expression on her orientalized face, she conveyed a lifetime of emotion: fear, grief, jealousy, devotion, resignation.

All over Europe sounded the tramp of marching boots. Every nation rearmed as fast as it could afford to. Mussolini renamed the Mediterranean "Mare Nostrum" ("Our Sea"). Hitler glorified a high Aryan birthrate in or out of wedlock. There were ominous rumbles of anti-Semitism, not only in Germany. Stalin conducted his bloody purges to purify the state. Japanese bombing of Chinese cities horrified the world.

In 1937 an American pilot set out on a round-the-world flight that ended in mystery.

Flying Feminist

News photographs of Amelia Earhart showed a tall girl with tousled hair, and though she always wore a polite smile, she had a look of such reserve that she seemed lonely. Her usual costume was jodhpurs and a wrinkled leather jacket. What the photographs didn't show was a woman quietly positive and ambitious.

Carey Thomas, a generation earlier, had battered her way into the ivy halls feeling that every scholastic victory was not just for herself but for all women who wanted higher education. It was much the same with Amelia Earhart. She had to set records. She had to prove herself as tough and capable as any man, not only because of personal ambition but because she was determined to blaze a trail for women in aviation.

"The public has no confidence in our ability," she said. "But if we had access to the equipment and training that men have, we would certainly do as well."

At the time of the first Women's Air Derby in 1929, usually called the Powder Puff Derby, she was outraged by slurs like that of a Los Angeles newsman who wrote, "Women have been dependent on men for guidance for so long that when they are put on their own resources, they are handicapped."

Throughout the race from Santa Monica, California, to Cleveland, Ohio, in which twenty women took part, Amelia Earhart hated the belittling, jocular names given them: ladybirds, flying flappers, bird-women, and so forth. At many of the overnight stops, the contestants were banqueted, and at the invariable witticisms of their hosts, Amelia always gave her stoic smile but pointed out firmly that the women had earned the dignity of being called flyers or pilots.

She would have won that Derby but for an accident to a rival's plane at Columbus, Ohio, on the seventh day. She and Ruth Nichols led the field in elapsed flying time, and the winner would be the one who made the best time into Cleveland. The contestants lined up on the runway. Ruth Nichols's plane, taking off first, suddenly dipped its wing and crashed into a tractor at the end of the runway. The plane flipped over.

Amelia immediately stopped her engines, jumped out of the cockpit and ran to the wreckage to pull the pilot free. Ruth was uninjured. Amelia took off for Cleveland, but by that time she had lost her edge over the others and came in third.

It seems that she did not have the usual youthful romances, but men had a comradely fondness for this serious, artless young woman. In any hangar Amelia, dressed in practical flying togs, would be closely surrounded by pilots and mechanics. In 1931, however, she married George Palmer Putnam, who had just divorced his third wife. Shortly before the ceremony she suffered the quakes and qualms not unknown to brides, but she coped with them in typical Earhart style. She handed the bridegroom a letter, a sort of marriage contract like that of Margaret Bourke-White.

It said in part, "You must know again my reluctance to marry, my feeling that I shatter thereby chances in work which means so much to me. . . . In our life together I shall not hold you to any medieval code of faithfulness to me, nor shall I consider myself bound to you similarly. . . . Please let us not interfere with each other's work or play, nor let the world see private joys or disagreements. In this connection I may have to keep some place where I can go to be by myself now and then, for I cannot guarantee to endure at all times the confinements of even an attractive cage.

"I must exact a cruel promise, and this is that you will let me go in a year if we find no happiness together.

"I will try to do my best in every way."

If the forebodings expressed in this letter became reality, no one ever knew. She always maintained a stony reserve about her private life. Incidentally, after the marriage the only name Amelia Earhart ever used was her maiden name.

But, in spite of her elusiveness, she knew exactly what she wanted. In 1934 she arranged to fly from Hawaii to California, a "first" for which a group of Hawaiian businessmen had put up a prize of $10,000. But rumors of political scandal began smogging around. It was said that Amelia's influence had been bought by island sugar interests to coax Congress into lowering the sugar tariff.

Sponsors lost their nerve and met to discuss withdrawing the prize. Amelia met with the committee in the dining room of the Royal Hawaiian Hotel. She went straight from Wheeler Field in her working clothes, jodhpurs and the leather jacket, and after listening to the discussion she stood up and in a level voice said, "Gentlemen, there is an aroma of cowardice in this air. You know as well as I do that the rumor is trash. . . . Whether you live in fear or defend your integrity is your decision. I have made mine. I intend to fly to California within this next week, with or without your support."

And she stalked out of the meeting. The sponsors plucked up courage and voted to award the prize money as planned. When the weather was right, Amelia took off from Oahu and made the first Hawaii-to-California flight in eighteen hours and fifteen minutes.

Prize money was never Amelia's objective. But that drive for recognition, that need to excel, were so compulsive that she had to enter every flying competition. She had to set records.

In May, 1935, she set out on her final conquest, a round-the-world flight from west to east. Forty days and twenty-two thousand miles later, she and her navigator, Fred Noonan, took off from Lae, New Guinea, on the last leg of their journey. They were never seen again. Did they fly hundreds of miles off course through instrument failure? If they were unable, then, to locate their next objective, tiny Howland Island in the Pacific, did they crash in the ocean when they ran out of gas? Or did they crash instead, as rumor persistently muttered, on the island of Saigon, to be executed by the Japanese military? And, if they were indeed over Japanese mandated territory, why? Was theirs an espionage mission for the government? Rumors, investigations, accusations, denials, all led nowhere.

However she died, Amelia Earhart's life is what matters, the life of a valiant pioneer.

Her Soul Was Anchored in the Lord

In the spring of 1939 Eleanor Roosevelt's syndicated column "My Day" read: "If you belong to an organization and disapprove of an action . . . should you resign or is it better to work for a changed point of view within the organization? . . . In this case I belong to an organization in which I can do no active work. They have taken an action which has been widely talked of in the press. To remain as a member implies approval of the action, and therefore I am resigning."

Everyone who read the column must have known that the first lady was talking about the refusal of the Daughters of the American Revolution to allow Marian Anderson to give an Easter concert in their Constitution Hall because she was black. Marian, however, had been so engrossed in her scheduled concerts, in rehearsals and travel, that she hadn't been reading the papers; and she left details of reservations to her manager and warm friend Sol Hurok.

Marian Anderson was deeply religious, as her mother and all the rest of the family were. This submissive faith helped her endure unpleasant incidents on tour, when a hotel, for example, denied her a room, or a cab driver refused to take her and her bags from the railroad station to the place where she was to stay. She did her best to avoid confrontations because she could not sing well if she was hurt by a feeling of being unwelcome.

Knowing that any Negro singer would find it difficult to win recognition in the States, Marian Anderson had gone abroad when she was twenty-nine, and her rich voice was well trained. She quickly won fame in Europe, and although life was easier there, where color was a small matter, she never considered any plan but to build up a reputation as an artist and then return to the United States, because that was home.

Little by little, when she returned in 1935 after four years abroad, she won an American following. A tall, broad-shouldered woman, she presented a majestic figure on the concert platform. She always wore a long gown of simple cut (so that it wouldn't soon go out of style), and the fabric was usually heavy satin or velvet or a brocade gleaming with silver or gold thread, in a tint that blended with her brown skin. She liked to dress richly because she had a flair for the dramatic, and also because she knew that Negroes in the audience, often poor people with high aspirations, liked to see one of their own, who had made it, magnificently turned out.

She stood quietly onstage beside the grand piano, hands clasped before her, and as she opened her lips for the first note, her eyes closed, her head lifted, and her face became a mask. Her very soul seemed to focus into a beam of sound that each listener felt was directed straight toward him. Slowly, the audience responded to the outpouring of glorious sound until they sat transfixed, uplifted. That strong, pure voice had an incredible range, "four voices in one," people said, though she called herself a contralto.

She sang Schubert (her favorite composer) and Brahms and Strauss and Debussy. Italian songs and Spanish ones and English and American. Audiences loved her "Ave Maria" and the deeply emotional "The Crucifixion." She ended every program with a group of spirituals, the most beloved one being "He's Got the Whole World in His Hands." Listeners often wept helplessly during this song, perhaps because they sensed that its message was the very essence of Marian Anderson's own humble and worshipful philosophy.

But suddenly this serious, courteous woman, who hated controversy, found herself at the center of a hurricane. All over the country members of the DAR resigned in protest at the ban on her use of Constitution Hall, and chapters telegraphed their indignation, but the Daughters' national board stood firm. Singers Kirsten Flagstad and Grace Moore protested. So did violinist Jascha Heifetz and conductor Serge Koussevitzky. Actors and churchmen and politicians and teachers all clamored their opinions. Editors, even in the deep South, wrote scornfully of the ban.

Columnist Westbrook Pegler, who could always be counted on for a contrary view, in this case was obliged to oppose the opposition. He wrote disdainfully of "a hitherto obscure Negro singer named Marian Anderson," thus stirring up a storm within a storm. Conductor-composer Walter Damrosch responded to Pegler: "This lady is one of the greatest artists of song that we have." Still others quarreled that the insult lay not in the fact of Miss Anderson's greatness, but in the injustice of a tax-free building's being closed to any citizen on the ground of color.

At last the controversy simmered down when Marian Anderson gave her Easter concert outdoors, at the Lincoln Memorial. The Gifford Pinchots (he was a former governor of Pennsylvania) were Marian's hosts, and it is fortunate that they were because the Washington hotels refused to rent her a room.

What an audience turned out that Easter afternoon! The crowd massed in a great semicircle from Lincoln Memorial around the reflecting pool and on to the Washington Monument. As she opened her mouth to begin the National Anthem, she felt a great wave of good will pouring out from all those people, almost engulfing her. It was such an emotional shock that for a desperate second she feared she wouldn't be able to sing. But she was a pro, and sing she did. Her concert included "America," "Ave Maria" and three spirituals, among them "My Soul Is Anchored in the Lord."

Later the DAR reversed its policy about black performers, and Marian Anderson sang in Constitution Hall several times.

Café Society

Doris Duke, heiress to the American Tobacco millions, and Barbara Hutton, the Woolworth heiress, had their coming-out parties in 1930, a tidy bit of symbolism, with that year marking the close-out of affluence. Both debutantes had a good deal of fond publicity, for America considered them romantic and the press considered them good copy. In 1933 Barbara Hutton married Alexis Mdvani, called Prince, although there were no princes in Russian Georgia from which he came. In the following year Doris Duke married socialite Jimmy Cromwell.

From that time on, the "Gold Dust Twins" had a bad press, in part because they had been darlings for too long, and Americans are perverse about their heroines. Miss Duke was canny about dodging publicity, but Miss Hutton was more naïve. She kept taking reporters into her confidence, and they kept gleefully making fun of her. "Now at last I have found happiness," she said on the occasion of one of her seven marriages. "My search is ended. I know that this is safe and sure."

But for Barbara nothing was ever safe, and her confused search for happiness and security never ended. The public grew to dislike and resent her so much that once as she entered a theater she was mobbed by a crowd that screamed and clawed at her, shouting insults. In the deep of the depression, Barbara could spend $10,000 to have an orchestra flown from London to Paris to play at her birthday party, and at that same time Woolworth clerks earned $11 a week.

"Why do they hate me?" cried Barbara helplessly.

Another debutante, with her background founded in theatrical fame rather than in great wealth, was, on the other hand, treated benevolently by the press. This was Diana Barrymore, daughter of John Barrymore and the beautiful Michael Strange. She was also smiled upon by society in the person of Mrs. Cornelius Vanderbilt. ("You are the living image of your mother, my dear!") A formal coming-out party for this child of a stage family dramatized a great change in twentieth-century mores: the new blending of society and theater.

Back in 1903, when the cast of the Broadway show *The Wild Rose* entertained at a Vanderbilt ball, the actors remained humbly apart from the guests. On a similar occasion a year or two before World War I, the dancers Irene and Vernon Castle were once engaged to perform after a society dinner at a Long Island estate. They arrived, after traveling by train, at the appointed time, then for a full hour they waited in a tiny room downstairs, having been greeted only by the servants, while the party upstairs leisurely finished dinner.

But now a dancer, actor, singer, author, columnist—anyone with a "name"—was not only admitted to society, he was sought after.

This easy blending of bluebloods and entertainers began during prohibition when everyone crowded into speakeasies. In the crush of bodies and the blare of music, those transparent walls between the classes dissolved in the flood of terrible bootleg liquor.

In the thirties the trend toward informality continued and Cholly Knickerbocker, who in real life was columnist Maury Paul, named the new conglomerate Café Society.

Elsa Maxwell, a lady who was nearly as broad as she was tall, was the great hostess of the new society. She had plenty of bluffs, but she never pretended to an aristocratic background. Before fame, she had been a pianist in a nickelodeon, an accompanist in a vaudeville act, half owner of a Paris nightclub, publicity writer in Monte Carlo, lecturer, and columnist. You could flip Elsa Maxwell like a coin: heads—a ruthless, malicious, ambitious snob; tails—a rackety, fun-loving, overgrown child with a hearty laugh and a contagious sense of gaiety. Both sides of the coin were genuine.

The press, including Elsa, played up the debutantes, naming the most conspicuous ones Glamour Girls. Brenda Frazier and Cobina Wright, Jr., were the most famous. Debuts, romances, freakish parties, quarrels, talents, wardrobes, and travels of all the Glamour Girls filled column after column in the newspapers and page after page in picture magazines. The most successful girls made the cover of *Life*.

Brenda and Cobina, Jr., were both backed by mothers as ferociously aggressive as any actress's mother. Cobina's mother wrote proudly that in 1939 her child was "the 'most' girl: most photographed, most publicized, most sought after." Brenda's mother hired a press agent to guide her daughter's publicity. But years later Brenda said bitterly that being a Glamour Girl was "the worst thing that could happen to a girl. . . . I wouldn't let it happen to my child at all."

The depression merged into a war boom and women found it easier to get jobs. But their position in society had not changed. A 1940 poll showed that the majority of Americans, nearly as many women as men, believed that women are not equipped for responsible and important positions in our society.

Judge Florence Allen, appointed early in the New Deal by President

Roosevelt to be Chief Judge of the U.S. Court of Appeals, Sixth Circuit, had a bitter time among her fellow judges, and they were men of cool judgment and high intelligence. These gentlemen avoided speaking to Judge Allen or looking toward her unless required to do so by the business at hand.

In 1937, New York University awarded Edna St. Vincent Millay an honorary degree of Doctor of Humane Letters, and a modest little dinner of recognition was arranged for her at the chancellor's home, hosted by Chancellor Shaw's wife and attended only by ladies. Later, however, she learned that male recipients of degrees were honored at an official awards dinner at the Waldorf Astoria, from which she was excluded by reason of her sex.

At Indiana University, a creative member of the English Department, named Cecelia Hendricks, determined to organize a really good writers' conference to be held during summer school. The president of the university was skeptical, but Miss Hendricks, a born executive, acquired financial backing, wrote hundreds of letters, lured big names as workshop leaders, drew in talented amateurs as students, and conducted a triumphantly successful conference.

When it was over, she faced the president with her achievement. To herself she must have been saying, "I've done it. I've proved that I can operate a writers' conference."

"You've made your point," the president conceded generously. "Now I am convinced that the university should have a writers' conference every summer. Now: what man in the English Department would you suggest as its director?"

Every year since then I.U. has had a writers' conference (one of the best in the country) and its director has always been a man.

In the late 1930s, however, women's rights were a small part of the nation's headaches. Americans were obsessed by events in Europe. People sat petrified in front of their radios to hear, not the comedians, but the news commentators. The decade that began in the cold grip of depression was ending in the glowering shadow of a world war.

The 1940s

ROSIE THE RIVETER

Frenzy of War

"God bless America," sang Kate Smith in her magnificent big voice, and millions of listening Americans were comforted and exalted. The song became an unofficial national anthem. Irving Berlin wrote it in 1918 but never used it, and twenty years later he gave it to Kate Smith. Song and singer were forever linked in the public imagination.

Everywhere people tensely discussed the war in Europe, and whether America could stay out of it. In 1939, 90 percent of the population wanted to keep out of the war, though 80 percent hoped the Allies would win. But little by little the voice of isolation lost its thunder and by late 1941 it had dwindled to a mutter.

The sorry old days of hysterical intolerance, familiar in World War I, dawned again. Anti-Semites, the KKK, America Firsters, all were poised for violence, but no major rioting occurred. Liberal magazines like *The New Republic* and the *New Leader* and *The Nation* froze into stances of anti-freedom of speech to anyone who disagreed with them. Even Dorothy Thompson, until now a fiery defender of liberty, said in a public meeting that freedom of assembly and freedom of speech should be allowed only to friends of democracy. The Bill of Rights must be temporarily nullified in order to save it. Her audience applauded patriotically.

People chafed for action. Home Guard units sprang up. In Chapel Hill, North Carolina, Mrs. Virginia Newell organized a thousand women into the Green Guards, who marched and drilled and sang, to "keep the beacons burning" for the lads who would someday go into battle.

Other women, particularly in the conservative Midwest, looked with gloom on this enthusiasm and stubbornly insisted that America could help the Allies without ever getting into the fight.

After Pearl Harbor, however, just as after the declaration of war in 1917, most of the nation had one single aim: victory.

Everyone wanted some part in the war. If family women couldn't be soldiers, they could save tin and fat. They made dresses, socks, and sweaters for refugees, and bandages for soldiers. They bought war bonds and gave blood. The best-selling publication of 1942, although not listed among the best sellers because it was classified as a pamphlet, was the *Red Cross First Aid Handbook*.

The government called for phonograph records in order to recover precious shellac, and hundreds of millions of records were turned in at once. The War Production Board asked for four million tons of scrap metal to be collected within two months, and in three weeks people had turned in five million tons.

There was a rubber shortage because the largest source of natural rubber was in Japanese hands, and the synthetic-rubber industry was in its babyhood. The U.S. Senate donated five hundred spittoon mats and the House twelve hundred. Balloon dancer Sally Rand gave fifty balloons, leaving her, so the story went, with only two to last her for the duration. "For the duration" became a byword, like "C'est la guerre" of a previous generation. And there was the other grim cliché, "Don't you know there's a war on?"

People who had never raised so much as a dandelion spaded up their backyards, and planted and fertilized and cultivated and reaped. The seed catalog became their favorite reading matter.

Big-time agriculture, meanwhile, suffered a manpower shortage in 1942. Hundreds of thousands of volunteers, chiefly teen-agers and women, went ardently to work and saved nearly all the harvest. In 1942, about 40 percent of the nation was busy with some kind of volunteer work.

And there was a new opportunity for women: military service. Young women rushed to join the WAC, the WAVES, the SPARS, and the Women Marines. They weren't always welcome. One Marine officer exploded, "Goddamnit! First they send us dogs. Now it's women!" Altogether, 350,000 women saw active duty, 65,000 of them overseas.

Some girls had to hurdle family objections to their joining up, because in America military service has never been held in high social esteem except for the elite, the graduates of West Point and Annapolis. Also, rumors of sexual promiscuity haunted the WAC. This kept interest high but approval low. Nevertheless, in wartime anything military has its glamour, and the girls signed up.

Originally it was supposed that women could do only a few modest jobs: typing, clerical work, switchboard operating, driving, and of course cooking. But the shortage of qualified men opened a few eyes, and presently female soldiers and sailors were mechanics, dieticians, physical therapists, medical technicians; they worked in personnel management, in supply, cryptology, radio, X-ray—in almost any job short of combat. Women Auxiliary Service Pilots—the original WASPs—ferried planes, towed targets, and flew weather observation flights.

All of these women served on a temporary basis, but in 1948 Congress rewarded them by giving military women regular status in their several services. Nurses and medical specialists had already, in 1944, been granted status on a par with men.

War is the great marriage catalyst. In 1941, one and a half million couples married—15 percent over the 1940 high. Thousands of brides were still in their teens, but they happily left school and set up housekeeping on minuscule budgets. Those who married servicemen followed them about the country from one training camp to another. Every seat in every dirty train and every unswept bus was taken, and aisles were occupied by weary, rumpled travelers who sat on the floor or on battered suitcases, because sixteen million civilians were on the move in pursuit of jobs or loved ones; these in addition to the millions in uniform who were also, it seemed, being constantly shuttled from post to post.

Arrived at their destination, enlisted men's wives were usually on their own in a search for quarters; never mind how ill-furnished, unkempt, or cramped, just so there was a bed large enough for two, for those nights when he was allowed off the base, and some kind of cooking arrangements, because on a soldier's allowance who could afford to eat out?

If a girl traveled with a baby or, after two or three years of war, with a toddler and a new baby, quarters were nearly impossible to find. Landlords, hardened to the sight of pinched, anxious young faces, said indifferently, "No children, no pets."

If the military wife was free of children, she went job hunting as soon as she'd unpacked her suitcase.

Traveling wives practiced a cheerful sisterhood, taking care of each other in sickness, looking after each other's babies, lending a coffeepot, a spare blanket, or a shoulder to cry on when a husband was ordered overseas.

Besides the boom towns created by military installations, there were the ones made by the presence of defense plants. Working-age people left farms and country towns and poured into these boom towns in the hundreds of thousands.

There was Cape Cod; Starke, Florida; Charlestown, Indiana; Seneca, Illinois; Salina, Kansas; Willow Run, Michigan; the dismal list could go on and on. Each town had once been peaceful, decorous, sometimes picturesque, and prosperous enough (especially by hindsight). When the war began, the towns swelled up as if in the last stages of a horrendous malignancy.

Strangers jostled for space on the sidewalks. They surged into the stores and bought everything in sight. (Merchants hid scarce items under the counter for their fellow townsmen.) The outsiders bought liquor as fast as it could be delivered, while the consumption of alcohol rose countrywide. Every hotel room was occupied every day, and with the shortage of janitors and chambermaids, hotel keepers almost quit trying to keep their places clean. Motels allowed guests to stay no longer than three days. Sewers could not keep up with the load. Five passengers shared every taxi. Restaurants were jammed and diners waited outside in long queues. One restaurant keeper put a sign in his window, "Please be polite to our waitresses. They are harder to get than customers."

Old residents scowled upon the intruders who turned their nice little cities into slums, and newcomers hated the locals for withholding the canned pineapple, the cold beer, and the teen-age girls.

Of all boom towns, Washington, D.C., was the worst. To buy a bottle of aspirin or a pack of cigarettes (a single pack to a customer, no more) one had to wait in a long line. Women helped to cram Washington. At the time of Pearl Harbor, 250,000 women worked for the federal government, but their number ballooned to more than 1,000,000 by the end of the war. One visitor, who left as quickly as he could, wrote, "Washington in wartime is a combination of Moscow (for its overcrowding), Paris (for its trees), Wichita (for its way of thinking), Nome (in gold-rush days), and Hell (for its livability)."

Nationwide, gasoline was rationed. So were coffee, shoes, meat, and sugar. If you absolutely had to have a new tire, you went to your ration board and got down on your knees. You could hardly find plumbing supplies, or glass to mend a broken window. Above all there was a shortage of living space and privacy. If you grumbled, you got the instant retort, "Don't you know there's a war on?"

The rubber shortage made a plump woman regard her girdle as her dearest treasure. She washed it tenderly and hung it to dry where the least possible light could reach it.

Women who wore out their last pair of stockings and couldn't find any in the stores—not even the baggy rayon hose—had to buy leg paint. Ads lyrically described "bottled stockings" as the smoothest, sheerest, most flattering leg wear ever invented, but in truth the bottled stockings streaked and ran if you sweated, and also rubbed off on the underside of your slip and on the trousers of your dancing partner.

As business and industry called for employees and as men were siphoned into the armed forces, women rushed in to fill the vacuum.

"The Manpower Question Has Been Solved by Womanpower"

So said President Roosevelt after Rosie the Riveter bustled into the shipyard and picked up her tools. When the war began, there were fourteen million women in the work force; when it ended, there were twenty million. At first most of them said they were working only for the duration, but by 1945 three out of four reported in an opinion poll that they'd rather stay on the job. They liked the independence and they liked the money.

Out of every five housekeepers who went to work, most of them previously untrained, two went straight into defense plants. One took up clerical work; and the other two found jobs in stores, restaurants, laundries, hospitals. The war opened up many new occupations for women, chiefly blue-collar. In shipyards, Rosie and her friends even took up repair, where before the war no woman had ever worked. In war plants, they worked at the assembly of small parts, inspection, packing, riveting, welding, blueprint reading; on drill presses, milling machines, lathes, punch and forming presses.

At first the factory manager looked lugubriously upon this swarm of women in pants with their hair tied up in bandanas. That old devil sex was sure to rear its head and make trouble in his plant. The women would want fancy rest rooms and special sick leave, they'd grouse if they chipped their fingernails, and they'd never get to work on time. To his surprise, Rosie's record proved to be as good as that of the man she replaced.

She didn't earn as much, though. It was government policy that women were to be paid the same wages as men, but somehow employers never got around to implementing the policy. Even in the eight government-owned shipyards, the most that Rosie earned was $6.95 a day; top pay for a man was $22 a day. Most women earned the minimum, $4.65 a day, and their chance for promotion was almost nil.

It wasn't only into war work that women stepped out brassily. The eight thousand reporters and editors in uniform were replaced by eight thousand women. Female musicians were hired by major symphony orchestras. The New York Stock Exchange hired the first woman clerk in all its dignified history and Wall Street nearly caved in.

The war allowed black women a small step upward. At the turn of the century, about 95 percent of those who worked for pay were farm workers or domestics, as they had been under slavery, but after the war the figure had dropped to about 53 percent. The women found jobs in factories, laundries, and hospitals, and in the North, doing clerical work and selling in stores.

Most women managed to do their jobs and also run their houses capably and even, if they were mothers, have their children suitably cared for. It wasn't easy under wartime conditions. One nonemployed mother, when asked why she wasn't out doing a job for the war effort, snarled, "Because I haven't got a wife."

But not all working mothers did their family job well. Hundreds of thousands of "eight-hour orphans" roamed the streets; some of them had latch keys hung on strings around their necks. Thousands of others were locked into the family car on the defense plant parking lot while Mother worked, or were chained like dogs to the family trailer. Horrifying stories of brutality and child molesting were told about the unlicensed child-care centers that sprang up. Not all of the stories could have been false.

Juvenile delinquency rose. Youth gangs formed in cities and waged zip-gun battles in the streets. Girls, some of them no more than twelve years old, sauntered through the dirty, crowded bus and railroad stations, helping "to maintain military morale." They were called Patriotutes, Victory Girls, and Cuddle Bunnies. The venereal disease rate rose hideously, and so did the rate of illegitimate births. Older workers resented their wartime competition. The little chippies, they said, worked for a beer and a sandwich and ruined the market.

Whatever became of these young war casualties?

"Teen Canteens" helped to neutralize vice and violence. They were established in hundreds of cities by concerned adults, and then operated by the young people themselves, who needed something positive to do. They held dances, jam sessions, table-tennis tournaments, beach parties. A new phenomenon had risen, a subculture: that of the teen-ager. Before the war there had been two generations, adults and children. Now there were three.

At school, teen-age girls wore saddle oxfords, thick bobby socks, pleated skirts, and tailored blouses. On their own time they wore a new uniform: loose blue jeans unevenly rolled up at the cuff, and an old shirt of Daddy's, the bigger the better. Its shoulder seams fell halfway to the elbow and the shirttail flopped around the flat little hips. In their untidy rooms they plastered the walls with American flags and pictures of Van Johnson and Frank Sinatra.

When Frankie sang, mobs of bobbysoxers screamed and gyrated, swooned and wept. At the close of a performance, he would stride rapidly offstage without warning and flee the theater under police escort to avoid a riot.

When they didn't have Sinatra in person, the bobbysoxers had their records. Not just Frankie's, but also "Pistol-Packin' Mama," "Jukebox Saturday Night," "Jersey Bounce," and "Two O'Clock Jump." The kids jitterbugged joyously while their money expanded the jukebox business into a vast industry. By the mid-forties, record companies were selling ten times as many records as they had a decade earlier.

While Sinatra was the bobbysoxers' idol, favorite pinup girls were Rita Hayworth, Hedy Lamarr, and Betty Grable—especially Betty Grable. Pink, plump, and pretty, she twinkled happily at GIs all over the world from her pictures pasted to a million walls and lockers on land and sea. In 1943 Betty was the biggest box-office draw of Hollywood. She stayed up there in the top ten for thirteen more years, and late in the forties she was the highest-paid woman in America.

From an unexpected source came a figure beloved of women. Mrs. Miniver of England, whimsical, tranquil, and loving, charmed readers of the book by that name. Dear Mrs. Miniver, so kindly and sentimental! An American girl—at the end of another day with no letter from Tom, who was somewhere in the Pacific; or at the end of a nerve-rasping day on the punch press; or a day spent with three children in a two-room flat near the army base—could turn the radio down low and curl up to read about this humorous and patient Mrs. Miniver and think that maybe tomorrow might be worth the fight after all.

Jan Struther was the Englishwoman who wrote the Mrs. Miniver sketches for the London *Times;* they were later collected into book form. After a year or two, the author was heartily sick of her creation, and especially sick of being addressed as Mrs. Miniver herself. When a rival newspaper offered a prize for the best parody on the fictitious lady, Jan wrote the cruelest possible parody, submitted it under a false name, and won first prize. No matter. The original Mrs. Miniver was such a morale builder in England that the *Times* insisted she be kept alive.

The book was made into an American movie, but as the book had no plot, being merely a series of little essays, a script had to be created. The movie was so gorgeously, dramatically Hollywooded and Greer Garson as Mrs. Miniver was so beautiful and stylish that book and movie met at only one point, the title.

During the war, women were not quiet politically. In 1944, more than one hundred of the Democratic party's county chairmen were women, compared to only twelve in 1940. At the nominating conventions of both parties in 1944, one-quarter of the delegates were women. Each party had the Equal Rights Amendment in its platform, but when the election was over, the amendment was quietly put to sleep again.

By the end of the war, one woman was in the Senate, twelve were in the House, and the representative who made the most stir was spectacular Clare Boothe Luce.

Woman without a Flaw

In a nationwide poll, the public voted that, after Marlene Dietrich, Congresswoman Clare Boothe Luce had the most beautiful legs in America. When a congressman jokingly remarked that such a distinction seemed beneath the dignity of the House, she retorted, "You are falling for New Deal propaganda designed to distract attention from the end of me that is really functioning."

Clare Boothe Luce was beautiful from end to end. And brilliant. And talented. And successful at anything she turned her hand to. And, besides all that, rich. An unloving analyst observed that Clare had everything and had it in superlatives. It is the superlatives that have won her all those enemies. She is too flawless.

Her first steps in public life were in the suffrage movement. Back in Woodrow Wilson's time, that belligerent dowager Mrs. Oliver Hazard

Perry Belmont seized upon Clare to take the place of the lovely Inez Milholland, who had recently died while campaigning for suffrage. Clare was to radiate beauty and sex appeal for the cause and also do a little office work for Alice Paul in Washington.

But, after women gained the vote, Clare gave up good works for marriage to millionaire George Brokaw. At a loose end after her divorce six years later, she tried for a job at *Vogue* but found that owner Condé Nast was in Europe. Walking down the hall, having failed to get an interview, she passed the open door of an editorial office. In it were six desks, two of them empty. She strolled in, and when she asked about the empty desks, one of the girls told her that two caption writers had left the staff to get married. Clare took off her gloves, settled herself at one of the desks, said briefly that this must be where she was supposed to do her work, and accepted an assignment writing captions for a *Vogue* article.

Easing her way into the competitive world, she was already, without knowing it, following a pattern of behavior that Sam Rayburn outlined for her years later: "Explain nothing. Deny everything. Demand proof. Don't listen to it. And give the competition hell."

At any rate, Clare's explain-nothing audacity gained her entrance to the magazine field.

She also wrote plays. She wrote easily, fluently, quickly. The director of one of her plays complained that if, during rehearsal, he suggested making a change in a line, she'd nod understandingly, take away the script, and come back after lunch with a whole new act. She was so prolific that she had no patience with authors who painfully ground out their work sentence by sentence, or who suffered blank, uncreative periods.

The Women and *Kiss the Boys Goodbye* were her most successful plays. *The Women* has played in more than a dozen countries, two movie versions were made of it, and since its opening in 1936 scarcely a week has passed without its being played by a road company or by amateurs somewhere.

In 1935 Miss Boothe married Henry Robinson Luce, potentate in the publishing world with his awesomely successful magazines, *Time*, *Life*, and *Fortune*. In the 1940s she was twice elected to the House as a representative from Connecticut, and later spent three years as ambassador to Italy, thus moving coolly from power to power.

All this versatility and success, combined with a certain chilly aloofness of Clare's, earned some hostility. Her friends, therefore, sometimes found themselves, backs to the wall, defending her. At a Hollywood dinner party, one of these friends told, defensively, about Miss Boothe's generosity, of how she helped less talented and less fortunate people. She wound down by saying (with an unfortunate choice of words), "Clare Boothe is always kind to her inferiors." But Dorothy Parker, master of the killing barb, was among the guests. She raised her big brown eyes. "Where," murmured Mrs. Parker, "does she find them?"

Use of the Parker poisoned dart was never part of Clare Boothe Luce's strategy. She employed only the blunt frontal attack. In Paris, when the humiliating defeat of 1940 was only weeks away and patriotic Frenchmen were heartbroken about it, Clare was invited to tea by the wife of the minister of labor, Mme. Pomaret. In characteristic Boothe style, Clare did not beat about the tea table. Or reflect on the pain of the Frenchwomen present. Sitting down and accepting a cup of tea, she looked her hostess in the eye and said, "Madame, we Americans who are friends of France feel that American opinion, which is largely isolationist, is partly so because we do not quite know what France's war aims are."

Mme. Pomaret, ruffling and flouncing like a pigeon in a cold wind, replied with some sharpness that France's war aims were no business of Miss Boothe's or of America's, and had the caller shown to the door.

At any dinner party Clare eyed the guests, decided which one could give her the most information, usually a man, and at the earliest moment closed in on him. But she not only fired relentless questions at him; she listened intently to the answers and remembered them. She had no time for people whose only talk was small talk, and she showed it.

Her mind seized so much material at one snatch, sifted it, and arrived at so quick a conclusion that people said her reasoning was intuition. But this is like saying that the flick of an electric switch lights a room by magic.

In August, 1941, she went to the Philippines as a correspondent for *Life* and returned convinced that the Japanese would attack Hawaii and the Philippines very soon; but though her husband, on her return, made an agitated appeal to the intelligence section, all he gained was the bland reply that the government would continue to depend on its established sources rather than on his wife's intuition, even though Mrs. Luce was a most beautiful woman.

In her personal life Clare Luce had a deep disappointment. She felt that both of her marriages lacked the warmth and interdependence that underlie happy marriages. She had, however, a warm relationship with her one child, Ann Brokaw. In 1944, the girl was nineteen and a senior at Stanford University. Then, between one moment and the next, she was killed in an auto collision. The mother's grief was so deep that she no longer had any desire to take part in life. Possessed of cold self-control, however, Clare continued to carry on her political duties exactly as if nothing had happened to her, and to the end of her career in the House she was a devoted foe of Roosevelt and the New Deal.

Another woman in Washington whose career overlapped hers was a contrast both in politics and in personality.

Nobody Called Her Frances

Even in the breezy, first-name New Deal atmosphere, she was Madam Secretary or Miss Perkins to all except personal friends. The small, dumpy secretary of labor with the bleak eyes and wintry smile was no favorite of the press. Reporters respected her organizing ability and her relentless work habits and party loyalty, but they grumbled about that clipped Boston accent and those frosty pronouncements, and they made fun, mildly, of the tricorne hat that she was never seen without. (Surely, during all those twelve years that she was in Roosevelt's cabinet, she bought a new tricorne *sometimes?*)

Frances Perkins had no flair for publicity. The child who had been so shy that she was unable to walk into the public library and ask for a book grew up to be a woman who hid her diffidence under a mask of austere dignity, and reporters never knew that facing a noisy, challenging press conference was her version of facing a firing squad. She spoke with chill brevity, trained by a New England father who used to rap the table and tell his children, "Don't waste people's time. If you have something to say, say it definitely and stop."

Miss Perkins took up her cabinet portfolio already well trained, having been New York's industrial commissioner under two governors, Alfred E. Smith and Franklin Roosevelt. As secretary of labor she set up the Federal Employees' Service, which selected the young men for the CCC, she urged the public-works program, worked on the National Industrial Relations Act, and worked for unemployment and old-age insurance.

Employees in the Labor Department she treated with stern formality, and they kept their jobs regardless of party, but only if they were competent. She cleaned up the Immigration Service ("It was in bad repute," she commented in her special style of frugal understatement), appointed Colonel Daniel MacCormack as its chief, and commanded that he was "so to administer the laws of man that the laws of God might have a chance."

When she retired in 1945, even those columnists who had opposed the New Deal heaped lavish praise upon her. One said that she had babied the unions and yessed the president, but on the whole we could have had a worse secretary of labor and probably would.

Throughout her career in Washington, Madam Secretary stepped lightly on the political eggshells, always remembering that, as the first woman cabinet member, she was a setter of precedents. Her behavior could make it easier, or harder, for women after her to step into the world of male politics.

No war is a good war. Win or lose, the cost in broken lives and broken bodies is too high. Nevertheless, the end of World War II found the United States fused as it had not been for nearly three decades. Aside from personal sorrow, America was happy knowing that it had firm, unified goals; happy in its fierce sense of achievement and victory.

The other side of the coin is less pleasing. More than 100,000 West Coast Nisei Japanese had been snatched from their homes and concentrated in camps for the duration. Jehovah's Witnesses had been mobbed and beaten because they took a stand against the war. And there had been vicious race riots. The Ku Klux Klan fattened on this intolerance like rats at a garbage heap.

At last the war ended. The GIs began to come home. Women quit their jobs to become wives and housekeepers again, or they were "let out" because the war plant was going to be converted into a peacetime plant. Naturally women were the first to be fired and the last to be rehired, and they accepted this as standard operating procedure. Two years after the war ended, three million women had been separated from their wartime jobs.

But the war had allowed professional women to make gains. During the 1940s the number of women physicians and surgeons jumped from 7,700 to 11,800—the largest single increase in any decade of American history. More than that: the number of social and welfare workers, religious workers, social scientists, teachers, and librarians increased.

Even for those who were married, work became a larger part of their lives, and those who had a foothold in an interesting profession were unwilling to give it up.

Men came back from the war to find that the girls were more like the hussies of the 1920s than like the little darlings of 1939. They were more positive, more independent. They were used to making their own decisions, and the workers were used to having their own paychecks.

The men had their own painful readjustments to make to civilian life. Some couples passionately devoted to each other before the GIs went overseas were unable to readjust to the new, difficult times, and the engagement was broken or the marriage thrown into the divorce court.

Many GIs had new thoughts about the ideal girl, too. Thousands of them married overseas: Oriental girls (so acquiescent, so smiling and agreeable!) or girls from Italy, France, or England. In March, 1946, the *New York Times* published a long article by an ex-GI who had been a correspondent for the army newspaper *Stars and Stripes*. This young man described afternoons in sidewalk cafés of Paris:

American WACs would insist on a loud and full share of the conversation with their escorts, while the French girls would let the men do most of the talking, adding only a word or two now and then to show their interest. Or they would go into appreciative peals of laughter at the right moment. . . . The Americans looked on their boy friends as competitors, while the Parisiennes seemed to be there for the sole purpose of being pleasant to the men. . . . Being nice is almost a lost art among American women. . . .

The franchise was given to Frenchwomen while I was in Paris last year, but they felt that running the government was chiefly men's affair, even if the men were running it badly.

For a feminine companion, what the young man really wanted was not a woman, but a pretty kitten on a stool at his knee. The postwar girl, catching on quickly, curled up and practiced her purring.

The GI Bill of Rights sent thousands of veterans back to high school for their diplomas, or into trade schools, or into colleges; some of them had interrupted their college careers to enter the armed forces. Many others now dipped into higher education who would never have had the means or the desire except for this opportunity. Altogether, 300,000 men took advantage of the GI Bill.

Single vets got $90 a month allowance, married men $120 a month.

These amounts would hardly cover the cost of rent and food, and so thousands of wives found jobs to help their husbands through school. This joint effort ought to have cemented the bond between them, but in too many cases husband and wife grew apart. She had her job, he had his scholastic pursuits, and by graduation time they were traveling on different roads entirely. In other cases, the wife too wanted a diploma. Then times were really tough, and money from one set of parents or the other had to be forthcoming. Especially if there was a baby, and somehow there always seemed to be a baby.

"That's my daddy!" was the familiar cry in a sweet, crowing voice as a haggard young man in black cap and gown trudged across the platform on commencement day to receive the hard-earned diploma. At every ceremony, the hall was packed with wives, their faces lined by anxiety, and with those plump, joyous toddlers.

Space was always a problem. Young couples crammed into Quonset huts, into auto trailers, into skimpy, prefab houses. The crib was crowded into one corner, and diapers were hung to dry over the furnace.

Grocery bills took the place of prom tickets. Husband and wife arranged their schedule not to take the classes they'd have liked best, but to accommodate the baby. Each hour, one or the other had to be at home to take care of him; he was tossed from Mother to Daddy like a basketball. The baby's pastime was chewing an old textbook and choking on bits of paper. A flash of nervous tension would cause a quarrel between mother and father. They ate their meals hurriedly, eyes on their texts.

Single men didn't have it so good, either. Schools were so crowded that not everybody could have a room. At Indiana University, unmarried male students slept on cots in dormitory halls, in gymnasiums, or in locker rooms.

But single girls wanted to go to college, too. More girls than ever before battered on college gates begging admission. A lot of them had to be turned away. In 1946, Mt. Holyoke closed its September list in February. The New Jersey College for Women had twice as many applicants as usual. It wasn't only classroom space that was pinched; there wasn't enough living space, either. In coeducational schools, the fraternity houses that women had occupied during the war now had to be turned back to the men.

College life for those who did enroll was not a time of frivolity, nor of idealism. The men, especially veterans, bore down grimly on one idea: I want training for a job; I want to make money; I want to have a family and provide them with all the things I've never had myself. These young people had spent their youth in the depression and had grown up in the ugliness of war. For many of them, their sights were set on material fulfillment and nothing else.

Most often, however, GI Joe opted not for college but for an immediate job. Married or still in the marketplace, he made it plain that he wanted a girlish girl. He recoiled from Rosie the Riveter with her careless slacks, her swinging stride, and her loud voice.

When Rosie laid down her tools and picked up her last paycheck, she reflected that she'd liked her job a lot, but she liked men better. Motherhood, that's what she wanted now. She panted for a husband as hard as Joe panted for a wife. And if Joe wanted her to be sweet and compliant, okay. She'd sweeten up and comply.

Fashion changed with Rosie's changing ideas. During the war, suits and dresses had been cut short and spare to conserve fabrics. Coats were straight-line and knee-length. The shoulders of all garments were broadened and padded to resemble men's. Women had even adopted a forceful posture, with chest out and shoulders back, to match their wartime lives.

But now the war had ended and a French designer named Christian Dior had coined a phrase for the English language: The New Look.

The new women appeared in long, loose coats of soft fabric, with full sleeves and big, luxurious collars. They cinched in their waists, accented their bosoms, flaunted their hips under peplums and panniers. They swished around in dirndl skirts, circular skirts edged with a ruffle, flounced taffeta petticoats, and undergarments lavishly trimmed with lace. The New Look was all part of the new joie de vivre.

Sheer black panties, slips, and nightgowns trimmed with black lace were big sellers. (This seductiveness had begun even ahead of the New Look.) Ladies who had been young girls at the turn of the century stiffened their spines and said, with flashing eyes, "Only a trollop likes black underwear!" In vain did their daughters plead that the most innocent virgins wore black simply because it was the style. Unbending, their mothers pronounced, "Any woman who wears black underthings is no better than she should be and don't argue with me!"

The swinging skirts were longer, but overall more skin was exposed. The bikini came to beaches and pools, and in dresses bare shoulders were the style. A strapless wired brassière was invented so that for both daytime and evening women could wear strapless gowns.

The American couturière Valentina designed the prettiest dress of the century, the full-skirted "ballerina" or cocktail dress, with hem about twelve inches from the floor. In it, a girl could be "dressed" after five o'clock even when her escort wore a business suit.

In this new spirit of gaiety, the taverns, bowling alleys, sports events, movies, legitimate theater, all were enthusiastically attended.

"She Wrote Like an Angel"

One of the finest playwrights of the period was Lillian Hellman. When her publisher brought out a new edition of her plays, and an editor invited her to write a new preface, she declined. In the former edition she had said that she wanted to live to be a better writer and "I still want just that," she said.

This devotion to the finest writing that she could command is the mark of her career. In every one of her plays, she wrote and rewrote. She took out two or three characters, put them back in, took them out again. She sharpened a line here, changed a scene there, and worked over each character until it stood out sharp and sound. Sometimes she spent as much as a year on one play. First of all, naturally, she researched her period or her subject, filling four or five notebooks of 8½-by-11-inch paper in single-space typing, her research covering customs, politics, dress and manners, anecdotes, statistics, possible names for the characters of the unwritten play, and their detailed biographies. At last came act one. When she finally handed her finished play to the director, it had such clarity, precision, and dramatic impact that only a word or a line here and there had to be altered during rehearsal.

In the fall of 1933, when Lillian had only one play in her trunk, and that one so unworthy that it had never been produced, she happened to attend a party given by Ira Gershwin, and there she chatted with Herman Shumlin. Shumlin was a producer with two glowing successes behind him, *Grand Hotel* and *The Last Mile*. She told him the theme of a play she was writing, to be called *The Children's Hour*, about two schoolteachers who are accused of lesbianism by one of the pupils. Shumlin shook his head. Forget it, he said, and he invited her to come to work for him as a play reader at $15 a week. To his surprise, she accepted.

What better playwriting school could she find?

In the producer's office she quietly, shrewdly studied her craft, and on her own time she worked on her play. After six months she marched up to Shumlin's desk, smacked a manuscript down on it and commanded him to look at it. Unaccustomed though he was to taking orders, he picked up the pages and began to read. She sat down in a corner with a magazine and pretended to study it. After reading her first act, Shumlin glanced up at her and said, "Swell." At the end of the second act he said, "I hope it keeps up." And when he finished the last page he said, "I'll produce it."

She was staggered. The most she had hoped for was a word of encouragement, a few suggestions for change.

The Children's Hour, a play of fierce intensity, was the hit of the season. It ran for twenty-one months in New York and hardly a day missed having a capacity house. It played another year on the road and was produced in London and Paris.

As a girl of twenty Lillian married Arthur Kober, a successful Hollywood script writer. The marriage lasted only seven years, but even after the divorce they remained friends. In fact, he was a frequent visitor at her New York farm, called Hardscrabble, and she dedicated one of her plays to him. Also, she was matron of honor at his second marriage.

By that time she was enmeshed in a deep love affair with the droll, melancholy, sensitive Dashiell Hammett. Their love continued until his death in 1961, though they chose not to marry. Hammett was author of best-selling detective novels, the most memorable being *The Thin Man,* which set a new fashion in detective fiction, the frivolous style. A whole generation of movie fans knew Myrna Loy and William Powell as the suave and witty Nora and Nick in *Thin Man* movies.

Hammett never tinkered with Hellman's plays—she was too strong-willed to accept that even from Dash—but he was an uncompromising critic, and she respected his praise or condemnation as final judgment. Once when she gave him the completed script of a play, he was exceptionally severe about it and said, "It's worse than bad. It's half good."

She was so crushed that she fled from Hardscrabble, spent a week alone in New York, and when she returned to the farm she deposited the torn-up manuscript in a briefcase outside Hammett's door. Then she started all over again on a fresh page.

When 1940 opened, Lillian Hellman's best-known play, *The Little Foxes,* was in its long Broadway run. Tallulah Bankhead starred as the ruthless and bitchy Regina, a role that she reveled in.

Foxes was a melodramatic play in the sense that it portrayed strong characters and strong action. But in Hellman's plays dramatic events are never falsely inserted merely to shock; when they come they are not jarring; they are the inevitable and horrifying climax of character and action already established. George Jean Nathan said about *Foxes* that it was a true and honest play in which there was no compromise.

It was after the success of *Foxes* that Miss Hellman bought her 130-acre farm. There she spent many of the happiest years of her life, and in the spacious main house she did much of her writing through the 1940s. Usually she wrote for three hours in the morning, two or three hours in the afternoon, and again from ten at night until one or two in the morning.

Many guests took refuge at Hardscrabble, some of them writers who, like their hostess, worked well in the atmosphere of earnest labor mixed with zany fun. When too many friends invaded her study and interrupted her work, Lillian posted this notice on her door:

This Room Is Used for Work
Do Not Enter Without Knocking
After You Knock, Wait for an Answer
If you get no Answer, Go Away and
Don't Come Back
This Means Everybody
This Means You
This Means Night or Day
By Order of the Hellman-Military-Commission-for-Playwrights. Court Martialling Will Take Place in the Barn, and Your Trial Will Not be a Fair One.

The Christmas Court-Martialling Has Now Taken Place! Among those:
Herman Shumlin, former *régisseur*.
Miss Sylvia Hermann, aged three, former daughter of a farmer.
Miss Nora, former dog.
Mr. Samuel Dashiell Hammett, former eccentric.
Mr. Arthur Kober, former itinerant sweet-singer.
Mr. Louis Kronenberger, born in Cincinnati, lynched by me.
Emmy Kronenberger, wife of Kronenberger, died with him.
Mr. Felix Anderson, former butler.
Irene Robinson, former cook and very pretty
Note: Mr. Max Bernard Hellman, father, is a most constant offender. His age has saved him. This sentimentality may not continue.

Miss Hellman loved the out-of-doors, particularly in spring, when she delighted in gardening. Sometimes she put out seeds on Monday, and, a friend said of her, if plants hadn't come up by Wednesday, she spaded everything up and started all over again with new seeds.

In the spring of 1941, Hellman's powerful anti-Fascist drama, *Watch on the Rhine*, opened on Broadway, with its strong message that in spite of hate and evil human decency can prevail. She did not consciously write a political document. Writers, she said, look at the world around them and then they write it down. But both her emotions and her intellect were painfully involved in the horror of death and destruction in war.

Later plays of hers were *Another Part of the Forest*, which took the *Little Foxes* family through a drama set twenty years earlier than the action of the original *Foxes*. Some critics consider this her finest play. Others give highest praise to *The Autumn Garden* or *Toys in the Attic*. Miss Hellman also did some adaptations, one of them being *The Lark*, in which Julie Harris sublimely played Joan of Arc.

With Lillian Hellman's insistence on getting the right words down in the right order, and with her use of strong themes and dramatic confrontations, she has few peers among American playwrights.

"Silence Gives the Proper Grace to Women" *(Sophocles)*

Owing to an accident of timing, Sophocles and Tallulah Bankhead never met. If they had met, however, the philosopher couldn't have got off that little nifty, because Tallulah wouldn't have stopped talking long enough. A friend of hers said that Tallulah not only talked until the cows came home, she could go on talking while they were milked, given their hay, put in their stalls, and when they gave the first *Mooooooo* the next morning, she'd still be at it.

Her husky voice was an octave deeper than a man's, but was so seductively sultry that she was never mistaken for a man.

No interviewer had a chance to ask questions. She began to talk while he was taking out his pencil and continued nonstop until he backed away with writer's cramp. She was always good copy. She worked at polishing her image as the wickedest woman on the public scene. "I'm pure as the driven slush," she said in that deep, rolling voice, and she loved her nickname, "Bawdy Bankhead." She made a show of being egotistical, and once inscribed a photograph of herself, "To Edie, the Miracle Woman, from Tallulah, the Miracle."

In youth she was as slim as a willow wand, and with those hollow cheeks and the voluptuous mouth she was so beautiful that John Barrymore called her the loveliest creature on earth. Though her height was only five feet, three inches, she seemed tall because she was so tempestuous. She slammed doors, stormed into rooms, hurled objects out of her way, sprang out of chairs, leaped into and out of cars, all with an air of rush, of violence.

She smoked from four to six packs of cigarettes a day, drank largely (anything but Scotch), and often stayed up all night, all the next day, and then gave an evening performance with her usual ebullience. No one ever saw her tired. When asked what she did to keep fit, she said, "I don't do anything to keep fit. I was born fit."

Her theatrical career began when she was fifteen, at the end of World War I. Her father, despairing of controlling her, gave her a fifty-dollar-a-week allowance and let her go to New York. There she took a room at the Algonquin Hotel, already beginning to be known as a gathering place for sophisticates, and hired a French maid, thus beginning as she continued, always in debt. Round Tablers Robert Benchley, Marc Connelly, Deems Taylor, Alex Woollcott, and the others took her to first nights, where she smoked cigars during intermissions. As the summer of 1919 was very hot, she went onstage in her small roles with bare legs, outraging the proper. They hissed the girl. Tallulah concluded that the quick way to fame was to break the rules.

At twenty, not having made the success she wanted in New York, except to be the most talked-about girl in town, she went to England, and there she repeated the story of Ethel Barrymore two decades earlier: she became the delight of the fashionable. London adored her southern accent, her arrogance and profane rudeness, her exuberance. And not only society London: the "gallery girls" were mad about her too. Fans lined up forty-eight hours before her openings to get tickets. Once two thousand of them stormed her stage door and the police had to be called to quell the riot.

She starred in *The Green Hat, Let Us Be Gay, They Knew What They Wanted, Camille,* and *Gold Diggers.* By now Tallulah was consciously learning to act, and in addition her powerful magnetism poured across the footlights to make every spectator lean forward in his seat and breathe a little faster. She spoke with a tremulous excitement.

At the same time her motions seemed completely unstudied. She walked across the stage, picked up a magazine, tossed a remark over her shoulder, all as naturally as if no one were watching.

But when she came back to the United States in 1930 she encountered more failure. It was not until Lillian Hellman's *The Little Foxes* came along in 1939 that actress and role blended like gin and tonic. As Regina, Tallulah fused strength, unscrupulousness, and cruelty into a brilliant performance, and she became a star of the first rank.

She and Lillian Hellman struck sparks over wartime politics, Tallulah being a middle-of-the-road New Dealer and a fan of FDR, while Lillian stood further to the left. "She'll never act again in a play of mine," wrote Miss Hellman, and Tallulah replied—in print, of course—"I say she's spinach, and I say to hellman with her." But Tallulah also said of the playwright, "She writes like an angel," and the author, in the same generous spirit, said, "Miss Bankhead is one of the great actresses of all time."

Tallulah cared hotly about politics—of course if Tallulah had an opinion about anything it was a burning opinion—and once in a restaurant when she overheard Vincent Sheean and a friend exchanging surly remarks about Winston Churchill, she marched over to their table and set them straight in a loud, firm voice.

Tallulah was no worshiper of things. She seldom bothered to wear jewelry, though she had a diamond necklace that was good for pawning. She told the story of a night when she and a group of friends were going to "some awful dive of a nightclub" and when the cab driver dropped them off in front of it, he said, "Better give me the diamonds, lady, before you go inna that place." Tallulah decided that he had an honest face and that inside the necklace would probably be stolen from her anyhow, and she handed it to him. After an hour or two she and her friends came out of the club to find that the cab was still waiting and so was the necklace. They all drove on to another nightclub, this time invited the cab driver to join the party, and all had a wonderful time together.

She was the fastest study on Broadway. Once, rushed into the lead of a Noel Coward play only a few days before the opening, she learned her part in forty-eight hours and had every line down cold.

A superstitious woman, she enacted a ritual before every performance. In her dressing room, she knelt in front of a picture of her father and mother, she said, and prayed, "Dear God, please don't let me make a fool of myself tonight." Then she drank a glass of champagne and was ready.

She never "got into her part" ahead of time, or even thought about it. Smoking a cigarette, she strolled around backstage or chatted with a stagehand until her cue came. Then, as she stepped onstage, the mass effect of the audience struck her. In that instant she was transformed into the stage character.

"You can't act on your emotions," Tallulah said. "Acting has to be deliberate and unemotional, or rather, the emotion you express has to be planned and deliberate so you can give an even performance every night.

"Acting isn't life, you know. Put a drunk onstage and he'd give a very unconvincing imitation of a drunk. . . . I dòn't lose myself in a part. . . . Suppose the character you're playing strangles another character. Where would you be if you lost yourself in the part and really strangled the character? On second thought, it might be a good idea with some actors I've played with."

Women in the Arts

When Agnes De Mille was ten years old, she saw Pavlova dance. "Across the daily preoccupation of lessons," she said, "lunch boxes, tooth brushings, and quarrelings . . . flashed this bright, unworldly experience and burned in a single afternoon a path over which I could never retrace my steps."

After that day, she too had to be a dancer.

Her dancing was splendid, but she won fame through her innovative choreography. One of the triumphs of her career came on the night in March, 1943, when the Rodgers and Hammerstein musical hit *Oklahoma!* opened in New York. Her choreography for that play was a Broadway revolution. Instead of the dance-line routine with its high kicks and mechanized movement, she created the most exhilarating dances that ever brought an audience to its feet, cheering. Dance and plot smoothly dovetailed, motion and song each abetting the other.

Oklahoma! was the greatest theatrical hit of the war years. In fact, it outlasted the war, with a run of five years and nine months in New York City. Besides that, a road company took it on tour for nine and a half years. It played in countries across the world. *Oklahoma!* popularized the full-skirted gingham dress and the flirtatious, swinging ponytail that was a fashionable hair style halfway through the fifties.

Supreme dancer, teacher, and choreographer of the half century was Martha Graham. Her achievement is all the more remarkable because her father forbade her to take dancing lessons, so that she was twenty-one before she had her first lesson—and Agnes De Mille's teacher had told *her* she was too old to begin dancing when she was only ten! Nevertheless, Miss Graham began by enrolling in Denishawn, the school headed by Ruth St. Denis and Ted Shawn.

She believed that expressive dance can expose the human heart and mind with power and eloquence, and her famous *Appalachian Spring* illustrates this premise. First presented in October 1944, it tells the story of a young pioneer and his bride: their wedding, the hellfire-and-damnation sermon that accompanied it, the bride's soft dancing that shows she believes in joy rather than in hell, the husband's solemn happiness. All these emotions of fear, hope, reverence, and love are portrayed by the dance.

At the beginning of the decade, a vivid new talent blazed into the literary world, that of Eudora Welty. Her first book of short stories, *A Curtain of Green,* was so dazzling that it merited a laudatory preface by that master of the short story, Katherine Anne Porter.

Miss Welty was then in her early thirties, but she had written many of the stories in that volume half a dozen years earlier. Before putting anything down on paper, "I sort of hang stories in my mind and let them hang there for a long time," she said. Often, so much additional time elapsed between writing and printing that by the time a story appeared in print she hardly felt that it was a work of her own hand.

She had been a voracious reader since she was a little girl, wolfing down Russian and French novelists, Shakespeare and Dante, history and legends, and especially fairy tales. Even as an adult she delighted in fairy tales.

During the 1940s Miss Welty published many short stories and four books, but could hardly be said to have had living quarters in the well-known ivory tower. She was, she said, "underfoot locally," meaning that she was involved in the civic and social life of her home town, Jackon, Mississippi. When her friends discovered still another book of hers in print, they exclaimed, "But, Eudora, when did you write that?" They didn't wonder at her talent; only, since they saw her about so much, they marveled that she found time to write.

Another southern girl, only twenty-three when her first book scattered sparks across the literary sky, was Carson McCullers, whose greatest work was done in the 1940s. Pain and spiritual isolation are the themes of her work. *The Heart Is a Lonely Hunter* and *Reflections in a Golden Eye* were followed by *The Member of the Wedding*.

In the last, teen-age Frankie Adams blunders unhappily toward maturity, innocently believing that she will go with her brother and his bride on their honeymoon, live with them afterward, and become a member of the real, outside world. Sad and sensitive Berenice, the family's Negro cook, is as baffled by life as Frankie is. "Things will happen," she said. "We all of us somehow caught."

Mrs. McCullers dramatized *The Member of the Wedding* and it played on Broadway starring Julie Harris and Ethel Waters. Later it was made into a movie.

The author had suffered three strokes before she was thirty, and spent much of her life thereafter in paralysis and pain. Her doctor, Mary Mercer, persuaded her to go on writing, one page a day, pecking away at a typewriter with one finger of her good hand. In this way she wrote *The Ballad of the Sad Café, Clock Without Hands,* and a play, *The Square Root of Wonderful*.

"Sometimes I think God got me mixed up with Job," she said. "But Job never cursed God and neither have I." She carried on sturdily until her death in 1967.

One day in 1915 a young art teacher named Georgia O'Keeffe locked herself into her room and held a private exhibition of everything she had painted. She looked at each picture. This painting had been influenced by that artist, that one by another artist. They were no good. Such work only "added to the brush pile." But this—and this—and this . . . those pieces represented herself alone.

When she unlocked the door, Georgia knew exactly what kind of work she wanted to do. She liked intensity and discipline. Bold, stark subjects. Strong colors. No prettiness and no imitations. She would find new ways of expressing her ideas.

Later that year she mailed a roll of drawings to a friend in New York, commanding that they be shown to no one. The friend took one look, and carried them straight to the studio of Alfred Stieglitz, pioneer photographer, who spread out the drawings on the floor and exclaimed, "At last! A woman on paper!"

He displayed them in a show, and within a few days a furious artist stamped into his gallery and demanded that her work be taken down at once. Stieglitz calmed her down, told her how much he esteemed the originality of her work, and the next year put on her first one-man show.

A few years later the two were married.

At first Stieglitz's friends didn't want her around. A *woman?* An *artist?* Let her keep busy framing pictures and hanging shows. But she went steadfastly on, painting her harsh, oversize flower cross-sections (Pornographic!" people said. "Female symbolism!"), bleached animal bones ("Brutal!"), stylized cityscapes ("Bleak!"), and wide expanses of clouds that looked like rocks. Her strong, severe nature shows in every painting. She liked best to work on huge canvases.

Her work is now displayed in London's Tate Gallery, the Metropolitan Museum, and museums of many other cities.

She was so independent that, when someone addressed her as Mrs. Stieglitz, she always corrected him: "Miss O'Keeffe."

She discovered New Mexico in 1929, and loved its landscapes with such passion that when her husband died in 1946 she moved there, bought an adobe house at Abiquiu, forty miles north of Santa Fe. Its roof was falling down and its doors falling off, but she remodeled and enlarged the house and lived there in contented solitude. "I don't need to see many people to live."

Her favorite time of day was early daylight, and when "the dogs started talking to her," she'd get up to make a fire and maybe some tea, and then sit in bed to look across the desert and watch the sun come up.

"Early morning is best," she said, "when there are no people around."

Her Spanish-Indian neighbors respected the stern, silent woman in long black skirts who, even when she was very old, climbed to the top of the highest mountain near her ranch, went alone on camping trips, raised the vegetables that she ate, ground her own flour, and built a $50,000 gymnasium for the young people of the little town.

The 1950s

THE CALM BEFORE
THE MARCHING

The Building Boom Was On

There weren't enough houses and apartments to go around, not with all those wartime marriages and postwar marriages. Many young couples were still living uncomfortably with one set of parents or the other, because few living units had been constructed during the war, when raw materials were sucked into the war effort.

But now the goods were available. So were the workmen, glad to get out of the armed forces or out of the defense plant. And there was the money. During the war, thousands of young people had stashed away their paychecks, or bonuses, or flight pay, to spend in the golden postwar world, and the postwar world was today.

"We want a place of our own," cried the young people. "Grass—trees—flowers—fresh air. Away from noise and dirt and traffic and landlords."

And so all over America new homes sprang up. New neighborhoods. Small cities, almost. Some houses were no more than boxes on slabs, put up in long rows, and some were split-level or Early-American-type mansions. But every house had that green space all its own, whether it stood on a fifty-foot lot in a neighborhood that numbered seventy-five children to the block or stood grandly on three landscaped acres.

Of course the new suburbia was automobile oriented. Few neighborhoods were served by public transportation, and even if city buses did trundle out to the most populous areas, they ran half empty. The great American love affair with the automobile continued as fervently as ever. A man might abandon his wife and children, but would he abandon a good car? Never.

The suburban woman soon found that she was immobilized without a car of her own, and as soon as possible two cars were parked in the garage or driveway.

It wasn't only cars that these tense and hard-working new home-owners strained to buy. They wanted goods of every kind. Follow them to the shopping center and watch them.

The shopping center, by the way, is a phenomenon of the 1950s. Trade drained away from the tradition-encrusted downtown stores to the shining extravagances on the outskirts of the city. Here, too, private transportation was of first importance. For every square foot of selling space, six square feet of parking space had to be provided.

But to return to the shoppers. A young woman is typically accompanied by one or two, or even three, young children who ride in the shopping cart or race through the aisles playing hide-and-seek with friends. The mother, somewhat disheveled, freely distributes slaps, jerks, and shrill commands, which the children cheerfully ignore. Better-groomed mothers slap less and command in lower voices and are ignored in the same cheerful way.

But, however ill-tempered she seems, the mother allows her young to throw a comic book, a plastic truck, and a small, ugly doll into the shopping basket without reproof. These toys, however, are not costly items. She may also buy a pair of matching lamps (because they are marked down for bargain days), an outdoor grill for the patio (all the neighbors have backyard cookouts), an electric toaster because the old one doesn't work anymore, two pairs of sheets (they come in stripes and flowers now), and a huge potted plant that takes her fancy.

Driving home, the young woman may worry about money. Installment payments will take up most of her husband's paycheck for the next two years, not allowing for loss of a job. But they had to have a TV, a range and refrigerator, and a washer and dryer. And an electric dishwasher as soon as possible. The kids needed that playground equipment so they'd stay in their own backyard. Besides that, she wanted a good camera for her husband's birthday, and ice skates for all of them if the city built that new ice rink, and she hoped she could talk her husband into buying the neighbor's dining-room set when they left town next month. . . . Yes, she spent too much. Everybody she knew spent too much.

Why?

Yesterday on TV she heard someone say that Americans suffer from consumerism. The great commodity scramble, he called it. When I was a kid, she reflected, people had to fight the depression, and next there was a war on. Now all that prosperity and peace we wanted are here, and it's not so wonderful after all. I don't know why!

Our young woman drives into a neighborhood of narrow lots, neat frame houses, and one-car garages. Pulling into her own driveway, she pauses to look fondly up and down the street. A nice place to live, better than the city, where she grew up. After four years, the new trees are beginning to look like something. And every house is a little different from the others. Only, she thought, sighing, this neighborhood used to be more fun. More friendly. Now there are just four or five of us to drink coffee together mornings.

Our friend's last comment tells us that her neighborhood has undergone the evolution common to all of suburbia—from modest areas like hers, through the ones where houses have from seven to ten rooms and where sons and daughters go to Yale and Smith; and on to the imposing areas with wrought-iron fences, where no car less haughty than a Rolls-Royce looks really at home in the three-car garage.

In every new neighborhood, as a family moves into its house it is greeted joyfully by earlier comers. For a time there is a great esprit de corps in the community, much partying, much eager putting forth of the best foot. Warm friendships develop. All is equality and fraternity, and everybody is delighted with the new suburban life.

Time passes. Slowly, people become identified with specialized interests in the nearby city, where all the men, but few of the wives, work. Intimacy dissolves. Small groups cohere. Some families withdraw entirely to themselves or make new contacts with groups at a distance from the neighborhood. Finally people begin to move away, through transfers to other divisions of corporations, or they move to classier neighborhoods. New families that replace them are greeted politely but without warmth. Now the suburb has evolved.

Suburban wives and their sisters in city, small town, and rural America had one problem in common. Each had to do the housework. In the 1900s, a modest household could hire a maid who lived in, at $3 a week. Half a century later, the girls were able to find jobs in factories, stores, and offices that paid as well as housework (now $5 to $10 a day) and gave them more social status.

In the 1950s, only opulent households could afford full-time, live-in maids. Affluent women hired a helper for one day a week, and the less affluent managed by themselves.

A Bryn Mawr report claimed that an urban household required

from seventy-eight to eighty hours a week of labor for cleaning, cooking, and other chores, but one cannot help looking suspiciously at these figures. Were housewives punishing themselves by keeping their houses shinier than necessary? Was it imperative that every child change all his clothes every day and sometimes oftener just because Mom had an automatic washer? Was it really important that the oven walls be as clean as a laboratory slide? Perhaps she was devoting herself to ceremonial nothingness, to the petty refinements of housekeeping that no one would ever observe except a fellow houseworker.

Woman's Place

It is all very well for some of us to boast about our magnificent indifference to propaganda. The humiliating truth is that all of us respond to it. And in the 1950s the movies, articles in women's magazines, platform speakers, pastors, and popular opinion carried a strong message to mothers: Woman's place is in the home. In fiction, story after story in the *Ladies' Home Journal* and the *Saturday Evening Post* had a protagonist who discovered in one way or another that she herself, the good man who had married her, and all of their children were happier when she devoted all her labor, her charm, and her love to their well-being.

Women believed this so fully that they felt guilty if they strayed outside the house unless all the children were along.

A woman's childhood training in docility helped her to accept the domestic role. It is true that American girls all through their school years are trained just as the boys are. They take the same classes and some of the same athletics, and they are expected to be as smart and as competitive as the boys. But all along the canny little girl knows that this training is only a kind of game; that someday she will fall in love, will drop all this pretense of being equal to the boys, and will adopt an attitude toward her husband simultaneously deferential and superior, just as her mother did. All her life, both parents have accented her femininity—with frilly underthings, girlish toys such as dolls, play dishes, and cookware, and dancing class, to which she wore her good shoes and white nylon gloves.

Boys, after they become men, are considered failures if they don't do well in their work. Girls fail only if they don't succeed in getting a husband. But after marriage a girl is sometimes bewildered to find that her seeming triumph is not enough. Thinking back to her school days, she realizes that she really liked that work in biology or geometry or business law; and that after all housework and baby care aren't enough. If she wants to stay married and stay at home, she has a number of options.

One, honored through the centuries, is to become a tyrant. She can domineer over her husband and be a terror to the children. The shrew earns plenty of hate, but she needn't feel abused. Second, she may, like the housewife of the Bryn Mawr study, make herself a martyr to housekeeping and child care. Or she can take to drink. Or hurl herself into PTA or other good works. Or she may engage in sexual dalliance. Last of all is the girl who isn't often heard from, the happy young woman who is really fulfilled by motherhood and wifery, and who may dip into one or all of the above five options from time to time, but only for fun.

Marriage was very much the fashion in the 1950s. A feeling of danger, of impermanence, was in the air. The bomb hung there, invisible, the bomb of Damocles. It gave young people a sense of quiet desperation. The only happiness they could count on, they reasoned, was what they could gather with their own two hands. If marriage seemed a way to happiness, they felt they had better take it now.

Many previous marriage prejudices melted away: (1) A man was no longer disgraced if his wife worked. She ususally did so until sometime before the first baby was born. (2) A man could help with the housework and diaper changing and still consider himself fully male. (3) Parents could help married children financially without being scorned by all their friends. The old rural concept came back into action: long ago it was customary for parents who could afford it to give their marrying children a few acres and a cow. Now they provided a temporary monthly income.

Girls married very young. In 1951, one girl in three had found a husband by the time she was nineteen. And they married in greater numbers than ever before. Fewer spinsters and fewer bachelors were on the scene. The census may have given statistically-minded girls a sense of panic because the 1940 census showed only half a million more males than females; in 1950, for the first time in history, there were actually more females than males, and by the end of the decade, 2,500,000 more of them.

Not all of the marriages took, but by mid-century divorce no longer carried a stigma. There was a rash of divorces soon after the GIs came home, then the rate leveled off again until the mid-fifties, after which from one-fourth to one-third of the total number of marriages ended in divorce. The divorce rate was higher in the blue-collar group and in the middle class than among the most prosperous and best educated. Perhaps the latter were perceptive enough to see (especially those who had already gone through one divorce) that their troubles were so complex that a mere reshuffling of partners wouldn't solve things anyhow.

The baby boom that got underway in 1946 continued to 1957. The national median was 3.6 children per family, though in suburbia the figure was a little higher. Who can explain that compulsion to have big families? Prosperity was naturally the basic factor. There was also a passion for nest building and nest filling brought on by years of poverty before the war and the separation of lovers during the war; a feeling that the outer world is full of trouble and danger that might be escaped by concentrating on one's own house and family—a safely hidden miniature world of one's own.

Then there was fashion. Americans tend to be conformists in any period, and the fifties was a decade of deep conformity. Even in the matter of fertility there's a certain desire not to be outdone by those Joneses.

Some experts also suggested that a suburban woman, tethered to home and neighborhood by prevailing social custom, and far from the city with its varied activities, feared the years alone when all the children would be in school; and she had another baby to give her an important, absorbing job to do.

A mother's activities were focused on the children. She was a Cub Scout den mother, a Girl Scout leader, and chairman of countless PTA committees. She worked at the school bazaar that made money for new band uniforms, she licked stamps for the school board, and she chauffeured the children to Little League games, to dancing lessons, to birthday parties, to baton twirling class, to the doctor and dentist, to basketball practice. At home she laundered the clothes, and sometimes made them as well, and she helped with the children's homework. Don't ask when she had time for the housework.

She was still a joiner, as the American woman has been since the first club was formed before the turn of the century, but in the 1950s she didn't work for social causes. Her clubs tended to be home-related and child-related.

While the typical mother concentrated on home and children, the father spent much of his free time doing the same. He was the handyman. He mended appliances, mowed the lawn, erected the basketball stand and the tree house, mixed the concrete for the new patio, and played ball with the boys. Togetherness was the slogan in the 1950s.

Ads in slick-paper magazines showed picture after picture of the well-groomed American family together: mother, father, and children smiling as they stepped into their shining new car; smiling at each other as they passed a tube of toothpaste from hand to hand; smiling happily as they looked at their newly painted house; smiling at the lawn made green with one application of the advertised fertilizer. How clean and wholesome they were! How totally devoted to themselves and their clean, wholesome, prosperous culture!

Religion flourished. (See ad picturing clean, happy family smiling its way up steps of Gothic cathedral to be welcomed by wholesome, contented clergyman.) Church membership rose: 63 percent of the population held formal church membership, an all-time high. Religion conformed to the times and became more bland. Instead of a bigoted, fiery belief in God, there arose an amiable believing in a belief in God.

At least three groups in America were not good conformists, but they hardly showed in the coast-to-coast picture. First, there was a sullen, anti-authoritarian youth subculture. Second, there were poverty-ridden groups that grew angrier and more audible as the decade passed, largely because they didn't seem to share in this prosperity that they heard so much about. And, third, there were educated men and women just too young to have served in World War II who disliked a lot of things about the country, but they didn't say much. The Silent Generation, they were called.

Sophisticates made a small cult of nonconformity and were pleased with themselves for their independence, even though they didn't take any action. In some circles the flaunt of disengagement was so much the style that a cartoon of the time showed a little girl, obviously a spawn of the upper classes, saying to her mother, "But, Mummie, why aren't you a nonconformist—like everybody else?"

All this may seem a weary pattern, but today's adults who were teen-agers in the 1950s look back upon the decade with nostalgia. How untroubled the country was then, they say. What gay, funny times we had! How we danced! How marvelous the music was! What a lot of things my little allowance would buy and how pretty the clothes were then.

The Middle-Class Woman Goes to Work

A poll of more than a thousand high school and college girls during the 1950s revealed that 80 percent of them believed that woman's place is in the home. These 80 percent expected to marry, have children, and stay at home with them in the best Victorian tradition. Few of them had definite plans for the future, or any professional ambitions.

And yet, after they became wives and mothers, hundreds of thousands of young women reversed their own plans, resisted the strong social pressure to remain in woman's place, and found jobs. Between 1950 and 1956, the female labor force rose by more than three million, or an increase of 17 percent. Why did they do it? Most of them defended themselves by saying that they worked because they needed the money. Those who said that they worked because they liked it were looked upon with a disapproving eye. More than half the working women were married. Early marriage and early childbearing sent mothers into the job market at about age thirty-five.

A working woman was usually aware that a show of lively competitiveness at work would result in her being labeled "hard-driving" and "aggressive," terms which are admiring when applied to men, but for her are downgrading, showing that she is overstepping the boundaries of approved behavior.

Most jobs of high school or college graduates were clerical. Women were added to the work force, but they didn't rise in the occupational scale. Girls in college saw where the jobs lay, and tended to limit themselves to secretarial, nursing, home ec, or education courses. Of all young women capable of doing college work, however, only one in four actually went to college.

During the 1950s, fewer than one out of ten doctorates were awarded to women, compared to 13 percent in 1940 and 15 percent in 1920. One educator observed that if the mid-century trend went on Americans would rank among the most backward women in the western world. While higher education for women increased in Britain, France, and Sweden, it diminished here. In the 1950s (to quote a showy pair of figures) 70 percent of the doctors in the Soviet Union were women, compared to 5 percent in the United States; and 75 percent of the dentists in Denmark were women, compared to 1 percent here.

The Eisenhower Years

The 1950s were the years of the Cold War in Europe and the shooting war in Korea.

The early part of the decade is sometimes called "the McCarthy era," that curious time of fear and moral confusion when the senator from Wisconsin was leading a campaign that blackened characters and blighted careers, often by nothing more than a charge of Communism, no proof being offered.

There were political scandals, and also that shocker called Sputnik, that panicked educators, parents, politicians, psychologists, columnists, and the school janitor into a furious scramble of quarrels about what's wrong with our schools and why can't Johnny read? When the tumult died down the result was a new, severe emphasis on science and math so that the United States too could rear a crop of Sputnik creators.

New slogans passed into the language. So familiar were the terms "the man in the gray flannel suit" and "the organization man" that anyone can tell how well known this figure was: the middling-young, conforming member of a corporation, subduing his individuality to the good of the firm. "Adjustment" was another of the words. To be well adjusted to society and family was to play the correct (conforming) part. "Insecurity" was the instant parlor diagnosis of any personality quirk.

The 1950s beheld the sorry spectacle of a Van Doren, member of the intellectual aristocracy, having to confess to a spectacular swindle in a radio quiz show. "The $64,000 question" was another of the decade's passwords.

If idealists felt depressed and let down by the quiz-show deceit, they were still more dismayed when the U-2 incident occurred. No one old enough to read the papers at that time has forgotten the spy mission that ended with Francis Gary Powers' plane being shot down over Russia. More important, he hasn't forgotten the fatuous lies, the various denials and retractions from the White House that finished forever the myth that *our* government is different from all those foreign governments that lie to *their* people. This incident caused the souring of the last bit of national idealism left over from the end of World War II.

Through these not-very-distinguished years, several women of distinction moved.

She Joined a Gentlemen's Club

Margaret Chase Smith was the first woman in the U.S. Senate not appointed to fill somebody's unexpired term, but elected on her own merits as a shrewd, hard-working politician. She had already served three and a half terms in the House of Representatives when Maine elected her to the Senate in 1948. There she remained for twenty-four years.

A member of that body called "the most exclusive gentlemen's club in the world," she walked easily between the extremes of masculine aggressiveness and feminine ingratiation. She was a pretty woman, trimly put together from her soft gray hair to her high heels, and she usually wore a fresh red rose at her left shoulder; but when she disagreed with the party and believed that more money should be budgeted for community services to benefit children, or felt that the rights of women in the armed forces were being overridden, or opposed the administration's Cold War policies, then she fought relentlessly for her convictions, even if she was one of a small minority.

She was a junior senator in the McCarthy era. One day she boarded the little subway that shuttles to and fro between the Capitol and the Senate Office Building. Senator McCarthy sat down beside her.

"I'm going to make a speech, Joe," she warned him. "And you're not going to like it."

Knowing something of her stance, he promised to ask her some very pointed questions after the speech, but he smiled. He was so agreeable. Such a nice guy!

Weeks passed before she was ready to make her move, because she always deliberated carefully over every vote she cast and every comment that she made publicly. But a day came when she was ready, and as word had gotten around that the senator from Maine, who seldom made a speech, was going to make one today, the chamber was well filled. When she rose to speak, senators on both sides of the aisle moved closer in order to miss no word. This speech was afterward known as her "Declaration of Conscience."

She looked cool and confident as she stood there in her greenish-blue silk suit, the red rose glowing at her shoulder. She cast her level glance over the Senate chamber and began, "I would like to speak briefly and simply about a serious national condition. It is a national feeling of fear and frustration that could result in national suicide and the end of everything that we Americans hold dear."

The Senate, she said, once the most admirable deliberative body in the world, was being "debased to the level of a forum of hate and character assassination sheltered by the shield of Congressional immunity."

The Constitution, she reminded her listeners, "speaks not only of freedom of speech but also of trial by jury instead of trial by accusation."

When she finished speaking, McCarthy did not rise to ask his pointed questions. Grim-faced, he strode from the chamber without a word. But other senators came over to congratulate her warmly, some of them men who, before her "declaration" would have hesitated to be seen talking affably with an enemy of the powerful McCarthy. Democratic Senator Stuart Symington of Missouri said that Senator Smith represented all that was best in American life—even if she was a Republican.

McCarthy did not take this humiliation meekly. For the next several years there was bitter political skirmishing between him and Margaret Smith; but in a poll of press and political scientists, Smith was among the top ten senators. McCarthy finished last.

Margaret Smith also took part in a later Senate battle, concerning the confirmation of Lewis L. Strauss as President Eisenhower's choice for secretary of commerce. Only twice in the past century had the Senate rejected a cabinet nominee, and at first Senator Smith saw no reason to object to Mr. Strauss. But as hearings went on and on and she found him to be evasive, nonresponsive, and careless with facts, she changed her mind. The quarrel in the Senate grew acrid and the voting was sure to be close.

At last, in the early hours one morning, after long days of wrangling, the roll call began. It continued as expected until Senator Smith's name was called. In her clear, level voice, she answered, "No." Senator Barry Goldwater of Arizona slammed a fist against his desk and swore. When President Eisenhower heard that Margaret Smith's vote was the one that had defeated his candidate, he was so enraged that his language was deep purple. Nothing that happened during his second term so infuriated him.

She was accused of getting even with the administration because she pulled little weight within the party, which was not ready to accept a woman politician on a par with men. There was talk of censuring her. But she held her cool. "I like integrity," she said. "I could not vote for that man."

This storm did not affect her popularity at home. In the following year—1960—when she ran again for her seat in the Senate, she received 61.6 percent of Maine's total vote, the highest percentage of any Republican senator that year.

She kept in close touch with the voters of Maine, visiting her state at least once a month, and she bargained for their advantages in fishing, agriculture, and air bases. Once when she was battling for lower prices on heating oil (important in a cold state like Maine), a Tenants Harbor housewife wrote to her, "We like the way you look out for the interests of us ordinary folks back in Maine. . . . As we see it, we have two choices: to switch back to the old wood-burning furnace or to write Margaret Chase Smith."

But she was human, too. In the 1960 campaign her Democrat opponent was Lucia Cormier, whom she defeated handily, five to two. Maine's junior senator, Edmund S. Muskie, a Democrat, had naturally supported the Democratic candidate. But Margaret did not forgive him. When she took her oath of office in 1961, instead of going down the aisle on the arm of the other senator from her state, according to Senate tradition, she was escorted by Maurine Neuberger, newly elected Republican senator from Oregon. The presence of another women senator, she explained, was "a historic occasion." But Edmund Muskie was neatly snubbed.

Glorious Eccentric

Margaret Chase Smith wasn't the only woman to be troubled by the free-swinging congressional investigation into private lives. The House Committee on Un-American Activities was conducting its first inquiries on the Hollywood scene when Frank Capra began to shoot *State of the Union,* a script with a left-wing slant. In this story, the protagonist is a burly, plain-speaking industrialist, wealthy and idealistic, who runs for president. Spencer Tracy played the part, and Katharine Hepburn was his wife, a subtle woman who sees through the plots laid by crafty politicians to use her husband. The third star was Adolphe Menjou, one of the politicians.

Reality elbowed its way into illusion, because Katharine Hepburn was a warm liberal and in real life she despised Adolphe Menjou for "naming names" at the House hearings, damaging many actors' careers in what she and many others called a smear campaign. Off-set they hardly spoke to each other, and some of the scenes in which they collided she played with exceptional sharpness even for Kate.

Though known as a left-winger, she was not intimidated by the possibility of being investigated herself. One regrets now that she was not summoned to the fearsome House committee of J. Parnell Thomas. That quick wit and lashing tongue of hers would have given the nation one of the liveliest performances of the 1950s.

Offstage, this lanky, imperious, gifted woman with the back as stiff as an Annapolis cadet's, the stern mouth and high cheekbones, wore slacks long before they were accepted as proper. At Claridge's, London's posh hotel, after she was told that slacks were not permitted in the lobby, she merely shrugged and used the servants' entrance. Atop the slacks she often wore an old sweater so much washed that it was baggy, and she held it together at the neck with a safety pin. Her life was strictly disciplined: hikes, tennis, golf, frugal meals, no parties, and lights off at ten o'clock.

Onstage and on film she delighted audiences as Eva Lovelace in *Morning Glory*, touchingly gentle, sensitive, and eager; or as Jo March in *Little Women*, noble, daring, and tender; as heartbroken Alice Adams; as the awkward, enthusiastic girl in *Stage Door*. One of her best-remembered parts, on both stage and screen was Tracy Lord in *The Philadelphia Story*. She played every part with radiant spontaneity.

One day during the filming of *Philadelphia*, director George Cukor became very nervous because the set was so noisy; hammering, sawing, banging footsteps, chattering, shouting, and Hepburn's laugh shrilling above all. Cukor rushed away to calm down in quiet. Katharine threw up her hands for silence. Everyone became dead still. She signaled everyone to follow and they hurried up to the flies above the stage, where they held themselves motionless. The director returned to an empty, silent stage. He looked all around, bewildered, and as he turned to leave, Katharine gave the signal and seventy voices, led by Hepburn, Jimmy Stewart, and Cary Grant, shouted, "QUIET!"

At other times, Kate was so domineering that if you weren't fascinated by her you had to hate her. She infuriated set decorators and cameramen and choreographers and costume designers and fellow actors and directors. She made it no secret that she knew everything. The trouble was that she did know everything about cameras and lighting and costumes and all the rest.

She was very rude. She pushed autograph seekers away. She hit a reporter with an umbrella when he got in her way. One day on the set of *The Lion in Winter*, she sent for the makeup man. (She was Eleanor of Aquitaine and Peter O'Toole was her husband, King Henry II.) The makeup man didn't come and someone told her he was with O'Toole. She rushed upstairs to Peter's room and screamed, "Why don't you let me have my makeup man!" and she whacked Peter a good one on the jaw.

But hear this: Peter O'Toole said about Katharine Hepburn, "Kate was the great experience of my life. . . . If it had been twenty-five years before, I would have broken Spencer Tracy's fingers to get her."

She was the essence of kindness to stagehands and to younger actors. In *Adam's Rib*, there was a scene in which she talked to young Judy Holliday at a table. Kate ordered that the camera focus the whole scene on Judy so that all the viewer saw of Kate was her shoulder.

During the filming of another picture, Kate's director was Vincente Minnelli, and she became acquainted with his wife, Judy Garland. Kate made Judy get up very early and take morning walks, and tried to distract her, to keep her from drinking and taking drugs.

In England, when she played *Much Ado About Nothing* with Alfred Drake, he would naturally have taken his bows before her, because she was the star, but she said, "Oh, no, none of that. We'll take our bows together." She firmly took his hand in hers, and they had their bows side by side, suggesting that they starred equally.

Hepburn seemed to be born without fear. While she was playing in *Coco* in New York, the building of the new Uris Theater opposite the one in which *Coco* played made a deafening noise. She strode across the street in her pants and sloppy sweater, rode the workmen's external elevator to the top of the Uris's metal framework, stepped out casually on a girder and asked the construction crew to lay off during matinees. Astonished by this red-headed, compelling woman, the workmen agreed.

Her long love affair with Spencer Tracy was the best-kept open secret in Hollywood. It was not until 1962 that an article in *Look* magazine mentioned the situation in print, breaking a reporters' silence of more than twenty years. Spencer was Catholic and would not ask for a divorce, but relations between Katharine and Spencer's wife, Louise, were gracious. His liver and kidneys were damaged beyond repair by years of heavy drinking, so that from the time Kate first knew him his health was in a dubious state. On two occasions when he collapsed and Kate believed he might not survive, she called Louise and the two women took turns standing vigil at his bedside.

In most of her roles, there was something of the real Katharine Hepburn: the maverick society girl, or the sensitive wallflower, or the eccentric rebel, or, as in *Summertime* and *The African Queen*, the harsh, disciplined woman with secret depths of gentleness and love. Some plays were even written with Kate and her special talents in mind. Garson Kanin and his wife, Ruth Gordon, wrote *Adam's Rib* for her and Tracy. They were cast as husband-and-wife lawyers opposing each other in a murder trial. In real life Kate was a militant feminist, and the real-life love story of Hepburn and Tracy was mirrored in *Adam's Rib*.

But if some aspect of the real Kate appeared in most of her roles, an exception was in Eugene O'Neill's *Long Day's Journey Into Night*. She played the tortured, morbid Mary Tyrone, a drug addict. The character was one that the actress had to study profoundly because it was against her own nature; yet she gave one of the most magnificent virtuoso performances of her career.

Except for great performances by actresses like Kate Hepburn, Hollywood stressed youth. Doris Day, Tuesday Weld, Debbie Reynolds, Sandra Dee, and others portrayed virtuous, vacuous schoolgirls in frivolous, vacuous stories. Audrey Hepburn was just as young but was awarded stronger parts.

In fashion, the accent was on femininity: hourglass shapes, cinch belts, bulky crinolines (three or four or five stiffened petticoats under full skirts).

Besides the pony tail, hair might be worn in a short and curly "poodle cut," a style made lovable by Mary Martin in *South Pacific*. In that gay and colorful musical, Mary Martin shampooed her hair onstage at every performance while she sang, "I'm gonna wash that man right out of my hair."

Girls wore soft ballet slippers called "flats" in pastel colors or they wore spike-heeled shoes with toes pointed like arrowheads. Fake furs were the style, some of them washable, and also the leotard, a stretch-nylon garment, usually black, that fitted like a second skin from neck to toe. A girl with a narrow, elegant figure could wear it as an outer garment, and other girls wore it under skirts, kilts, or skiing togs. Maternity dresses were chic; the pregnant woman no longer had to remain in modest seclusion. Most memorable of all was the breast fetish of the fifties. Huge bosoms were the very symbol of sex. Girls with fried-egg-type fronts wore falsies. All brassiéres were uplift.

All in all, fashion as usual reflected the mood of the times: in the fifties, this was an arch seductiveness, a take-me-I'm-yours, I'm-panting-for-love expression.

The report of the Kinsey team, *Sexual Behavior of the Human Female*, which appeared in 1953, surprised nobody by reporting that women have the same sexual drives that men have, but it was news that their urges begin later in life, rise to a peak at thirty or forty, and then begin tapering off. Men, on the other hand, are most ardent for sex at twenty or before, and lose interest younger. Thus a graph of male and female desire shows separate curves. As hers rises, his is already falling; the lines cross; hers goes up while his declines.

But women, Kinsey concludes, are seldom the passion flowers that men wish they were. Most of them can take sex or let it alone. Husbands are often surprised at how little their wives miss them sexually while they are separated. The venerable myth of the single woman who looks hopefully under the bed every night, alert for the waiting rapist, is only that—a myth.

To many (especially parents of teen-age girls) it came as a shock to learn that 50 percent of the women interviewed had had premarital sexual relations, and 40 percent of the married women had had extramarital affairs. In both categories, men scored higher.

The great sexual revolution took place in the 1920s. Kinsey's team—which spent forty man-years compiling their statistics—discovered that of the women who grew up before the 1920s, 86 percent were still virgins (if unmarried) at age twenty-five. But of the women who grew up after the 1920s, only 36 percent (if unmarried) were still virgins at twenty-five. Sexual behavior flipped into its new pattern at the end of World War I. The end of World War II created no such change. People just hopped in and out of beds (and cars) in the nimble style that was already established.

The revolution of the 1920s had this effect on class behavior: early in the century a young man would usually find his premarital partner among prostitutes or among factory girls. But by 1930 the girl-next-door or his classmate at college was his mate.

Following Kinsey's report on woman as a female, a second milestone book appeared, this one about woman as a social being. It is Simone de Beauvoir's *The Second Sex*, translated from the French. Without emotion but with elegant logic Mlle. de Beauvoir developed her thesis, that because woman is not considered as an individual, but is simply The Other, she is pushed into a secondary, inferior position, causing severe alienation in herself and in society. De Beauvoir's comprehensive work, which has become a classic, was a startling first. It was a forerunner of Betty Friedan's *The Feminine Mystique* and the flood of feminist books that would pour into the bookstores in the sixties.

The popular reader who may never have heard of the Beauvoir book almost certainly has heard of one called *Peyton Place*. Grace Metalious wrote a story of poverty, incest, illicit love, bigotry, and violence, a tale so lurid that the school board in her town of Gilmanton, New Hampshire, since it was unable to punish her, fired her husband who was principal of the grade school. Townspeople fumed, feeling that the author held up to the world a reflection of their town as seen in distorting, sideshow mirrors. The public, however, was so diverted by *Peyton Place* that it grew into a popular TV series.

A very different writer was the complex and subtle Flannery O'Connor of Georgia. Her work too contains horror and violence, but nothing in it is merely sensational. Ugliness is there only to illuminate the revelation that the protagonist must face. Like Carson McCullers, also of Georgia, Flannery O'Connor died tragically young, but she had already produced an impressive body of work.

Gwendolyn Brooks, poet laureate of Illinois since Carl Sandburg died, and recipient of two Guggenheim fellowships for creative writing, was the young black woman—only thirty-two at the time—who won the 1950 Pulitzer Prize for poetry. *Annie Allen* was the volume for which she was awarded the prize, and later in the decade her prose book *Maud Martha* was published.

Whether poetry or prose, the author writes with brilliance, with originality, with a keen ear and eye for the life of Chicago blacks, and with a compassion that warms every line.

She herself, growing up, did not share in the harsh, bitter life of the streets, for she was reared in a good and careful home where the parents and her brother, too, were all artists. But, as the years passed, she became more and more sympathetic toward militancy, and now writes only for a black audience. Whites may listen in, to their enlightenment, as white music lovers a generation earlier listened to Bessie Smith, who also chose to perform for fellow blacks. The poet now permits her work to be put out only by a small publishing house that specializes in promoting black authors.

All her works are a glory to read.

Harden Your Heart

"The Cross is the symbol of torture, of the sacrifice of the ideal to the non-ideal. I prefer the dollar sign, the symbol of free trade and therefore of the free mind."

So said Ayn Rand. (Pronounce "Ayn" to rhyme with "mine.") Displeased with "Alissa," the name her parents gave her, she invented her own name in 1926 when she came to America from Russia as a bitter anti-Communist. She might be tagged a radical capitalist.

One of the original, creative thinkers of the century, she authored several books, among them *The Fountainhead,* in 1943, and *Atlas Shrugged,* in 1957. *Atlas* sold nearly 1,000,000 copies and the earlier book, 1,250,000.

The novels—though they are works of philosophy as much as works of fiction—have intricate, skillfully woven plots. The characters, however, are stick figures, all the capitalist heroes being grand, statuesque inventions, while their socialist antagonists are unwholesome weaklings. The two parties engage in unlikely dialogue, with the philosophy of self-interest coming out on top.

In *Atlas Shrugged,* one of the characters is a philosopher turned pirate, who preys only on ships engaged in nonprofit ventures such as ships loaded with food for starving Europeans. He says, "I am a man . . . who robs the thieving poor and gives back to the productive rich." One speech in the book occupies sixty closely written pages. Through, 1,168 pages all told, the author never cracks a smile.

So revolutionary were Ayn Rand's ideas that they roused a fury of rage on one hand, and on the other created a cult of devout followers who called her philosophy "Objectivism." According to this system of belief, man's highest purpose is his own happiness. The concept of God is insulting and degrading to man, because it implies that man is an inferior being who can only worship an ideal without hoping to achieve it. *Atlas Shrugged* says, "As a man is a being of self-made wealth, so he is a being of self-made soul."

Ayn Rand in debate on her favorite topic was a formidable figure. A sturdy, erect woman in plain blouse and skirt, her straight dark hair cut in a Dutch bob, she would fix a glacial stare on her opponent until he quailed, then smash his silly argument with a hot rush of words.

She was a chain smoker. She didn't make jokes, go to parties, or waste time talking trivialities. She traveled only one road, and she charged down that one with mighty strides: the road of Objectivism.

Objectivists affirm that the only proper department of government is the police function: to prevent people from initiating physical force against one another. Force by wealth, power, color, intelligence, or other weapon doesn't count. All government activities except for this limited police action must cease, leaving each citizen free to survive or expire according to his energy or shrewdness.

Once in a TV interview with Mike Wallace, he remarked that she sounded strangely like Cain crying, "Am I my brother's keeper?" And Mike asked her, "Aren't you your brother's keeper?"

"I am not," she snapped. "I do not believe in the sacrifice of one man to another."

But Wallace pursued, "If you saw a man, starving, lying in the street, ill, would nothing move you to give him help?"

"If I can afford it, and if I know nothing evil about the man," she conceded, "yes, in an emergency I would help him."

No pussyfooter, she said at another time with a superb absence of modesty, "I challenge the cultural tradition of two and a half thousand years."

Ayn Rand's philosophy appealed to many Americans who were bewildered by the complex society they lived in, who growled at the cost of the welfare state, objected to paying taxes, and felt guilty about the suffering all over the world, but would have liked to harden their hearts and feel no pain. Most people, however, brought up in the Judeo-Christian tradition, were not ready to accept Self as their highest ideal.

Gift from Anne Lindbergh

In the 1950s one of America's favorite people produced a book that made thousands of women exclaim, "But she's writing about me! Yes, this is so true!"

For two weeks Mrs. Lindbergh took a vacation from family (she had five children), from household and social obligations, and lived alone in a sparsely furnished cottage on an island. Through long, contented days of solitude, she paced the beach, gathered shells, and reflected on their symbolic meanings in her life—in woman's life. All this in quiet search for a pattern that would allow outward simplicity, inner integrity, and the fullest possible relationship with other people.

Her questions have been pondered and discussed by thousands before her; but this gentle and thoughtful author had answers that reached out uniquely to the American woman.

In *Gift from the Sea*, Mrs. Lindbergh writes in simple, poetic style about the need of stilling the soul, about the ever-changing faces of love, of growth toward wisdom, about the need for uncrowding the spirit, "For it is only framed in space that beauty blooms."

Ever since her marriage to the flyer Charles A. Lindbergh in 1929, she had had to be on guard against the glare of publicity. Her photographs show a small, neat woman standing with feet side by side and one hand clasping the other hand in front of her; a composed, shy, modest woman, ready, one feels, to slide out of sight at the first seemly moment.

She has written many books: *North to the Orient, Listen! the Wind, Dearly Beloved, Earth Shine, Bring Me a Unicorn*, and others. She never wrote about the shattering experience of 1932, when her first child, eighteen-month-old Charles Lindbergh, Jr., was kidnaped and killed. A recent book, however, *Hour of Gold, Hour of Lead*, is a collection of her letters and diaries from that period, and they reveal a young woman of courageous poise in the face of horror. Probably every woman alive during that time grieved for the young mother and identified with her.

Two years after *Gift from the Sea*, her book *The Unicorn and Other Poems* appeared, and John Ciardi reviewed it for the *Saturday Review* not only unfavorably but with explosive disapproval, even scorn. Mr. Ciardi did not criticize the poet, only her poetry. But the reaction from his readers! One would have thought he had condemned her morals and her loyalty to the Union. Women (most of Mrs. Lindbergh's defenders were women) wrote to him in furious protest. They accused him of brutality, of ignorance, of insulting a great American. This raging storm proved, as nothing else could, how highly venerated Anne Lindbergh was. What of the lady herself during the battle of people *vs.* critic? She declined to make any comment at all.

STORM AND STRUGGLE

The Black Rebellion

Many leading ladies of the 1960s were revolutionaries. It was a stormy, passionate decade, marked by an ugly war abroad, rioting in the streets at home, a rising crime rate, a frightening drug problem, defiance of the young toward the old, a deteriorating environment. Would you expect such revolutionary times to produce only women who were charming actresses, cheerful wives, and chairmen of PTA bazaars?

At six o'clock one December morning in 1955 a young housewife stood at the window of her darkened living room watching for the first bus of the day to stop in front of her house. It rumbled down the street, headlights blazing in the winter darkness. "Martin! Martin!" she called. "Come quickly!" Her husband ran to stand beside her, both their faces shining with excitement. Not one person rode that usually crowded bus.

This was the first day of the bus boycott in Montgomery, Alabama, a dramatic day in the long fight to achieve equal rights for black Americans. And the boycott was working.

Coretta Scott King, the wife of Martin Luther King, Jr., was totally dedicated to that movement.

Coretta King was a strong character. She was still a college girl, studying music on a scholarship at the New England Conservatory in Boston when she decided to marry the young minister. After careful reflection, she determined that, no matter what happened after she married him, she would adjust to the new conditions. Wherever Martin lived, she would live there too. Whatever he did she would be involved in.

These were not the exaltations of an emotional girl dazzled by love.

They were the decisions of a young woman who had, after thoughtful inward debate, chosen her path. Deliberately, she turned her back on a career as a concert singer to become the wife of a man she knew was even more dominant than she was.

Do not think because she was deliberate that she was cold. Coretta loved her husband, their four children, her close-knit family, and his, and many friends. A strong woman, she loved strongly.

She and Martin were both deeply religious. They believed that God was infinite and also personal, a loving father who strives for good against evil in the universe. They believed that they were His instruments in a divine plan and purpose. Again and again in the fifteen years of their marriage, as the freedom struggle moved from one phase to the next, Coretta had the sense of being propelled by God in a positive direction.

The King family and all their co-workers in the Southern Christian Leadership Conference, of which Dr. King became the first president, believed in nonviolence because of their dedication to the teachings of Christ. From the first, it was a church-oriented movement. But they were not, they said, "passive resisters." They were a militant organization which believed that the most powerful weapon was nonviolence. Gandhi was their model.

Young Mrs. King worked in every department of her husband's two churches, first in Montgomery, Alabama, and later in Atlanta, Georgia, and with her well-trained voice was especially active in the choirs. She also worked beside Martin in every facet of the fight for equal rights.

First there was the Montgomery struggle to desegregate buses; then sit-ins in Atlanta and in Albany, Georgia, to desegregate restaurants; "freedom rides" all over the South to integrate interstate buses; and protests in Birmingham.

In the summer of 1963 the great March on Washington took place, when 250,000 people, one-fourth of them white, assembled near the Lincoln Memorial. What an inspiring sight that was! Lovely Camilla Williams began the ceremonies by singing "The Star-Spangled Banner." Marian Anderson was to have sung it, but to her disappointment her plane was delayed. There were many speakers and Mahalia Jackson sang with much "soul." Lena Horne too was among the notables. It was an afternoon of heart-stopping emotion, when millions of people believed that integration was almost won.

By now Coretta and Martin Luther King, Jr., had been married for ten years, years of continuous effort and turmoil. Coretta, brimful of energy and idealism, loved being at the heart of one of the great movements of history, whether her task was to make a speech, to parade in a freedom march, or to visit Martin in jail. Though never arrested, she would have been fiercely glad to serve time in jail, too.

Her unique contribution to the movement was a series of programs that she called Freedom Concerts. She invented the format. It alternated between narrative and song, and she performed solo with a piano accompanist. The opening number was a talk entitled "The American Dream," followed by a song; then narration again, "The Dream Blighted," followed by another song. Orally, she carried the story of the freedom movement from 1955 to 1965, interspersing narration with such numbers as "He's Got the Whole World in His Hands," "Lord, I Can't Turn Back," "No Crystal Stair," and always ending with the stirring "We Shall Overcome."

At first Dr. King did not believe that her concerts would succeed as a fund-raising effort, but in fact she earned more than $50,000 for the SCLC and its affiliates. One hopes that after the last concert she looked him squarely in the eye and said, "I told you so."

Her life as a housekeeper was hectic. The phone rang all day and most of the night, some calls being obscene hate calls. The house often boiled with people there for meetings, or to spend the night, or to have a meal. There might be no dinner guests, or there might be a dozen unannounced. She learned to cook in quantity, and to be cheerful about it when the food, instead of being served when ready, stood on the stove for hours drying out and "waiting," as she said, "for slow-moving history."

She gave close attention to her children. As black children and as children of a famous father, they faced special problems. Jail, for example. She carefully explained that their father's imprisonments were not a disgrace, as some of their classmates thought, but a mark of honor. When the father was jailed in Albany, Georgia, Coretta was deeply touched to hear four-year-old Marty consoling his older sister, who was six. Christened Yolanda, her pet name was Yoki. Marty sat on the edge of her bed with one leg folded under him and said, "Don't cry, Yoki. Daddy will be back. He has to help the people. He's already helped some people, but he has to help some more, and when he finishes he'll be back. Don't cry."

The mother also carefully schooled all the children to have a healthy attitude toward the color of their skin. She seemed to have succeeded, but one day Yoki, then seven, remarked plaintively that white people are pretty and Negroes are ugly. Coretta exclaimed, "But, Yolanda, that's not true! There are pretty people in all races." She picked up a copy of *Ebony* that happened to lie on a table and sat down with the little girl to look through its pages. "See her," said the mother. "See how beautiful she is." Or, "Isn't he handsome?" Yoki agreed to every comment. When they finished the magazine, Yoki said, "You know, colored people are pretty and white people are ugly."

"Oh, no!" cried her mother. "That's not right either!" She had to start all over again.

The Kings had gay and loving times together, but on the day that President Kennedy was shot and the parents sat side by side watching the events on television, Martin said somberly, "This is going to happen to me also." Coretta could not say, "It won't happen to you." For a long time she had faced the possibility that he would be murdered. She could only move closer to him and hold his hand tightly in hers. For the rest of their time together, the specter of assassination was always with her.

Shortly after Easter in 1968, King and other SCLC leaders met in Memphis to plan a protest march in that city. Tragedy struck April 4, when Martin Luther King, Jr., was shot as he stood on the balcony of a motel in Memphis.

Coretta accepted her loss with deep grief but with no bitterness, because she believed that to the end her husband was an instrument in the hand of the Lord. The funeral took place in Atlanta on the following Tuesday, but so strong was this woman that on Monday, the day of the scheduled march, she traveled to Memphis with Harry Belafonte, other friends, and the three oldest King children to represent her husband. (Bunny, then five, was too young to go.) She and the children marched a mile to City Hall at the head of a crowd of between 25,000 and 50,000 people.

Many speeches were made, all on the theme of Martin Luther King's life. Coretta, when it was her turn to speak, talked firmly and quietly about his qualities as a husband, a father, and a leader.

Nonviolence was the keystone of all King's plans. For ten years he was able to hold his followers to the Gandhi principle. But in 1965 he had chosen Selma, Alabama, as the target for demonstrations that he hoped would lead to voter registration rights. There violence erupted.

From that time forward, the protest against blacks became more and more violent. Homes of black leaders were bombed (including the Kings' house) and a bomb exploded in a Birmingham church during a

Sunday-school session and killed four little black girls. Marchers were murdered. In some counties, there was unconcealed collusion between white hoodlums and law-enforcement officers.

Now the blacks struck back. There was rioting in the Watts section of Los Angeles, in Chicago, in Detroit, in Newark. White backlash followed. The year 1969 was the bloodiest of all the years of the black struggle.

Civil rights are not yet won. Pessimists say that the position of the black was worse in 1970 than in 1960. Optimists point instead to these figures:

In 1960, nonwhites earned 52 percent as much as whites. In 1968, 63 percent.

In 1960, 39 percent of nonwhites finished high school. In 1968, 58 percent did.

A Gallup poll showed that 54 percent of blacks were satisfied with their work in 1960, but in 1968, 76 percent said they were satisfied.

In 1960, 22 percent of blacks lived below the poverty line. In 1968, 12 percent.

Freedom Singer

Erect and motionless, Joan Baez stood in the spotlight at Madison Square Garden and in her sweet, pure soprano sang to a packed audience. With two accompanists behind her, she sang Negro spirituals, political songs, and love songs, all with the seemingly effortless control and the purity of tone and phrasing that one usually expects only from an accomplished classical singer. Her listeners, however, mostly people under thirty, clad in jerseys and bell-bottom jeans, probably were there less because of her voice than because they believed in the messages expressed in her songs. She was the passionate advocate of peace, love, and freedom.

Between numbers she stood there on the stage in her purple maternity smock and talked to the audience in a simple, direct fashion as if she were talking to a friend. She had a recent letter from David, she said. David, as all of them knew, was her husband. He was serving a jail sentence for refusing induction into the army. She was proud of him. "If we are going to have the revolution in this country that we need," she said, "we have all got to be willing to go to jail."

For her last number she sang "We Shall Overcome," and invited the audience to join in. After the few first notes, all the people in the Garden quietly got to their feet as if the song were their national anthem.

Photographs of Joan Baez never do her justice. They emphasize the length and narrowness of her face, and a certain Indianlike stolidity. People are surprised, meeting her face to face, at the delicacy of her features and at her shining, candid expression.

Older people withheld approval of that Baez woman. "Rabble rouser," they said darkly. "Narrow-minded—arrogant—a violent hater." They were quite right. She saw little but the evil in society. "Takes drugs, I bet, like all those hippies." There her critics were wrong. She spurned all copouts, whether they were silent-generation consumerites or flower children who dreamed along on LSD. She said she chose to get high on natural things, like the earth, trees, the blue sky, friends.

Al Capp, creator of the *Li'l Abner* comic strip, introduced into his cartoon sequence a guitar-playing, folk-singing grotesque named Joanie Phoanie, who twanged such songs as "A Molotov cocktail or two / Will blow up the boys in blue." Joan Baez was huffy, considering herself ridiculed, but the cartoonist replied blandly, "Protest singers don't own protest. When she protests others' right to protest, she's killing the whole racket."

Joan was the leading female exponent of the anti-war movement (unless you put Jane Fonda first) and Joan led the cheering whenever draft-card burning made the news. But, "I'm not a pacifist," she would say. "I am a nonviolent soldier who refuses to use weapons. Nonviolence is confronting violence and coming up with something better, such as submitting to prison." She was jailed many times.

Young people flocked to hear this militant singer at rallies, at protest meetings, at sit-ins and love-ins, and they bought her records, especially "Where Have All the Flowers Gone?," Pete Seeger's wistful anti-war ballad. She was so popular that on one tour abroad she earned $8,500 for each appearance, and that was nice for her because, she naïvely confessed, she enjoyed luxury. Often, however, she refused to charge high fees. At Madison Square Garden, for example, she insisted that every ticket be priced at $2, though she was urged to ask more.

A book she wrote, entitled *Daybreak*, reduced her stature rather than enhancing it. Her written message, sentimental and naïve, lacked the power of her singing.

In the fall semester of 1964, she took part in the campus revolt at Berkeley. Wearing a jeweled crucifix and strumming her guitar, she led a thousand University of California students into Sproul Hall, all of them lustily singing "We Shall Overcome." They carried in books, food, and sleeping bags.

For fifteen hours the students camped in corridors, played jacks, watched old Charlie Chaplin movies, and had a boisterous good protest. They also filled staircases and held "freedom classes," most of them taught by graduate students on standard academic subjects; but there were some fanciful classes too.

The protest, led by a group called the Free Speech Movement, had grown as naturally as milkweed in the prevailing 1960s climate of unrest, discontent, and idealism. Many participants had been active in civil rights movements, some of them in the Bay Area, while others had gone south to take part in the freedom marches. The immediate cause of the Berkeley protest, or revolution, as the university's chancellor and the governor of California called it, was the university's objection to the students' taking active part in politics. Less specific was a disgruntled feeling that the whole university was dehumanized, that students were no more than IBM cards in a mechanized bureaucracy.

At any rate, Governor Edmund G. Brown ordered police to clear Sproul Hall. It took twelve hours, because most prisoners went limp and had to be dragged off. Eight hundred of them were arrested, not gently, and they were hauled away in paddy wagons. Faculty members already had $85,000 bail bond money collected. It was gratifying to the Free Speech activists that so large a part of the faculty was staunchly behind them. Eventually the protestors won their demands from the school administration.

The Berkeley revolution was only the first in a series of campus uprisings across the nation. One summer a few years later, the National Students' Association met in Manhattan, Kansas. This was a students' group that had been, up to this time, as sedate as any PTA, but like other young people its members hated the war in Vietnam, and they struggled with the feeling that their lives were totally controlled by inhuman agencies—the Pentagon, the draft board, the government, the multiversity—which cared nothing for them as human beings, and on which they had no influence.

When, in the course of their conference, a senior from the University of Hawaii borrowed a cigarette lighter and, with shaking hands, burned his draft card, they stood up and cheered. To show their defiance of materialistic values, they set fire to dollar bills, and then enthusiastically passed a resolution condemning the criminal action of the government against the people of Vietnam.

One of the most widely publicized revolts on campus was at Columbia University. During a sit-in, the call went out for women volunteers to cook for the hungry strikers. One young female revolutionary jumped up and protested that women hadn't joined the movement just to work in the kitchen; and the call was amended for *people* to help prepare food.

Protest groups usually assigned typing and mimeographing jobs to the girls, while the men were busy in policy meetings. Old stereotypes die hard.

"You Can't Trust Anyone Over Thirty"

The term "hippy" is not easy to define because hippies came in so many shapes and sizes. The young drug addict who freaked out on the sidewalk and let his friends provide enough food to keep him alive was a hippy, and so was the hard-working member of a farm commune who got high only on rock music. There were weekend hippies, too, who worked for a living Monday through Friday; then on Saturday and Sunday cast off their disguises, put on faded pants and torn shirts, and mingled happily with their dissociated kindred.

But three things seemed common to all: rejection of society's values; a deep need to live in a close-knit group; and the wearing of weird garments.

The girls wore shapeless granny dresses that reached the feet (bare feet unless the weather was very cold), or they wore tight jeans and sleeveless jerseys that never looked quite clean. (No shaving of the armpits—razors aren't natural.) A feather boa or a soiled velvet cape might add variety to the costume.

The young people lived in families or tribes and looked after each other with passionate care as if, in their alienation from their past, they feared loneliness above death. In 1965 and 1966, at the height of the Haight-Ashbury concentration in San Francisco, tribes would live together—as many as fifteen or twenty in one small, half-furnished apartment, sharing clothes, food, and mattresses. One member, or perhaps two, would assume responsibility for feeding the others and providing grass, LSD, or speed. Jobs were easy to find. The post office employed hippies for semi-skilled jobs, and there were always calls for unskilled labor. The workers, who were also of course the leaders, willingly shared all they earned with the family. Other members panhandled from tourists who came to gawk. "How about a quarter, lady, to support my habit?" Or "Got a loose dollar, fella?" The beggar had no sense of shame. He expected to share whatever he got, so why shouldn't outsiders share with him?

In Haight-Ashbury days, there was an organized group called the Diggers, who took their name from a seventeenth-century organization which seized crown lands and cultivated them to provide food for the poor. The Diggers bought or begged food in quantity and distributed it every evening to the nonworking hippies.

One conventional young family of mother, father, and children, who farmed on a hill outside San Francisco, expected the Diggers to call at the farm once a week for a supply of vegetables and fruit. The young mother said sharply, "Of course I want those hippies to be fed. I understand why they've copped out. But me? I'd rather make beautiful children than beautiful dreams."

Naturally the hippy families were fluid. Members drifted away and new ones attached themselves to the group. Sex played its part in the cohering and melting away, but drug users are not very sexy. The group seemed more important to them than any one lover.

About four people a day were taken from Haight-Ashbury to the emergency ward of San Francisco hospitals, gone completely awry on a "bum trip." One distraught girl, supported on one side by a nurse, on the other side by a white-clad male attendant, lurched down a hospital corridor calling piteously, "But where are my friends? Do my friends know where I am? Where are my friends?"

Instead of merely drifting like the much-publicized Haight-Ashbury group, some hippies went to the land, determined to found a small, nonviolent, nonhypocritical society. No two communes had exactly the same ideals. Few survived more than a few years, but they provided earnest young people with enough time and space to puzzle out their own life patterns.

Parents, abandoned by sons and daughters, were sorely wounded. Young people laughed at the sacrifices made for them, sneered at the dreams dreamed over them, and shrugged away the importance of those years of care devoted to them. The young people, in their bigotry, thought they were free of the vices they saw so clearly in others: bigotry, selfishness, and the arrogant uses of power.

The alienated young might be divided into three classes, with the hippies in the middle. On one side there were the political activists, the New Left, who believed that with strenuous effort they could correct the evils of society. Some hippies were dropouts from this group. On the other side were people in mystical, religious groups—here again is that desperate need to belong to something.

Conventional churches had no answers for these young intellectuals. Each had to search out a personal meaning to life. They longed for a deity, not sure they would ever find it. They explored Eastern religions, the occult, witchcraft, astrology. Some consulted *I Ching*, the Chinese book of divination, before making any decisions.

Most of these bright young men and women hated science. What had science achieved except smaller souls and bigger wars? Science was anti-life. Faith in their instincts, faith in their emotions, that was a quality shared by many of the young. Loud music, dancing that resembled the ecstasies of old-time revivals, even uncouth manners and uglified clothing were "natural" and therefore good.

The performer who typified this life style was Janis Joplin.

When Janis sang into the mike, she sang with every limb, every muscle, every emotion. She poured out a river of energy that made her radiant and magical to her audience. She was unattractive, really: she had coarse skin, a big nose, and uncombed hair that tumbled down her back. She wore dozens of jangling bracelets, rings on every finger, bright blue hose—or red, or green—and a loose velvet blouse, or a skintight sheath.

When someone asked her what she made of her life, she said, "Getting stoned, staying happy, and having a good time doing just what I want." She was a blues singer, and you can sing the blues to a lover, to the sky, to an enchanted audience, to the moon. Janis shouted her blues to the whole world—loud, sad, angry, spontaneous, turning blues into screaming, wailing nightmare.

"When I get scared and worried, I tell myself, 'Janis, just have a good time!' So I juice up real good and that's just what I have. Whatever I do, I do a lot, and whatever it is, it's a damn sight better than being bored."

She gloried in self-destruction. "Sure, I could take better care of my health. It might add a few years, but what the hell?"

At twenty-seven, she died of an overdose of drugs.

Meanwhile, what of the young people who were not hippies? Of course they rebelled against their parents' way of life, but only in a ritual fashion. The new dancing represented the change. "The twist" it was called at first, and as the decade passed the twist went through a number of variations. Boys and girls could dance as partners or alone or in a mass, the only rule being to dance hard, with the whole body, feet kicking, arms waving, hips gyrating. Each dancer was doing his thing, but all of them were doing it together.

Costumes had never been so interesting. Unconsciously, every woman demonstrated her life style by her clothes. The conservative lady wore a neat dress not much above the knee, or a tailored pants suit. The flashy woman wore green eyelids, heavy false eyelashes, and built up her hair tall and elaborate, like Marie Antoinette's. The fat old lady recapturing her youth wore skin-tight shorts, brilliantly figured shirt, and vivid yellow hair cut short. Girls who were with it wore broad, thick shoes, steel-rimmed spectacles, frayed pants, and the inevitable long, straight hair. Many of the girls were as clean as spring violets, but they didn't want that to show. The young also wore narrow skirts up to mid-thigh (mini) and for a winter or two they wore heavy, dark coats that went down to the instep (maxi).

Every generation of the century was different. In the twenties, young people were pleasure-oriented. In the thirties they were economically austere (not by choice) and politically radical. Political and social apathy marked the youth of the forties and fifties, but in the 1960s there was a widespread and wonderful sense of social commitment. Young men and women wanted a better world, and many of them worked for it, in the Peace Corps or VISTA, in community involvement, in church affairs.

Scientist and Poet in One Package

The most revolutionary woman of the decade was a slight, gentle person with a quiet smile. Her incendiary weapons were binoculars, microscope, and hundreds of written records that she studied in preparing the most influential book of the century, *Silent Spring*.

Rachel Carson's book altered the course of history by turning the direction of man's thinking. A number of scientists had been uneasy for years about damage to the planet and all its occupants, inflicted by lavish use of pesticides; but not until *Silent Spring* came out in 1962 did the average citizen learn of the possible doom of the world as we know it.

What fury and uproar when that book appeared! Some experts damned it as hysterical and half-baked. Others praised its careful scholarship. The suburban flower gardener stood on one foot, spray can in hand, afraid to go after the bugs and unwilling not to. A cartoon of the sixties showed a lugubrious customer at a bar, staring into his drink and muttering, "Just when I get used to the Bomb ... along comes Rachel Carson."

She was born in 1907 in the tiny town of Springdale, Pennsylvania, in the lower Allegheny Valley. A shy and solitary child, she was allured by two ideas: to become a writer and to know the ocean, which she never saw until she was nearly grown up. Fascinated, she read all the sea literature she could find. At college she majored in marine zoology and then spent summers at the Marine Biological Laboratory at Woods Hole in Massachusetts. There she not only drudged through hundreds of dry and technical papers in the library to answer all the questions that teemed in her mind, but also spent happy hours sloshing through barnacle-covered tidepools, scooping up specimens from the icy water to examine them with a hand lens, and watching the racing tidal currents pouring through the "Hole."

In her free time, Rachel Carson loved to slip away from the world of men into the secret world of the small, wordless creatures who inhabit the globe with us. Once she became enthralled by the night sounds of insects in her own back yard and wrote: "Most haunting of all [of the crickets] is the one I call the fairy bellringer. I have never found him— I'm not sure I want to. For his voice, and surely he himself, are so ethereal, so delicate, so other-worldly, that he should remain invisible, as he has through all the nights I have searched for him."

In a letter to a friend, written during a summer holiday in Maine, she wrote: "There is a wonderful pine woods up over the hill, all carpeted with reindeer moss and full of the most wonderful smells when the sun is hot on the evergreens. It is a happy hunting ground for warblers, and you can almost always hear their lispy little voices in the trees overhead."

In 1936 Miss Carson went to work for the U.S. Fish and Wildlife Service, and became director of its publishing program. The service issued many booklets on wildlife refuges, bird migrations, and similar topics, so that she and her six assistants actually did the work of a small publishing house.

It was a demanding assignment, but she had such zest and humor that she was never bored. She and her colleagues had a good deal of quiet fun on the job. A group of them usually met for sandwiches at noon and for tea during breaks, and their droll discussions turned stuffy official methods and solemn stupidities into matters of gaiety.

Her civil service pay, however, had to be stretched to the snapping point. Besides herself, she had a family of three to support: her mother (who, to the end of her life at eighty-nine, was one of Rachel's dearest companions) and two little nieces, whose mother, Rachel's sister, had died. To earn more money, she turned to her cherished pursuit of writing. In 1941 she published her first book, *Under the Sea Wind.* Though it had good reviews, it was a disappointment financially, bringing her less than $1,000. Magazine articles paid better, but she felt impelled to do something more lasting and important than short pieces, and spent three years writing *The Sea Around Us,* though in a sense she had been working on it all her life. In the course of the writing, she consulted more than one thousand separate printed sources and corresponded with oceanographers and other specialists all over the world. She wrote painstakingly both for scientific accuracy and for perfection of style.

The Sea Around Us was a triumph. *The New Yorker* published about half of it in a three-part series called "Profile of the Sea" and the public response was greater than it had been to any previous material in the magazine. The *New York Times* voted it the outstanding book of the year, it won the National Book Award, and it stayed on the best-seller list for eighty-six weeks.

As for money—its astonished author never again had to be anxious about pennies. She was even able to gratify the longing of years: she bought a bit of land on the coast of Maine and there built a house, where she spent every summer for the rest of her life. She also retired from government service to devote full time to writing.

A modest woman, she was surprised at the interest her readers had in Rachel Carson the person, just because they liked her book; and she quietly declined to open the door to her private life, though she accepted many speaking engagements and worked arduously at answering all of the flood of letters from around the world.

Many people were charmed by the lucid and beautiful style of *The Sea Around Us;* the author was equally scientist and poet. "If there is poetry in my book about the sea," she said, "it is not because I deliberately put it there, but because no one could write truthfully about the sea and leave out the poetry."

But she could not settle into repose merely because she had become successful and famous. As early as 1945 she was troubled by the insect-control programs instituted by the Fish and Wildlife Service, and in the late fifties when DDT and other miracle sprays began to be used over wide areas, often distributed by airplane, she felt it imperative that someone protest, not only for the welfare of wildlife but for the sake of public health. Indiscriminate killing of insects, followed by the death of insect-eating birds, was upsetting the delicate balance of nature.

DDD, when applied to a lake in California in order to kill gnats, resulted in a house-that-Jack-built sequence. Large carnivorous fish ate smaller carnivorous fish that had eaten herbivorous fish that had eaten plankton that had absorbed the poison from the water. All of their bodies contained concentrations of DDD greater than the concentration originally applied to the water. What of the human fisherman at the top of the chain, who caught a string of fish from this lake and took them home to fry for supper?

A story made the rounds of a cannibal king who forbade his people to eat any more Americans because their fat was contaminated with chlorinated hydrocarbons.

Rachel Carson herself was reluctant to take on the project of publicizing the dangers of widespread insect spraying. This was partly because she knew she would be ridiculed and attacked for taking an unpopular stand; and also because her private life was complicated.

Marjorie, one of the nieces whom she had reared, fell victim to pneumonia and died, leaving a five-year-old son. Miss Carson felt that she was the logical member of the small family to adopt Roger and rear him, though by that time she was just short of fifty. In addition, she suffered severe sinus infections, developed a heart condition and an ulcer, had arthritis in her hands, and was soon to learn that she had an inoperable cancer.

Nevertheless, she concluded that there would be no peace for her if she kept silent about this matter of pesticides, which she believed was a danger of the grimmest kind.

Consequently, she set to work on her long task. It took four years to complete. The writing of *Silent Spring* required an enormous amount of correspondence and the study of innumerable records, and ill health often slowed her progress so that she would nearly despair of finishing. She once said that she felt like the Red Queen in *Alice*, who had to run as fast as she could just to stay where she was.

The time came, however, when the manuscript was completed, and one night after Roger was asleep she took her pet cat into the study, turned on the record player and listened to her favorite record, Beethoven's violin concerto. Suddenly the tension of four years broke and she wept. Next day she wrote to a friend, "I had said I could never again listen happily to a thrush song if I had not done all I could. And last night the thoughts of all the birds and other creatures and all the loveliness that is in nature came to me with such a surge of deep happiness, now that I had done what I could."

One of the basic conflicts of our time is involved in the challenge of *Silent Spring*. The chemical industry considers that it is all right to use poisons unless danger has been proved beyond all reasonable doubt. Rachel Carson's argument is that chemicals must not be used unless their safety has been proved.

Pesticide manufacturers paid for research on chemicals in universities. The food industry supported research on nutrition in many other university laboratories. Consequently, heavily sarcastic reports from these labs belittling *Silent Spring* have to be suspect. In the same vein, the American Medical Association, during the conflict that followed publication of the book, referred its members to an information kit compiled by the National Agricultural Chemicals Association.

On the other hand, specialists in public health supported Rachel Carson's position. So did the press. So did the public which had no financial stake in pesticides.

The author was scoffed at as a sentimental bird lover and a bleeding heart obsessed with the romance of the balance of nature. She never replied angrily. She did point out that you can no more ignore the balance of nature than a man on the edge of a cliff can ignore the law of gravity.

Rachel Carson died in 1964, but lived long enough to see her position vindicated. She did not live to see the full power of the environmental revolution. It was one of the great movements of the 1960s, and she had played a major part in its beginning.

Articulate Professor

From the time her first book was published in 1928, no American woman has had so much to say about so many things, or said it so positively, as anthropologist Margaret Mead. She has poured out magazine articles and letters to the editor, served on countless scientific panels, and delivered lectures all over the country, sometimes as many as eighty in one year.

She is a woman of inexhaustible energy. Short (five feet two) and broad, she swings her arms like a member of the Cold Stream Guards when she walks, and in talking makes spirited gestures with both hands.

She wears plain, undistinguished dresses, parts her curly hair in the middle, and often wears prim, rimless glasses. She cares a lot less about how she looks than about what she and those about her think. In unprofessional hours she enjoys science-fiction books, the theater (she has gone to as many as forty plays in one season), lives in Greenwich Village, and attends St. Luke's Episcopal Chapel regularly. She is bossy and excited about life and fun to be with, and she is a disciplined scientist.

She made eleven voyages to the islands of the far South Pacific to study the disappearing life-styles of the occupants. Her books, a dozen of them, are written with a beautiful clarity and simplicity seldom reached by scientists, this lucidity being the reason they are so widely read by the nonscientific public. Fellow anthropologists, who disapprove of the popular approach, hurl at her the vilest epithet known in scientific circles. "Journalist!" they hiss.

In her lectures she is a spellbinder like a politician of old. Her language is precise, but idiomatic. She does what few other scientists do: she makes anthropology relevant to today's society. She says, for example, that Americans might well study the easy, unstrained life of Samoans to learn how adolescents can survive without the trauma common in our culture.

Studying today's American youth, she says that we are faced with the first generation of students who feel involved in war and politics. She predicts that they will now take more responsibility for the policies of their universities, and will involve themselves in civic and government affairs.

Retiring in 1969 as curator of ethnology at the American Museum of Natural History, and as professor of anthropology at Columbia University, she is one of those rare and wonderful people who will never slow down until the clock stops entirely.

Rebel in the Theater

Judy Garland was seventeen and looked twelve when she made *The Wizard of Oz* and immortality.

Millions were captivated then by Judy's childlike grace, by the huge dark eyes, wonderlit and innocent, and by the tender, vulnerable mouth. Not to mention that clear, sweet voice that expressed everyone's longing to go "Somewhere over the rainbow."

Millions more are captivated every year when *The Wizard* reappears on television. Judy Garland as Dorothy of Oz is as much a part of Americana as homemade quilts, the story of the Pilgrims, and San Francisco cable cars.

She made her first public appearance at the age of four, when a relative pushed her onstage to sing "Jingle Bells." Her two older sisters, doing a song-and-dance act in their father's Grand Rapids theater, backed off, because who can compete with a curly-haired moppet piping away? Judy sang chorus after chorus while her mother played the theater piano and the audience laughed and applauded. That day began Judy's lifelong love affair with an audience.

Soon after that, probably, she began her lifelong hate affair with her mother. Mrs. Gumm (Judy assumed the name Garland later) was grimly determined that all three of her daughters were going to become actresses. The youngest was the most marketable, and the mother soon concentrated on her. The family broke up, leaving the other two girls with their father (whom Judy adored and longed for), and Mrs. Gumm pressed Judy into vaudeville and finally into the movies at MGM. But, though she loved the profession, and though during her stardom she and Mrs. Gumm shared a mansion in Hollywood, Judy always spoke with bitter vindictiveness of her mother, who never showed her any tenderness.

She also hated Louis B. Mayer, the stern, tyrannical chief of MGM. All her life she was in revolt against authority. MGM exploited her as a commodity because, an executive said, the studio "had $14 million tied up in her" and couldn't afford to risk their investment in protecting the mere health of a human being. Judy made fifteen movies before she was twenty.

The girl with the fresh, young voice was already on pills by the time she was fourteen. To begin with, she had a difficult weight problem, and took amphetamines as appetite depressants. They made her jittery and hyperactive, so she took sleeping pills at bedtime.

She and Mickey Rooney were America's favorite teen-age sweethearts in the "Andy Hardy" series. Though they never had a love affair, Mickey remained a staunch friend to the end of Judy's troubled life.

She said that MGM kept both of them at work days and nights on end, feeding them pep-up pills to keep them on their feet when they were exhausted. Then they'd be taken to the studio hospital and knocked out with sleeping pills, Mickey collapsing onto one bed and she on another. After four hours, they would be awakened, given more pep pills, and put back to work. "Half the time we were hanging from the ceiling, but it became a way of life for us."

In later years, a nurse or physician stood by on the set to give Judy a "pop" of morphine in the arm to help her complete a day's shooting schedule. But it was probably not until she made *A Star Is Born*, when she was past thirty, that Judy slipped over the thin line into drug addiction, against which she had to struggle for the rest of her life. A few years later, she had a physical checkup in a hospital. Chronologically, she was relatively young, but the medical reports showed that physically she was already an old woman.

Victim of drugs and alcohol, victim of her own confusion and despair, she lacked the stern self-discipline of a Katharine Hepburn (another loyal friend), which might have saved her. But, as Judy saw it, all her troubles were the fault of her enemies, or of circumstances she was helpless to control.

Lonely and afraid of life, she kept seeking love. "I can never feel complete when I'm not in love," she said. Yet she divorced four husbands. Always she craved more of a person than he could give; she was never fully gratified. When she married for the fifth time, only a few months before her death at forty-seven, she announced jubilantly, "Finally, finally, I am loved! This is it, I *know* this is it! For the very first time in my life I'm happy, really happy! I have never *been* so happy!"

Though many men loved Judy and left her, three people in her life remained steadfast in their affections: her three children. Liza Minnelli, a handsome and talented actress herself, is the child of Judy's second husband, director Vincente Minnelli. Lorna and Joey are children of her third husband, Sid Luft. Judy kept the three children with her when she traveled and she lavished on them all the tenderness that she had longed for and been denied by her own mother.

Theirs was an unusual childhood: always moving from place to place; witnessing scenes of temper, melancholy, and wild joy; as familiar with backstage shadows as with playground sunlight. Yet they say that they knew the essential stability: they could always depend on their mother's interest and concern.

Judy's friends did not fare so well. Bitterly she said she had few friends that she hadn't paid for, and that when the money ran out, so did they. She failed to remember the times when in her cups or in one of her black moods she shrieked at them, insulted them, broke her promises to them, failed to turn up for rehearsal with them, forced them to waste hours waiting for her; she forgot the times she refused to act when it didn't suit her. Some friends were alienated by the fact that while she had the manners of a duchess (when she chose) she also had the vocabulary of a stevedore.

But how this woman could sway an audience! In 1951, when her career was on the rocks, she went to London and appeared at the Palladium. She was scared to death to face a live audience. But she strode to the microphone, opened her mouth, and let that golden voice pour forth. How they applauded! Presently, as she sang on and on, jubilating in the love that poured forth to her, she began tapping her feet, she twirled, and fell flat on her back. Judy's accompanist rushed to pull her to her feet and found her laughing. She seized the mike again amid a roar of cheers: "Go on, Judy! We love you!" When she finished the concert, they gave her a standing ovation.

She made comeback after comeback like that one.

In 1963 she starred in *The Judy Garland Show* on TV. It was canceled after twenty-six weeks. At one performance she announced that her next number would be a song she very much wanted to sing and she hoped they would understand. It was only a few weeks after President Kennedy's assassination. Then, after no rehearsal with the orchestra because CBS executives had already turned down her idea of doing a concert of great American songs, and she was defying them, she sang "The Battle Hymn of the Republic." Psychologically, her timing was perfect. She stood with head thrown back, eyes shining. The studio audience wept. The cameraman cried and so did the crew and the staff. Everyone who heard Judy Garland broke up, remembering the loss of their president.

Many great performers have had ardent followers. But Judy Garland had a cult. Those who worshiped her loved both the sweet, serious little girl singing "Over the Rainbow" and they loved the sad and broken woman up there on the stage.

All those comebacks helped to create the Judy Garland cult. And the fact that she could fall down flat in public and then jump up and sing again. Further, everybody knew that she was a victim of drugs and drink and a life without discipline. They knew she loved and lost and loved again. She was battered and despairing and laughing and rebellious. She was the very symbol of failure and defiance.

And so the defeated old, and the homosexuals, and the alienated young, and those with insoluble problems, and those with pain greater than they knew how to bear identified with Judy Garland. They flocked to hear her sing, and they mourned when she died of an overdose of drugs, probably accidental, in June of 1969.

First Lady

The most admired and most disliked woman of the 1960s was Jacqueline Kennedy.

What style she had! She stood erect, head poised elegantly, hands relaxed at her sides. Public admiration is proved by the way young women imitated her bouffant hairdo, pillbox hats, sheath dresses, short white gloves.

The John F. Kennedys' informal style of entertaining was copied, too. All of their social affairs were gayer, younger, more fun than had ever been seen at the White House. For the first time, cocktails were served before dinner and smoking was permitted. The presidential couple never had a formal receiving line except at state dinners. At receptions they mingled with the guests, shaking hands here and there, chatting casually.

Jacqueline's voice was so soft it seemed almost a whisper, but what she said was never lost. People leaned closer and listened more intently to her than to other women. But, though she spoke gently, those who wished to be her friends or to continue in her employ learned not to cross her.

Mrs. Kennedy had no close women friends except her sister Lee. Kennedy sisters-in-law did not drop in at the White House for a chat, nor did wives of government officials. Unlike Rose Kennedy, who was always out among people, Jacqueline kept to her own quarters when she was in Washington. At White House events, she was unfailingly gracious and poised, but aloof.

In private, however, she romped with the children, Caroline and John, as gaily and easily as if she were a child herself. With the White House staff she loved to tease, to exaggerate, to make fun of everything including herself; yet there was a line against familiarity that no one dared cross.

Coming from a background of wealth, she dealt easily with the large staff of servants. She knew them all by their first names and spoke to them pleasantly; but she knew exactly what standard of service she expected from each. She kept a watchful eye on every detail of housekeeping and sent out a stream of notes from her desk to the chief usher, the housekeeper, the chef, the secretaries.

After one dinner party, she sent a note to Anne Lincoln, the housekeeper, complimenting her on the fact that the food was "fantastic" and the service "in record time." Then she went on to point out that there was a ten- to fifteen-minute wait for the first course, and in consequence a drop in the spirit of the party; that the wine was not served until the diners had finished their fish; and last, that the name of the dessert was misspelled on the menu. "It is Surprise, not Suprise. If this is your spelling, take note. If it was Sandy Fox [who wrote out the menus] tell him nicely."

She saw to it that everyone on the staff had a well-organized schedule and adhered to it rigidly. For herself, she refused to be fenced in. A secretary, looking over the first lady's engagements for the day, remarked that Mrs. Kennedy "had to see" a certain person that afternoon. With a spark of fire in her near-whisper, Jacqueline replied that she didn't "have to" do anything she didn't want to do.

Politics bored her and so did most politicians. In this she differed from practically every other Kennedy. In fact, though she made all the correct family gestures in public—holiday visits and so on—she resisted being absorbed by the clan as other Kennedy in-laws were.

Her interests lay in the arts and in artists, and she liked to invite to the White House such men as Leonard Bernstein and Pablo Casals. She determined to make the White House "a truly historic house," and for that purpose assembled a Fine Arts Committee, which brought in money and peerless antiques. She named experts to head restoration projects.

No detail of color for wall paint, weave of upholstery fabric, or curve of table leg was too small to merit her attention. No conception of altering entire rooms was too great for her ingenuity to cope with.

She and her committee acquired rugs, fine paintings, priceless art objects, and early nineteenth-century furniture until, under her direction, the White House became in itself a magnificent state treasure.

Jacqueline Kennedy had not only the executive ability to oversee this big operation; she was shrewd about financing it. She watched every state dollar with a miser's eye.

In private life, however, she had an extravagance that infuriated the public. In one year, it was said, she spent $30,000 for clothes. "I'd have to wear sable underwear to spend that much," she scoffed. But a secretary, writing some years later, said that her wardrobe expenditures for 1961 were actually more than $40,000.

She resented the press that avidly reported such private details, that prowled close to photograph her in unguarded moments, that published nationwide debates about whether her dresses were or were not too short.

But she would have been more than human if she hadn't enjoyed her popularity abroad, especially in France, from which the founder of the Bouvier family had emigrated. During a trip to France with President Kennedy, he said to an audience, which roared with laughter, "I do not think it altogether inappropriate to introduce myself. I am the man who accompanied Jacqueline Kennedy to France."

When President Kennedy was assassinated, her courage and patrician good taste made her the most beloved figure in the nation. Reserved though she was throughout that affair, the stunned expression of her face told that she was among the walking wounded. She was the symbol of the national grief that united the country for a time as it has not been united since the mid-1950s.

This affection continued throughout the next five years, cooling slowly. A few spiteful stories made the rounds, best known being the ones based on money. Jackie expected, so the reports went, to pay less than other women paid for furs, jewelry, expensive gowns, and so on, because of the publicity value of her name. It was said that she preferred to pay bills with gifts of objects, which might be valued as souvenirs, rather than to pay cash.

But, when she married Aristotle Socrates Onassis, the Greek shipping tycoon, then envy boiled up as true venom. People could have forgiven her beauty and aristocratic background, and even, to some degree, her cool aloofness, if there just hadn't been so much money involved. But for a wealthy woman, widow of a wealthy man, to marry one of the richest men in the world . . . it was too much. If Jacqueline Bouvier Kennedy Onassis had any virtues at all, after that marriage the American public did not want to hear about them.

On the Literary Scene

One of the great literary events of the 1960s was publication of Katherine Anne Porter's only novel, *Ship of Fools*. It had been twenty years in the writing, and during those years its imminent appearance was announced from time to time, and its name even appeared now and then in the publisher's catalog. At last the actual volume was in the book stores.

Of course she hadn't worked on it continuously. There were long interruptions, and during those twenty years she published four volumes of short stories and essays.

A small, beautiful, very feminine woman of seventy-two, Katherine Anne Porter said, "It's my last novel, of course. At my age, what do you expect?"

She was nettled by the mixed reviews that *Ship of Fools* received, because she was accustomed to being considered America's finest writer of prose, and being praised, as she deserved to be, for the purity and precision of her writing. But now, while some critics hailed the book as the great novel of the twentieth century, others said coolly that it was the longest short story in literary history.

The novel tells the events in the lives of twenty or more passengers and crew members of a ship that sailed from Vera Cruz to Bremerhaven in 1931. She writes about these people with remarkable insight.

She said defensively, "Of course *Ship of Fools* is not about nice people. It is about ordinary people who just muddle through the best they can. . . . They are a sorry lot, by and large . . . but they are the sum of what I know about human nature."

She described the voyage as the story of the criminal collusion between good, harmless people, and evil. Disaster occurs through inertia and through their lack of seeing what is going on before their eyes.

Born in Texas in 1890, Miss Porter went to Mexico as a young woman and lived through the revolutions there. They were "mild revolutions," she reflected, compared to today's wars, but people laid their lives on the line. Some of the young men she danced with and went horseback riding with were stood up against walls and shot. There was reality in that experience, so that when she went to New York to the F. Scott Fitzgerald world of jazz and bathtub gin, she felt oddly out of place.

From the age of sixteen she intended to become a writer, but she learned her craft. She wrote for fifteen years before she dared submit her first manuscript to an editor. In writing, she always brooded over a story until, when she finally put pen to paper, it was in nearly perfect form in her mind. Speaking of one of her most famous short stories, she said, "I started 'Flowering Judas' at seven-thirty P.M., and at one-thirty I was standing on a windy, snowy corner, putting it into a mailbox."

Ship of Fools was originally intended to be a short book, but it developed, she said, like a coral formation. It ended as a long, carefully plotted major work of art.

The sixties also saw Mary McCarthy's novel *The Group*, a funny, outspoken, and, she hoped, shocking story of the lives, loves, and hates of eight Vassar graduates, class of 1933. Jacqueline Susann's *Valley of the Dolls,* on a lower literary level, outshocked and outsold *The Group.* Distinguished historian Barbara Tuchman brought out two master-pieces, *The Guns of August* and *The Proud Tower,* which gave a dramatic, wide-sweeping picture of the political and military world before 1914.

The Women's Revolution

The shot that was heard around the nation was a book called *The Feminine Mystique,* which asserted that women are unfulfilled and exploited. It took most people by surprise and made them say, "What a crazy notion! What could women want that they haven't got already?"

This mystique is a conviction, grown especially powerful since World War II, that women find total fulfillment in having babies, loving their husbands, and staying in their beautiful houses to enjoy all those beautiful labor-saving devices. Most American women subscribed to the mystique, and if they weren't as happy as they thought they should be, they felt properly guilty. If they sneaked out of the house and got a job, they felt twice as guilty because that meant they were neglecting the children.

The book didn't sell especially well until its second year, when it came out in paperback. Suddenly in 1964 it became the most widely read book in America. It made converts and enemies by the hundreds of thousands, because if this subject arouses any response at all, it is a highly emotional response.

Author Betty Friedan argues vehemently that "the problem without a name" is suffered by millions of trapped housewives, but can be solved. Is her solution to take every married woman out of the kitchen and put her to work doing the jobs that men now perform and some of them hate? No, nothing so simple.

Each woman who feels smothered by witless household drudgery has to struggle toward her unique solution. She needs to see herself as a person—not just somebody's wife and somebody's mother—but a productive, creative, self-respecting individual. After that she has to find what work she needs beyond housewifery to fulfill herself as a person. It may be a job as a cashier at the supermarket, or it may be a return to piano playing or entrance into politics as precinct committeewoman.

This Betty Friedan who startled the whole country into seriously thinking about the problem of woman's individuality—or, on the other hand, into laughing hilariously at the whole idea—was a woman in her forties when the book came out, a dumpy, fierce-looking suburban housewife, mother of three, graduate of Smith *summa cum laude.* She is abrupt, quick-tempered, and often rude. She has the energy of a whole basketball team. She dresses as if she bought her clothes while thinking about that morning's headlines. In excited moments she runs a hand through her already rumpled gray hair. She answers such mail as she happens to open, ignores the rest, never stops talking, and hasn't time to finish a sentence.

She is a woman of fiery convictions. "What I think you are supposed to be," she says, "is passionate, fanatic, and crusading." She was horrified by the word "cool," so fashionable in the sixties. "Coolness is an evasion of life! I'd rather be committed than detached! ... I like revolutions! Revolutionaries are my kind of people! ... Some people think I am saying, 'Women of the world, unite! You have nothing to lose but your men!' It isn't true! You have nothing to lose but your vacuum cleaner!"

When *The Feminine Mystique* had earned thousands of fervent advocates, she founded the first women's liberation organization, called NOW—National Organization for Women. Compared to later women's lib groups, it is very conservative, so conservative that it has been likened to the NAACP. It appeals to middle-class, middle-aged business and professional women, most of them white. Crusading black women spend their ardor on the civil-rights movement. NOW grew so swiftly that by the end of the decade it had fifty chapters in twenty-four states. Most college campuses had a chapter.

NOW has two horns. The first is reformist, and attacks job inequalities through court action. It lobbies in legislatures and strives to bring more women into public office.

The other horn is composed of little rap groups all over the country. Five to fifteen women meet weekly in each other's homes to exchange ideas and experiences. In their sessions, anxieties are dissected and the members learn from each other how similar their problems are. Women who have never done so before learn to like women. Many marriages and nonmarriage relationships are broken through the insights gained in these encounter groups. Other relationships are made more firm.

One militant group of women demonstrated in Atlantic City at the time of the 1968 Miss America Pageant. They picketed the convention hall, carrying signs that read, MISS AMERICA SELLS IT, I AM A WOMAN—NOT A TOY, A PET, OR A MASCOT, and MISS AMERICA IS ALIVE AND ANGRY—IN HARLEM.

One of the demonstrators told a reporter, "The winner tours Vietnam entertaining the troops as a murder mascot." (One of the signs read GIRLS CROWNED—BOYS KILLED.) "The pageant," this demonstrator continued, "is one commercial shell game to sell the sponsors' products. Where else could one find such a perfect combination of American values: racism, militarism, and capitalism—all packaged in one ideal symbol—a woman."

The serious demonstration against the pageant drew a good deal of laughter. The women's liberation movement has to fight the concept that has plagued feminists for a hundred years: feminism is funny. If the believers wax sarcastic or dramatic or violent, they meet the same old response that their suffragist grandmothers knew when they marched up Fifth Avenue in their big hats and flopping black skirts: uproarious laughter. It is hard to convince the uninvolved that they are engaged in a revolution as serious as the civil-rights fight, the youth culture, or the ecology battle.

In the late sixties, a forum was held by the *Ladies' Home Journal* and Kelly Girls, the well-known placement agency for female office workers. In this forum a panel of five men and five women agreed enthusiastically that women have never had it so good. They hadn't been reading Betty Friedan. Women, the speakers proclaimed, have all the privileges that men have, and a few of their own. They are free to enter any profession, business, or job they like; they can earn any salary they are capable of, and rise to any position they choose.

At about the same time, Mrs. Nixon, then first lady, was asked her opinion of women's position in society, and she replied, quite sincerely, "Women have equal rights if they want to exercise them. Women who are really interested should just go out and pitch. I do not feel there is any discrimination."

But when President Nixon filled more than three hundred administrative posts in Washington, only thirteen of them went to women, and three of those were stenographic jobs in the White House.

On college campuses, the job recruiters who interviewed senior women were looking for airline stewardesses, nurses, and bank tellers. Senior men were interviewed for a variety of professional and management positions.

A study in the 1960s showed that one year after graduation from law school male graduates earned 20 percent more in salary than their female classmates. Ten years later, the male lawyers earned 200 percent more than female graduates.

The Opposition

Light-hearted and witty, poet Phyllis McGinley led the defense of the American homemaker. "There are still rewards to be found," she said, "in woman's noblest and most venerable role as keeper of the home. . . . By and large the world runs better when men and women keep to their own spheres, but more important, we who belong to the profession of housewife hold the fate of the world in our hands. It is our influence which will determine the culture of coming generations. We are the people who chiefly listen to music, buy the books, attend the theater, prowl the art galleries, collect for the charities, brood over the schools, converse with the children. Minds need to be rich and flexible for those duties."

Miss McGinley, or Mrs. Charles Hayden as she also likes to be known, is called a writer of light verse, but her topics are sometimes serious, and so excellent is her technique as a poet that in 1960 she won the Pulitzer Prize for poetry.

By the time she faced Betty Friedan in good-humored battle, she had authored nine volumes of poetry, two books of essays, and fifteen children's books. She wrote with pleasure, thinking out her verses as she hung curtains or scrubbed floors, because the housewife firmly dominated the poet.

Women who liked their feminine role within the home were fortified by such stanzas as these:

> . . . (T)hough aware that life is what
>   One ought to view with wrath and gravity,
> I live delighted with my lot,
>   Sunk in content as in depravity.
>
> Less woman, I expect, than mouse,
>   To alter fate I would not bother.
> I like my plain suburban house.
>   I like my children and their father.
>   . . . .
> Trapped, tricked, enslaved, but lacking sense
>   To enter in the conflict single,
> I wear my chains like ornaments,
>   Convinced they make a charming jingle.

THREE-QUARTER MARK

Stars of the Seventies

The witchery that can turn the dingiest stage lights into twinkling stars and turn ordinary songs into music of the soul is a magic wielded by few actresses. Pearl Bailey is one of them.

When the curtain goes up, her audience may be only a few hundred separate cells of anxiety or weariness or even indifference, but as that rich voice, the shining eyes, and the radiant smile reach them, people respond. Their enjoyment flows up toward the stage. It warms her, and her excitement and pleasure flow back to them. By the end of the show everybody is glorified into loving Pearl Bailey, loving color and music, loving life.

Besides several movies, she has had many Broadway successes: *St. Louis Woman, Arms and the Girl, God Bless You All, House of Flowers,* and the best known of all, *Hello, Dolly.* She was such a perfect Dolly the show might have been written for her. The finale was always so stirring that people left their seats to run up to the stage. They shook her hands, they kissed her, they were so enraptured that they shouted, "God bless you!"

She is an emotional woman, strongly charged with resentment or protectiveness or laughter or love or whatever has her aroused. She can be aroused to anger, too, especially when she is on the street or having dinner in public and people stare rudely or, as they sometimes do, make insulting remarks. Naturally she is touchy and defensive on the score of color. Even in her position she still meets people who think that blacks should "know their place."

She is a versatile woman. Once when she was having lunch at Wolfe's in Miami Beach, a woman came up to her and said, "Pearl Bailey, I love you. I am your biggest fan. I've always wanted to meet you." She raved on in this vein and then said, "What is it you do?" Startled, Miss Bailey answered, "I do what I've been doing all my life. Do you mean you came across this restaurant and gave me the great greeting and you don't even know what I do?"

The woman replied, "Well, Pearl, I've been out of town for three or four months."

The point was made. Pearl acts, sings, dances, composes music and poetry, expresses her political opinions, has written two autobiographical books, and recently put a cookbook into print. But most of all she is the woman with the magnetism that pulls people right out of their theater seats with love for Pearl Bailey.

"Bilge water," said Catherine Drinker Bowen.

The eminent biographer was referring to sanctimonious praise of humble housewifery.

She herself had a son and a daughter, but observed that no woman can make a lifetime occupation of rearing two children. With the smaller families of the future, she predicts that the mother image will lose its sanctity and something else will take its place.

When young women ask her the age-old question of how to cope with a husband, children, and a career, she gives the hoary old answer, unchanged by labor-saving devices or the women's liberation movement, that they must do double the work that housewives do and use twice the energy. Even in old age, Mrs. Bowen's eyes flash and her lips turn up in a lively grin.

In gathering material for her books, she reveled in studying for them and then delighted in the writing. "With my hands on the typewriter," she once wrote, "I feel like the war-horse in the Bible that smells the battle far off and saith among the trumpets, Ha ha."

She had to overcome difficulties in her work that a man would probably not have met. One of her most famous books is *Yankee from Olympus*, the biography of Oliver Wendell Holmes. The Holmes papers were guarded by two executors, one of whom was Felix Frankfurter, justice of the United States Supreme Court. The executors were astonished that the first person who requested access to the papers was a non-Bostonian and a nonlawyer, and worst of all, a nonman. At first she was given all she asked to start her studies—five hundred Holmes letters—from which she was told she could take any notes she wished.

But two months later came a letter explaining that Holmes's legal friends, in talking it over, felt that nothing in her experience equipped her to write about a great American, and denying her access to any further unpublished material on the great jurist. Obviously, the executors expected to stop her from going on with her project. Was she discouraged? No, she was embattled. She determined to leg it, questioning everybody alive who had known Holmes. It added a year to her labor.

When the book was finished and the Book of the Month Club chose it for a club selection, Felix Frankfurter—who had made the job as difficult as possible for her—sent her a telegram of congratulation. Ten years later he made a point of asking to be allowed to introduce her when she was to speak during a literary program. He sat on the platform with her, and she had no idea what his intentions were. When it was time to introduce her, he got up and told the audience that he had done all he could to stop Mrs. Bowen from writing *Yankee from Olympus*, but that some people work best under difficulties, and she was one of them. He made a handsome public apology.

Catherine Drinker Bowen says she is not sure how much of Frankfurter's attitude was based upon her sex, but she certainly met the same rebuffs when, some years later, she searched out material for a biography of John Adams. Again she was refused access to unpublished material. As before, she was not crushed, but only made more combative than ever. This time her material had to be obtained in research libraries, and it took five years.

In the 1950s she set out to write a biography of Sir Edward Coke, distinguished jurist in the time of James I. It was the familiar old story: with the pleasantest of smiles, she was denied access to the papers at Cambridge University that she wished to study. Her finished book, *The Lion and the Throne*, won the National Book Award (in America) and it also won a gracious letter from one of the Englishmen who had tried to stop her from writing the book. He asked if he might be permitted, next time she was in Cambridge, to give a small celebration in her honor.

Catherine Drinker Bowen enjoyed the triumphs but, born to battle, she also loved the challenges.

Mrs. Bowen says that in private life she enjoys housekeeping, by which she means that she likes living in an attractive house and entertaining friends, and considers her house and garden most delightful toys. But she adds that if house and garden should seriously interfere with her writing, house and garden would have to go.

Every weekday morning millions of women have breakfast with Barbara Walters. Well groomed, alert, and poised, she gives watchers of the TV *Today* program a sense of being part of the sophisticated, fast-moving world of New York and Washington, the world of politics and science, of letters and the theater. Barbara interviews Golda Meir and Henry Kissinger, Ted Kennedy and Mrs. Eisenhower, authors and athletes and composers. She and her co-host Jim Hartz, the witty, mustachioed Gene Shalit, and newscaster Lou Wood exchange quick, funny ad-libs in leftover seconds between features so that you sense that they enjoy each other, and you, the viewers, are caught up in that brisk, clever life, so different from your own.

Barbara Walters also appears in weary minutes of taped commercials during which even her fondest admirers have to go to the kitchen for another doughnut or a recheck of the grocery list. She has been moderator for her own thirty-minute show, *Not for Women Only* and has now become the first anchorwoman on a national evening news show.

No other woman in television has reached Barbara's eminence. Probably no other works so hard. And none has so many detractors.

Why is the beautiful and successful Walters disliked by so many? Because she breaks the mold of the feminine ideal. She is aggressive. This quality, respected in successful men, is abhorred in women. Betty Furness and Dinah Shore, among others, waft beguilement like perfume. Barbara Walters, in spite of her grace and humor, is sometimes accused of being cold.

If Carl Stern or Edwin Newman fails to exude sexual allure on TV, no one makes a case of it. But let a woman be serious and unsexy for a moment and she is "cold." If Mike Wallace asks a tough question in a TV interview, he's doing his job. If Barbara asks one, she's ruthless.

After graduating from Sarah Lawrence in 1958, the young Miss Walters considered teaching, but instead became a secretary at NBC, taking the well-known typewriter route into a career. For most girls, the typewriter proves to be the end of the road, but for her (because she was more aggressive than most girls?) it led instead to a job as publicity assistant, then producer of a local show, next a writer on the network shows, and at last to a berth on the *Today* program, of which Hugh Downs was then host.

Now divorced, she is the mother of a little girl, Jacqueline, born in 1969. Her hectic life permits little time with the child, but the love and warmth that she craves are gratified by motherhood.

Hectic is the word for the life style of this hard-driving, ambitious woman. Up before five o'clock each morning, she dives into the clothes laid out the night before, hurries to the studio, has her hair done and makeup applied while she sips coffee from a paper cup and reviews the morning's program. At seven o'clock the two-hour show begins.

Her working day after nine o'clock is a river in flood: phone calls, script writing, appointments, background study for tomorrow's interviews, dictation (she tries to answer all her letters, whether approving or critical), arrangements for interviews. She is highly organized and emotionally controlled so that she can accept interruptions without excitement, then return undisturbed to a former train of thought.

NBC seldom assigns her interviews. She pursues "the leaders, the legends, the beautiful, the infamous, and the just," to use her own words, whom she proposes to interview. Then she carefully plans the questions she will ask. In spite of her reputation for asking turn-of-the-knife questions, she says she tries to avoid subjects that will cause pain or embarrassment, and only approaches intimate or scandalous ground if the interviewee has already discussed his dubious situation in public. Easily hurt herself, she is sensitive to others' feelings.

Some critics, even among her admirers, say that she talks too fast; sometimes they can scarcely follow her rush of speech. Occasionally, during an interview, she talks too much. She has a horror of permitting a moment's silence, so that there is often a nervous sense of speed and tension. But would the viewer lift a finger to switch off the TV? No, she might miss a flash of the wit or the originality of the talk. (Most of Barbara's fans and defenders seem to be women.)

She is the kind of agonizer who bites the blanket during the night because she forgot to ask the crucial question.

Her childhood she considers an unhappy one. Her father, Lou Walters, was the nightclub entrepreneur who started Boston's famous Latin Quarter. As the child of show-business parents, she moved from city to city so often that she had no time to form close friendships. She saw the famous people of the theater, but longed for an ordinary, unglamorous family life. But now, a woman in her forties, she is repeating the childhood pattern: all the glamour and excitement of show biz but none of the tranquility she thought she wanted.

Political Women and Church Women

Unlike Barbara Walters, the congresswoman from Manhattan couldn't care less if she's called aggressive. For Bella Abzug, "the lady in the big hat," "aggressive" is a mild term. She's been compared to a Mack truck, a screaming tornado, and a cannon. She works sixteen hours a day, most of the time at the top of her voice. She wins elections by tramping the sidewalks campaigning, wins her constituents' affection by shouting for their rights, wins enemies by her inflexible opposition. An admirer said of her that Congress needs fifty new voices, and when Abzug walks in, it gets ten of them. A nonadmirer said that she has the effect in Washington of a splash of pickled beets on a white dinner jacket. She is the Ethel Merman of politics.

In the early seventies, Bella Abzug was a hard campaigner against the war, and later, as head of the House Subcommittee on Government Information and Individual Rights, she raged against the illegal and "police state" files of secret information on private citizens collected by the CIA.

An explosive advocate of women's liberation from the movement's earliest days, she said recently about women: "Our time has come. We will no longer content ourselves with the leavings and bits and pieces of the rights enjoyed by men. . . . We want our equal rights, nothing more but nothing less. We want an equal share of political and economic power."

Shirley Chisholm, also of New York, was the first black woman ever elected to Congress, and later, she ran for president. In 1972 the equally able Barbara Jordan of Texas joined her in the House. A lawyer from Houston, Congresswoman Jordan works vigorously in the minimum wage and fair employment controversies. Her party recently named her Democratic Woman of the Year.

Quietly but persistently, with none of the Abzug turbulence, women have been knocking on church doors asking for a larger share in religious life. As early as 1970 the Lutheran Church of America and also the American Lutheran Church sanctioned the ordination of women as pastors. In that same year, the more conservative Episcopal Church voted to permit the ordination of women as deacons. The Episcopal ministry is composed of three orders: deacons, priests, and bishops. Written church discipline fails to specify sex. Whoever expected the question to arise?

The Catholic Church, much liberalized during the past decade, now allows women to be lay readers, to lead a congregation in singing, to take up the offering, and to serve as ushers. Church law, however, flatly states that an ordained priest must be male, leaving no room for quarrels about interpretation.

Several Jewish women have become rabbis.

Many Protestant churches have permitted women's ordination for years, but in the early seventies Dr. Cynthia Wedel, president of the National Council of Churches, observed wryly, "I have yet to hear of a woman holding a permanent post as minister in a good-sized parish which could afford to hire a man."

Against women in the pulpit there is a profound prejudice. Some people point for authority clear back to Paul, who said, "Let your women keep silence in church: for it is not permitted unto them to speak, but they are commanded to be under obedience, as also saith the law. And if they will learn anything, let them ask their husbands at home: for it is shame for women to speak in church."

Rudely disregarding Paul, in July, 1974, eleven young women were ordained as Episcopal priests, and in September four more were ordained. One faction in the church maintains that they were "validly ordained" because the ritual was conducted by three bishops, and many women of the church rejoice at the reversal of the old "always a bridesmaid, never a bride" syndrome.

Alison Cheek, one of the newly ordained priests, said that God has always been regarded as masculine, but with women in the priesthood, "the femine aspect of God's nature will receive more attention."

Angry opposition to the ordination, however, came from the House of Bishops, which declared that all fifteen young women are in defiance of the will of the church. Their stand is that priesthood is not a right to be claimed by any individual who simply asserts that he (or she) has a "call."

In rebuttal, one of the women said that when doctrine and discipline come face to face with a personal call, "you can't continue to put up with the church's complicity with being untrue to the Gospel."

One archdeacon spluttered, "These women are no more priests than [are] monkeys in the trees!"

Nonchurch people, able to enjoy a good row since they have nothing at stake, regret that the next Episcopal convention, with its nine hundred delegates both lay and priestly, will settle the dispute.

Women's Liberation Movement

The movement was at its noisiest in the early 1970s. There was a spate of angry books by highly articulate young women. *Sexual Politics* by Kate Millet is one of them. By "politics" she means the struggle for power between the sexes. Women, she says, have always been the humiliated, the subordinated sex, sometimes pampered, sometimes patronized, but always exploited. She writes with irony which is funnier to her women readers than to men, and she develops her thesis through more than 350 small-type pages. "Thesis" is the exact word, because this book grew out of her Ph.D. thesis at Columbia.

A vivid, handsome girl, she was once called "a brilliant misfit in a man's world." She is a sculptor herself, and is married to Japanese sculptor Fumio Yoshimura. After the book came out she admitted that it might contain some exaggerations, but, she explained cheerfully, she had to write forcefully because nobody was listening.

What critics focus upon is her slapdash assumption that male and female are created exactly alike in personality, intellect, and emotion, and that society creates *all* the differences, manufacturing artificial stereotypes.

Cautious scientists say that male and female genes are different, but that we do not yet know the exact extent of these differences. However, they hesitate to admit that sex genes can be left altogether out of our thinking.

Scientists tend to speak in carefully qualified language, but a California plumber, not skilled in scientific circumspection, expressed the idea in his way. "If women want to be equal, let 'em. If they want to be plumbers, let 'em. But when they go out on a job, they're going to have to lift two hundred pounds of pipe like any other plumber." Blue-collar workers are possibly more hostile to change than professional men. Fortunately for women, machinery makes muscle less and less important as a job qualification, and in many occupations it never was important.

Returning to the output of books, Australian Germaine Greer wrote *The Female Eunuch*, and again the title is significant. Her theme is that woman's sexuality is not merely passive, but is that of a castrate: timid, languid, delicate. Further that women have been forced into this artificial pattern by men who took the leading role for themselves and belittled heterosexual contact to a sadomasochistic design.

A third book, most impressive of the three, is *Sisterhood Is Powerful,* a fiery collection of writings by many women in the movement. The editor is Robin Morgan. In the acknowledgments section, she gives warm thanks to many sisters who gave her information, material, encouragement, and editorial suggestions. She names more than thirty of them. Last, she writes, "Some mention, albeit brief, should also go to three men," whom she names. "Without such men 'this book would not have been possible.' On the other hand, it would not have been necessary."

Gloria Steinem, one of the key figures of the women's liberation movement, began publication of a magazine, *Ms.,* the organ of the movement, staffed entirely by women.

At the same time, women's groups formed as quickly and naturally as mercury flowing together, groups as varied as human personalities themselves. Betty Friedan's National Organization for Women had five thousand members by 1970. There were also Redstockings (the name is a takeoff on the derogatory old term "bluestocking"), Radical Mothers, Radical Women, the National Women's Political Caucus, the Coalition of Labor Women, and WITCH. These letters stand for Women's International Terrorist Conspiracy from Hell, and are a reminder that all women who have dared to be different have been persecuted by society, including the women of Salem who were labeled witches. Members of WITCH like to dress in spectacular rags, rush howling into a university building, a bank, or a store that displeases them, scream curses, and storm away again, leaving their shaken victims uncertain whether they have been fearfully damned or only spoofed.

Other women, less frivolous, gather in rap groups to discuss women's lib and their special problems as women. By the way, people inside the movement never, never use the term "women's lib." They refer to the "women's liberation movement," a serious name for a serious campaign.

Wide publicity has affected the thinking of Americans. "Why aren't my opinions as valid as his?" asks a young wife. "Shall we have a girl for club president and a boy for secretary?" asks a nominating committee. "What's wrong with promoting a woman to be supervisor over men?" asks an employer.

Liberal young men can accept women as equals in a way their fathers would have found painful if not impossible. A young woman was offered an appointment as assistant professor in a renowned university in the city where she and her husband lived, but at almost the same time his company offered him a transfer out of town to a better job. He declined the transfer. He said he did not want to deprive his wife of her big chance. As a man he would have more opportunities for advancement than she would.

Thanks to all the agitation, some jobs are now open to women that were formerly marked "for men only." A few women work as air traffic controllers, project engineers, bank managers, sheriffs, electricians, die makers, TV cameramen, truck drivers. In an eastern city a group of women set up as furniture movers, and they do all the lifting and hauling themselves. They call their company the Mothertruckers. In the world of music Sarah Caldwell made a great breakthrough when she conducted orchestra and opera at the Met, first woman ever to do so.

This isn't a long list, and before women begin to congratulate each other on their achievements, they had better observe how few women hold key positions. Bank presidents, boards of directors of large corporations, and university presidents are nearly all men. Most women who operate newspapers inherited or bought their posts instead of rising by promotion. Though most elementary schoolteachers are women, four out of five principals are men. The House, Senate, Cabinet, Supreme Court, and state offices are staffed entirely or largely by men.

Geri Josephs, a former vice-chairman of the Democratic National Committee, found that political parties have habitually practiced discrimination. "Men want women to do the kitchen work of politics," she said. The man on the street, however, is less biased. A 1970 Gallup poll (how could we know what we think if we didn't have those polls?) showed that 83 percent of voters were willing to vote for a qualified woman for Congress, and 13 percent were not. In this, men voted the same as women. But here is the stunner: When asked if they would vote for a woman to be president, 58 percent of the men said Yes, whereas only 49 percent of the women would do so.

The women's movement hasn't made much difference in paychecks. As late as 1973, women in professional and technical jobs earned only two-thirds as much as men in similar jobs. For every dollar that a working man earned, the Department of Commerce reported, a woman earned only 58 cents. The lowest-paying jobs, such as household, clerical, and service, were still performed chiefly by women.

But women have poured into the labor market. During the 1950s and 1960s, fifteen million women joined the work force, while only ten million men joined. About 40 percent of all workers are now women. In bad times, they are still the first to be fired, just as they were first back in the 1930s.

Government, however, is putting the pressure on employers to give equal rights to women. Under the Equal Pay Act, courts have ordered that millions of dollars in back pay be given to employees, most of whom were women; and discrimination against women can cost an employer his federal contract.

That Equal Rights Amendment

The House approved the ERA in 1970. It had been pending for forty-seven years. Soft-voiced Representative Martha W. Griffiths of Michigan marshaled three hundred fifty votes; only fifteen votes were cast against the bill. After the Senate passed it also, it went to the states, where it has had, as they say in show business, mixed reviews. All the women's liberation people backed it, including the highly organized League of Women Voters. At this time the outcome is not certain.

"What do [women] want liberation from?" asks Phyllis Schlafly of Illinois. She is leader of the National Committee to Stop the Equal Rights Amendment. "What they call the imprisonment of the home, the slavery of marriage, the tedium of caring for children? . . . For most women fulfillment is in the family. . . . I'm a free and happy woman, and I'm able to order my life the way I want. Freedom to me means that I have the love and companionship of a wonderful husband, six beautiful, healthy, and successful children. And I am able to do what I want in my free time."

On the East Coast, men established a protest group called M.S.— Male Supremacy. Its founders claim that women's clubs, policemen, and firemen have rallied round to help defeat the ERA, and that their ideal is to reunite the family. The father chapter in Brockton picketed the Massachusetts General Hospital sperm bank, and a spokesman declared, "If women ever get control of the sperm banks, men have had it. There'll be no need to have men around at all. We want to eliminate the sperm banks."

Other antis say they don't want unisex rest rooms, legalized homosexual marriages, and conscription of girls. They fear that rape will no longer be a criminal offense, that child-support laws will evaporate, and that there will be no all-female DAR or all-male Rotary.

ERA supporters reply that what the women antis really fear is responsibility, and that the fortunate cherished woman (highly vocal, but a minority) doesn't want to give up her childlike status.

How these arguments resemble the ones that preceded passage of the Woman Suffrage Amendment!

Gloria Steinem, in her TV appearances and platform speeches, argues often and eloquently for the women's liberation movement, and never raises her gentle voice. Slender and poised, usually dressed in neat but sexless clothes, her even-featured face is calm. She likes to wear large, slightly tinted glasses, parts her long, straight hair in the middle and lets it hang loose, covering a third of her face. She gets letters all the time from people who detest her hair style.

"You call for a revolution," she observes, "and people want you to comb your hair."

Speaking more seriously, she points out that a caste system operates in America, with nearly all decision-making roles taken by white males. Women, blacks, Spanish-speaking and Third World people form an under-caste. Discrimination against women and against racial groups go together, she says, "in a very, very deep way. Wherever there is one kind of caste, the other group is always in danger. . . . These problems can only be attacked together."

Over and over again she explains that the movement (in spite of Mrs. Schlafly) is not trying to force every married woman out of the kitchen and into a job. "We want to increase everybody's options," she says. "Choice," that's the key word; freedom to choose one's life pattern.

On her speaking tours, Gloria faces up to press conferences, taping sessions, lectures, receptions, and continuous conversation on women's liberation. Calm and tireless, she goes through whole days of this. She thrives on contacts with new people and their interest "gets my adrenalin flowing. It all becomes new to me again."

The United Nations named 1975 International Women's Year, and sponsored a conference in Mexico City. It was attended by 2,000 official delegates from 150 nations. In spite of the gorgeous background, the splendid costumes, and the gallantry exercised in official social gatherings, Americans came away from the conference in disgruntled mood.

It was specified in advance that there were to be six women to every man, but this, as one of the reporters said bitterly, was only a body count, not a power ratio. In committees, where the resolutions and declarations and the World Plan of Action were hammered out, there the men took over. In their home countries, it was these men who held official positions. The unskilled female delegates, especially from Asian countries, did not know how to wrest authority from the men.

Rather than a conference "for women" it appeared to be a world-wide political convention, and a hostile one at that, with Communist delegates scowling upon non-Communist, a show of anger against the West by Third World people, and much parading of nationalism. Delegates from developing countries were so intent on the redistribution of resources between rich and poor that the redistribution of power between men and women hardly interested them.

American delegates, who knew their history lessons and all the economic statistics, were nevertheless startled to see at first hand how heavily the burden of disadvantage presses upon women in poor countries. Most of the poor live in small villages where infant mortality is higher among females, where girls are not welcome in the family, where women get the smaller share of food in time of famine, where medical care if any goes to men ahead of women, where heavy work loads, constant pregnancies, and malnutrition all result in physical exhaustion that keeps women from having enough energy to improve themselves and acquire basic skills. As a university study expresses it, "Work, hunger, ignorance, and infirmity remain [women's] constant familiars."

At a pre-conference meeting in a Latin American country, a group of women who expected to attend the conference asked a peasant woman what she needed most to come out of the international meeting. She remained timidly silent until the moderator asked the question again and held the microphone closer to the woman's mouth. "Well ... fields," she whispered. "The rains are coming and we need land to plant."

American women recognized their sisters in distant lands as "the slaves of slaves" and saw a reflected image of themselves as unduly prosperous.

The Turn of the Century

What of the American woman in the year 2000? (Everyone's entitled to take part in guessing games.) Plainly she will be a very different creature from the dear little woman of 1900. A girl born in the 1970s will grow up to be two inches taller than her grandmother. She will be healthier, stronger, and thinner.

She and her male counterpart will dress more nearly alike than they do today, and their behavior will be more similar. Manners and social life will continue their trend toward the casual and informal.

Marriage will survive, though more couples in love will live together without marriage until they become parents. Having a baby out of wedlock, however, will be socially acceptable. Working mothers will suffer the same anxieties and frustrations about their children's welfare that they suffer today, even though day-care centers will be more numerous.

Tomorrow's young people will accept a variety of life styles. It will be honorable to remain single, or to live in a group, or to be openly homosexual or lesbian.

The ERA will have been ratified, and all the dissension over it be forgotten.

The sexual, racial, and anti-authoritarian revolutions of the 1960s and early 1970s will rumble into semi-quiet as their gains are consolidated and new, small advances made. By the end of the century, it will be time for new and probably more violent eruptions. What form will they take? The one sure prediction is that women will be even more involved in the history of tomorrow than in that of the present.

The environmentalists, heirs of Rachel Carson, will be there still slugging, with every round fought against an antagonist that has a financial stake in the outcome.

As for jobs, it is too much to hope that man and woman will be equal as early as 2000. Men are so reluctant to acccpt women as professional peers that it will be far into the twenty-first century before universities, industry, and government are staffed by as many women as men. But the time will come at last when sex will not be the determining factor in job distribution.

However, two centuries from now, or three centuries, or five, if there should be a gigantic overthrow of civilization and our social structure should topple like a falling skyscraper, then the position of the sexes will revert to its historic norm, with men the upper-caste people; and the struggle will all have to be started from the beginning. If this prediction proves to be wrong, how embarrassed I shall be.

Index

Abzug, Bella, 238
Adams, Franklin P., 83, 99, 104
Adams, John, 235
Adams, Maude, 37-38, 113, 116, 137
Addams, Jane, 31-34, 63, 71, 91, 146
Agar, Eileen, 146
Aherne, Brian, 135
Akin, Stella, 143
Allen, Florence, 143, 159, 160
"Amos 'n' Andy," 139
Anderson, Felix, 178
Anderson, Marian, 129, 155-57, 207
Anderson, Mary, 68, 69-70, 71
Anthony, Susan B., 49, 50, 51, 58, 59, 67
Arden, Elizabeth, 107
Arlen, Michael, 95
Arnstein, Nick, 116
Arthur, Jean, 141
Asquith, Cynthia, 116
Astaire, Fred, 140
Astor, Mrs. John Jacob, III, 12
Atherton, Gertrude, 19, 105-6
Augusta Victoria, Empress, 25

Baez, Joan, 210-11
Bahlman, Anna, 80, 82
Bailey, Pearl, 233-34
Balch, Emily Green, 64
Banister, Marian, 143
Bankhead, Tallulah, 177, 179-82
Bara, Theda, 87
Bard, Josef, 144, 145
Barnes, Margaret Ayer, 124-25
Barrie, James Matthew, 37, 137
Barrymore, Diana, 158
Barrymore, Ethel, 15-16, 24, 41, 87, 90, 116, 180
Barrymore, John, 15, 158, 180
Barrymore, Lionel, 141
Barthelmess, Richard, 114
Bayes, Nora, 87
Beaton, Cecil, 85
Belafonte, Harry, 209
Belmont, Mrs. O.H.P., 59, 60, 169
Benchley, Robert, 100, 180
Benny, Jack, 139

Bentley, Irene, 17
Bergen, Edgar, 139
Bernhardt, Sarah, 139
Bernstein, Leonard, 226
Berry, Walter Van Rensselaer, 80, 81
Besier, Rudolf, 135
Blatch, Harriot Stanton, 55-56, 59
Boissevain, Eugen, 58, 109, 110
Bok, Edward, 27
Bourke-White, Margaret, 147-49, 152, 154
Bow, Clara, 90
Bowen, Catherine Drinker, 234-35
Brice, Fanny, 87, 116
Brokaw, Ann, 171
Brokaw, George, 169
Brooks, Gwendolyn, 202
Broun, Heywood, 83, 100
Brown, Catherine, 137
Brown, Edmund G., 212
Buck, John, 123
Buck, Pearl, 122-24, 125, 127, 152
Byington, Spring, 141

Cahill, Marie, 17
Caldwell, Erskine, 148, 149
Caldwell, Sarah, 242
Campbell, Alan, 102
Campbell, Mrs. Patrick, 87
Canby, Henry Seidel, 83
Capp, Al, 211
Capra, Frank, 197
Carnegie, Hattie, 138
Carson, Rachel, 216-20, 246
Caruso, Enrico, 88, 89
Casals, Pablo, 226
Castle, Irene and Vernon, 85, 158
Cather, Willa, 77-79, 83, 108
Catt, Carrie Chapman, 52, 53-55, 56, 63, 65, 71, 91
Chaplin, Charlie, 140, 212
Chatterton, Ruth, 87
Cheek, Alison, 239
Cherry, Charles, 16
Children's Bureau, 71
Chisholm, Shirley, 238
Churchill, Winston, 150, 181

Ciardi, John, 205
Claire, Ina, 87
Clark, Marguerite, 87
Cleveland, Grover, 12
Coke, Edward, 235
Colman, Ronald, 115
Connelly, Marc, 180
Coolidge, Grace Goodhue, 112
Cooper, Gary, 137
Cooper, Miriam, 113
Cormier, Lucia, 197
Cornell, Katharine, 96, 116, 125, 129, 134-36
Coward, Noel, 116, 181
Cowl, Jane, 87, 125
Crawford, Joan, 140
Cromwell, James, 158
Crothers, Rachel, 106
Cukor, George, 198

Damrosch, Walter, 157
Daniels, Bebe, 87
Davis, Bette, 129
Davis, Richard Harding, 41
Day, Doris, 200
de Beauvoir, Simone, 201, 202
Dee, Sandra, 200
de Havilland, Olivia, 129
De Mille, Agnes, 182
Department of Labor, 69, 70, 71, 171
De Selincourt, Hugh, 76
Dewey, John, 56
Didrikson, Mildred (Babe), 129-30
Dietrich, Marlene, 141, 142, 168
Dionne quintuplets, 152
Dior, Christian, 175
Dodge, Mabel, 84
Dos Passos, John, 93, 122
Downs, Hugh, 236
Drake, Alfred, 199
Drew, John, 137
Duff, Juliet, 116
Duke, Doris, 158
Duncan, Deirdre and Patrick, 36
Duncan, Isadora, 34-36
Durbin, Deanna, 142

Earhart, Amelia, 153-55
Ederle, Gertrude, 111
Edward VII, 17-19
Edward VIII, 149-51
Eisenhower, Dwight D., 196
Eisenhower, Mamie Geneva Doud, 98, 236

Eliot, T. S., 110
Elizabeth, Princess, 152
Elizabeth, Queen Consort, 132, 152
Elliott, Maxine, 17-19
Ellis, Havelock, 76
Etting, Ruth, 87

Fairbank, Janet Ayer, 124
Fairbanks, Douglas, 86, 87
Farley, James A., 132
Farrar, Geraldine, 24-26, 137
Farrar, Henrietta, 24, 25
Farrington, Nina, 17
Faulkner, William, 93
Ferber, Edna, 102-4, 105, 146
Ferber, Fannie and Julia, 103
Ferguson, James and Miriam, 98-99
Fish, Mrs. Stuyvesant, 17
Fitzgerald, F. Scott, 96, 122, 228
Fitzgerald, Zelda Sayre, 96, 97
Flagstad, Kirsten, 142, 157
Fonda, Jane, 211
Fontanne, Lynn, 115-16, 138
Fox, Sandy, 226
Foy, Eddie, 17
Frankfurter, Felix, 234, 235
Frazier, Brenda, 159
Friedan, Betty, 202, 229, 230, 231, 232, 241
Fullerton, Morton, 83
Furness, Betty, 236

Gable, Clark, 129
Gale, Zona, 83
Gallico, Paul, 130
Galli-Curci, Amelita, 107
Garbo, Greta, 96, 141
Garden, Mary, 107
Garland, Hamlin, 79
Garland, Judy, 142, 199, 221-24
Garrett, Mary, 23
Garson, Greer, 168
Gatti-Casazza, Giulio, 88
George V, 150
George VI, 132, 152
Gershwin, Ira, 176
Gibson, Charles Dana, 41, 95
Gilbert, John, 115
Gillette, William, 137
Gilman, Charlotte Perkins, 72-73, 74
Giraudoux, Jean, 116
Gish, Dorothy, 112, 113, 114
Gish, Lillian, 87, 112-15, 116
Glasgow, Ellen, 12, 127-28

Glyn, Elinor, 90
Goelet, Bertie, 28
Goldman, Emma, 68
Goldwater, Barry M., 196
Gordon, Ruth, 200
Grable, Betty, 167
Graham, Martha, 183
Grant, Cary, 198
Greer, Germaine, 240
Griffith, D. W., 113, 114
Griffiths, Martha W., 243
Guinan, Texas, 105
Gumm, Ethel, Marian, 222
Gustav V, 123

Hackett, Francis, 33
Hamilton, Edith, 125-27
Hammett, Dashiell, 177, 178
Harlow, Jean, 140
Harriman, Mrs. J. Borden, 12, 60, 143
Harris, Julie, 179, 184
Hart, Moss, 141
Hartz, Jim, 236
Hayes, Helen, 115, 116, 134, 137-38
Hayworth, Rita, 167
Hegger, Grace, 146
Heifetz, Jascha, 157
Held, Anna, 87
Held, John, Jr., 95
Hellman, Lillian, 176-79, 181
Hellman, Max Bernard, 178
Hemingway, Ernest, 93, 102, 122
Hendricks, Cecelia, 160
Henie, Sonja, 152
Hepburn, Audrey, 200
Hepburn, Katharine, 129, 197-200, 223
Hill, Grace Livingston, 122
Holliday, Judy, 199
Holmes, Oliver Wendell, 234
Hoover, Ike, 131
Hope, Bob, 139
Hopwood, Avery, 106
Howard, Leslie, 129
Hurok, Sol, 156
Hurst, Fannie, 83
Hutton, Barbara, 158

International Ladies' Garment Workers'
    Union, 143
International Women's Year, 244
Irwin, Mrs. Richard, 12

Jackson, Mahalia, 207
James, Mrs. Arthur, 18, 19

James, Henry, 82
Janis, Elsie, 87
Johnson, Hugh, 132
Johnson, Van, 167
Joplin, Janis, 215
Jordan, Barbara, 238
Josephs, Geri, 242

Kanin, Garson, 200
Kaufman, Beatrice, 104
Kaufman, George, 104, 116, 141
Keller, Helen, 71
Kelley, Florence, 71-72
Kennedy, Caroline and John, 225
Kennedy, Edward M., 236
Kennedy, Jacqueline Bouvier, 86, 225-27
Kennedy, John F., 209, 224, 225, 227
Kennedy, Minnie, 117
Kennedy, Rose Fitzgerald, 225
Kent, Elizabeth, 58
Keyser, Mary, 32
King, "Bunny," 209
King, Coretta Scott, 206-10
King, Martin Luther, Jr., 206, 207, 208,
    209
King, Yolanda and Marty, 208, 209
Kinsey, Alfred Charles, 201
Kissinger, Henry, 236
Kober, Arthur, 177, 178
Kopf, Maxim, 146
Koussevitzky, Serge, 157
Kronenberger, Louis and Emmy, 178

Lamarr, Hedy, 167
Landon, Alfred M., 132
Lathrop, Julia, 71
Lawrence, Gertrude, 107
LeGallienne, Eva, 87, 138-39
LeGallienne, Richard, 56, 138
Leigh, Vivien, 129
Leslie, Mrs. Frank, 54
Lewis, Michael, 146
Lewis, Sinclair, 83, 145, 146
Lewis, Wells, 146
Lillie, Beatrice, 107, 116
Lincoln, Anne, 225
Lindbergh, Anne Morrow, 204-5
Lindbergh, Charles A., 111, 205
Longworth, Nicholas, 28, 30
Longworth, Mrs. Nicholas. *See* Roosevelt,
    Alice Lee
Loos, Anita, 107
Lowell, Amy, 106
Loy, Myrna, 177

Lubbock, Percy, 82
Luce, Clare Boothe, 168-71
Luce, Henry R., 148, 169, 170
Luft, Joey, Lorna, and Sid, 223
Lunt, Alfred, 115, 116

MacArthur, Charles, 100, 138
MacArthur, Mary, 138
McCarthy, Joseph R., 194, 195, 196
McCarthy, Mary, 228
McClintic, Guthrie, 135, 136
McClure, S. S., 77
MacCormack, Daniel, 172
McCullers, Carson, 183, 184, 202
McCutcheon, George Barr, 39, 122
MacDonald, Jeanette, 142
McGinley, Phyllis, 232
McKinley, William, 46
McMein, Neysa, 100, 104
McPherson, Aimee Semple, 117-19
March, William, 112
Margaret Rose, Princess, 152
Marsh, Mae, 113
Martin, Mary, 200
Massey, Park, 48
Maxwell, Elsa, 159
Mayer, Louis B., 222
Mdvani, Alexis, 158
Mead, Margaret, 220-21
Meir, Golda, 236
Mencken, H. L., 107
Menjou, Adolphe, 197
Mercer, Mary, 184
Merman, Ethel, 238
Metalious, Grace, 202
Metropolitan Opera Company, 25, 34, 88, 142, 242
Milholland, Inez, 57, 58, 109, 169
Millay, Cora, 107, 108, 110
Millay, Edna St. Vincent, 107-10, 160
Millay, Norma and Kathleen, 107
Miller, Alice Duer, 100
Miller, Marilyn, 87
Millet, Kate, 240
Mills, Mrs. Ogden, 17
Minnelli, Liza, 223
Minnelli, Vincente, 199, 223
Mitchell, Margaret, 128-29
Mitchell, Dr. S. Weir, 20
Moore, Colleen, 129
Moore, Grace, 142, 157
Moore, Owen, 86
Morgan, Anne, 60, 65
Morgan, Helen, 104, 105

Morgan, J. Pierpont, 65
Morgan, Robin, 241
Muni Paul, 152
Murray, Mae, 87
Muskie, Edmund S., 197

Nast, Condé, 169
Nathan, George Jean, 107, 112, 178
Nation, Carry, 46-49, 51
National American Woman Suffrage Association, 46, 50, 52, 53, 64, 65
Nazimova, 87
Negri, Pola, 87
Nesbit, Evelyn, 26
Neuberger, Maurine, 197
Newell, Virginia, 161
Newman, Edwin, 236
Nichols, Ruth, 153, 154
Nixon, Patricia Ryan, 231
Nixon, Richard M., 231
Noonan, Fred, 155

O'Connor, Flannery, 202
O'Keeffe, Georgia, 184-85
Onassis, Aristotle Socrates, 227
Onassis, Mrs. Aristotle S. *See* Kennedy, Jacqueline Bouvier
O'Neill, Eugene, 116, 200
Ormiston, Kenneth G., 118, 119
Ostenso, Martha, 106
O'Toole, Peter, 199
Owen, Ruth Bryan, 143

Palmer, Mrs. Potter, 33
Parker, Dorothy, 100-102, 109, 170
Parker, Edwin Pond II, 101
Parrish, Anne, 107
Paul, Alice, 56-59, 66, 67, 146, 169
Paul, Maury (Cholly Knickerbocker), 159
Pavlova, Anna, 182
Pegler, Westbrook, 157
Perkins, Frances, 70, 143, 171-72
Perkins, Mary Westcott, 72, 73
Perkins, Mrs. Thomas H., 12
Peterkin, Julia, 106
Phelps, William Lyon, 137
Pickford, Jack, 87
Pickford, Mary, 86-87
Pinchot, Gifford, 157
Pinero, Arthur Wing, 15
Pons, Lily, 142
Ponselle, Rosa, 87-89
Porter, Katherine Anne, 183, 227-28
Powell, William, 177

Powers, Francis Gary, 194
Prince of Wales. *See* Edward VIII
Putnam, George Palmer, 154

Radziwill, Lee Bouvier, 225
Rainer, Luise, 152
Rainsford, Mrs. W. S., 12
Rand, Ayn, 203-4
Rand, Sally, 162
Rattigan, Terence, 116
Rayburn, Sam, 169
Red Cross, 64, 65
Reynolds, Debbie, 200
Rice, Grantland, 130
Rinehart, Mary Roberts, 106
Robins, Margaret Dreier and Raymond, 71
Robinson, Anna, 17
Robinson, Irene, 178
Roche, Josephine, 143
Rogers, Ginger, 140
Romani, Romano, 88
Rooney, Mickey, 222
Roosevelt, Alice Lee, 16, 28-30, 41
Roosevelt, Anna Eleanor, 121, 129, 131-34, 155
Roosevelt, Elliott, 134
Roosevelt, Franklin D., 131, 132, 133, 134, 142, 143, 148, 152, 160, 165, 171, 181
Roosevelt, Theodore, 17, 28, 29, 30, 134
Ross, Harold, 100, 104
Ross, Nellie Tayloe, 99, 131, 143
Round Table, 99-100, 102, 104, 180
Rubenstein, Helena, 107
Russell, Lillian, 17

St. Denis, Ruth, 183
St. Johns, Adela Rogers, 128
Sandburg, Carl, 202
Sanger, Margaret, 73-77
Sanger, William, 74, 76
Schlafly, Phyllis, 243, 244
Schneiderman, Rose, 143
Seeger, Pete, 211
Shalit, Gene, 236
Shaw, Anna Howard, 50-52, 53, 56, 64, 71
Shaw, George Bernard, 87, 116
Shawn, Ted, 183
Shearer, Norma, 106, 140
Sheean, Vincent, 181
Sheldon, Edward, 124, 125
Sherwood, Robert, 100, 116
Shore, Dinah, 236
Shumlin, Herman, 176, 177, 178

Simpson, Ernest, 149, 150
Simpson, Wallis Warfield, 149-51
Sinatra, Frank, 167
Singer, Paris, 36
Slee, J. Noah H., 77
Smith, Alfred E., 171
Smith, Bessie, 202
Smith, Kate, 161
Smith, Margaret Chase, 195-97
Stanton, Elizabeth Cady, 50, 55
Starr, Ellen Gates, 31
Steinbeck, John, 140
Steinem, Gloria, 241, 244
Stern, Carl, 236
Stewart, Donald Ogden, 100
Stewart, James, 141, 198
Stieglitz, Alfred, 184, 185
Strange, Michael, 158
Strauss, Lewis L., 196
Struther, Jan, 167, 168
Susann, Jacqueline, 228
Swanson, Gloria, 87
Swarthout, Gladys, 142
Swope, Herbert Bayard, 100
Symington, Stuart, 196

Taft, Helen, 65
Talmadge, Norma, 87
Tarbell, Ida, 83
Tarkington, Booth, 63
Tashman, Lilyan, 87
Taylor, Deems, 109, 180
Taylor, Elizabeth, 86
Teasdale, Sara, 106
Temple, Shirley, 140
Thaw, Harry K., 26
Thomas, J. Parnell, 198
Thomas, Martha Carey, 21-24, 39, 50, 71, 91, 124, 153
Thompson, Dorothy, 129, 143-46, 149, 161
Tracy, Louise, 199
Tracy, Spencer, 197, 199, 200
Triangle Shirtwaist Company, 60, 61-62
Tuchman, Barbara, 229

Valentina (couturière), 175
Valentino, Rudolph, 96
Vanderbilt, Grace Wilson, 16, 158

Waldron, Charles, 135
Walker, James J., 111
Wallace, Mike, 204, 236
Walsh, Raoul, 113

Walsh, Richard, 124
Walters, Barbara, 236-37, 238
Walters, Lou, 237
Waters, Ethel, 184
Wedel, Cynthia, 239
Weld, Tuesday, 200
Wells, Herbert George, 76
Welty, Eudora, 183
West, Mae, 142
Wharton, Edith, 79-83
Wharton, Edward, 81, 82, 83
White, Pearl, 87
White, Stanford, 26
Wilhelm, Crown Prince, 25
Wilhelm II, Emperor, 24, 25
Williams, Camilla, 207
Wills, Helen, 111, 112
Wilson, Edmund, 109
Wilson, Lois, 83
Wilson, Woodrow, 57, 58, 59, 66, 67, 168
Windsor, Duke and Duchess of. *See* Edward VIII, *and* Simpson, Wallis Warfield

Wise, Stephen, 56
Wister, Owen, 29
Woman's Christian Temperance Union, 46, 47, 62
Woman's Party, 58, 59, 67
Woman's Peace Party, 63
Women's Bureau, 69, 70
Women's Liberation Groups, 230, 241
Women's Trade Union League, 60, 61, 69, 71
Wood, Lou, 236
Woollcott, Alexander, 99, 104, 180
Wright, Cobina, Jr., 159
Wynn, Ed, 139

YMCA, 64, 65
Yoshimura, Fumio, 240
Young, Clara Kimball, 87

Zaharias, Mrs. George. *See* Didrikson, Mildred (Babe)
Ziegfeld, Florenz, 87, 104